THE GOLDEN STATE

THE GOLDEN STATE

A History of California

Second Edition

Andrew F. Rolle
Occidental College

John S. Gaines
King College

Harlan Davidson, Inc.
Arlington Heights, Illinois 60004

ISBN: 0-88295-797-X, paper
ISBN: 0-88295-796-1, cloth

Library of Congress Card Number:
79-84210

PRINTED IN THE UNITED STATES OF AMERICA

85 86 87 BC 10 9 8 7

CONTENTS

PREFACE

The authors are grateful for the success of the first edition of *The Golden State.* Without the support of the many high school teachers and college professors who have adopted this book, thirteen printings would not have been warranted, nor would it now be ready for this second, revised edition. Also, we thank those persons whose suggestions have helped in the preparation of this revision.

The new edition is needed, not only to deal with events of recent years, but also to update the original chapters in the light of recent research. We have attempted to give greater emphasis to a number of topics: particularly, ecology, culture, sports, and the roles of women, blacks, and Chicanos. We have included new illustrations and have prepared up-to-date bibliographies for each chapter.

We continue to be amazed at the challenge involved in preparing a brief readable history of this complicated state. While stressing what is new in this volume, we also want our readers to know that virtually all of the familiar material has been retained.

Among the persons who have aided in this revision are Professor Robert F. Heizer, Professor Richard Orsi, Rosalind Isuji, Roy Hayes, Sydney Allen, William Schroeder, and Robert Garland. Special commendation goes to Mrs. B. L. Griffin, our typist.

Andrew F. Rolle
John S. Gaines

ILLUSTRATIONS

•1•

THE LAND
AND ITS
PEOPLE

The history of California begins with the remotest of epochs and encompasses hundreds of millions of years. According to native folklore, the sky was fashioned of whale skins while the earth was made from a basket, the Sierra Nevada range was built by a small duck, and the Coast Ranges by a crow. The differences among Indian languages were explained in a fable which said that some of the animals could not speak properly because they had to sit so far from the fire that their teeth chattered from the cold. Charming as these quaint legends are, they cannot substitute for a serious examination of the origins of both the land and its people.

OVERALL DIMENSIONS AND
CHARACTERISTICS

California spans the Pacific seaboard between the 32nd and 42nd parallels, a distance of 1,200 miles including coastal indentations. Maximum length of the state is 824 miles, while its width is 252 miles. California is third in physical size among the states (after Alaska and Texas). Since the early 1960s, when it overtook New York, it has been the largest state in population in the Union.

The contrasts in climate, topography, flora, and fauna all contribute to the state's unique character. California offers virtually every physical, climatic, geologic, and vegetational combination: the wettest weather and the driest; some of the hottest recorded temperatures on earth and also the coldest; poor sandy soil in the southeastern desert regions and rich loam in the great Central Val-

1

ley; the highest mountain in the United States outside Alaska and the lowest point in the country, only sixty miles distant; scrub brush in southern California and the world's largest trees in the rugged High Sierra. The state has more land area, more population, and more natural resources than many of the nations of the world. Lord James Bryce, the nineteenth-century British commentator, dubbed it an "Empire."

THE LAND

California's richly sculptured landscape has provided geographers and geologists with more questions than answers. Recently, however, the science of plate tectonics has developed a theoretical framework that offers a tentative explanation of the complex processes that, over eons of geological time, have shaped the landforms of California into their present configuration.

The principal elements of this new theory are (1) the earth's crust is divided into huge continental and oceanic plates that drift about on top of the earth's molten interior; (2) the sea-floor spreading along oceanic ridges is the principal force behind the movements of these plates; (3) massive folding and faulting occurs when the plates collide; and (4) deep ocean trenches and intense volcanism occur wherever one plate overlaps another. California sits astride one of the most active geological zones in the world, where the "east Pacific rise" intersects the "North American plate." The geomorphic regions of California are the product of such interaction.

The Mountains of California

Heaved up by primordial forces, the mountains of California occupy a little over half of the state's surface and make up six of the twelve geomorphic regions within the state boundaries. The oldest of these are the Klamath Range, which extends from Oregon into the northwestern corner of California. Over 100 million years ago they were offshore islands. Their jagged terrain, with peaks over 8,000 feet in elevation, is composed of heavily faulted and folded metamorphic and sedimentary rocks. Richly forested and intersected by the deep canyons of rapidly flowing rivers, this region has some of the highest rainfall figures in North America.

Its granite core formed by the melting of sedimentary rock pulled downward by crustal action and then pushed back up into the sedimentary layers of the ocean floor, the Sierra Nevada is geologi-

California landforms

Each of the regions identified is relatively uniform in surface features and has its own geological history. This map demonstrates the diverse and complex geography that has exerted a tremendous influence upon the history of California.

50   0   50   100
Scale in miles

Klamath
Mountains
Mt. Shasta

Cascade Range
Modoc Plateau
Mt. Lassen

Coast
Mt. Linn

Central Valley

Sierra

Nevada

Basin
and
Range
Country

Mt. Tamalpais
Mt. Diablo

Ranges

Yosemite Valley

Mt. Whitney

Death Valley

Tejon Pass

Mojave
Desert

Mt. Pinos

Santa Cruz I.
Santa Rosa I.

Transverse

Cajon Pass

Ranges

Mt. Wilson

San Gorgonio Mt.

N

San Nicholas I.
Santa Catalina I.

Peninsular
Ranges

San Clemente I.

Mt. Palomar

Imperial
Valley

Colorado
Desert

3

Located in the Klamath Range, these redwood trees are in Jedediah Smith State Park in Del Norte County. *(Redwood Empire Association)*

cally young, emerging from the sea about 100 million years ago. Long periods of erosion, volcanism, and glaciation produced its craggy features. The range has been in an "uplift phase" for at least 3 million years. By far the largest mountain system in California, the Sierra consists of a huge block that tips gently to the west and abruptly to the east. Almost 400 miles long, and between 50 and 80 miles wide, it is larger in area than the French, Swiss, and Italian Alps combined. Its central area is capped by Mount Whitney's 14,496 feet, while its northern crest is closer to 8,000 feet and its southern end at Tejón Pass descends to about 5,000 feet. The north-south orientation of the range and the west-to-east direction of most rain-bearing weather systems create a rain-shadow effect on the eastern slope and beyond. Although not heavily glaciated since the ice ages that occurred between 3 million and 10,000 years ago, the Sierra contains about seventy small glaciers of quite recent origin. At present, most of each winter's snow pack melts during the summer; this runoff is a major source of the state's water supply. The western foothills of the Sierra are coursed by many west-flowing streams, including several that flow through the Mother Lode country. Although the beauty and accessibility of such mountainous locations as the Yosemite Valley and Lake Tahoe attract millions of tourists, vast reaches of wilderness are still available to the seeker of solitude.

The Cascade Range of north central California overlays the northern portion of the Sierra's core and extends northward into Oregon and Washington. Of recent volcanic origin, this spectacular series of peaks and lava flows includes majestic cone-shaped Mount Shasta, which reaches an elevation of over 14,000 feet, as well as Mount Lassen, a 10,000 foot peak which produced a spectacular series of eruptions between 1914 and 1917, California's only volcanic disturbance ever witnessed by scientific observers. Indian stories tell of periods when ashes and smoke blackened the sky and the sun burned blood-red.

The Coast Ranges are over 400 miles long and average 20 miles in width. Consisting mostly of faulted and folded sedimentary rock, they are lower and younger than the Klamath Range. They first emerged from the sea as a series of islands parallel to the coast. The portion to the west of the San Andreas Fault has drifted northward from its former location along the west coast of Mexico. Through a complex series of events, this crustal fragment was detached from the North American plate by a similar process to that which separated Baja California from the mainland. It now rides on the Pacific plate. Made up of gently rolling hills covered with grass and live oaks,

5

Floor of Yosemite Valley before silting of Mirror Lake.
(From Dr. Rolle's collection)

it was particularly well suited to the needs of its dense native population.

The Transverse Ranges are the only mountains in California that have an east-to-west axis. Formed where the northward moving Pacific plate meets the firm resistance of the Sierra block, this youngest of California landforms is characterized by massive folding and complex fault systems dominated by the intersection of the Garlock and San Andreas faults. This landform also includes the Channel Islands and the Tehachapis as well as the Santa Monica, San Gabriel, and San Bernardino mountains.

The Peninsular Range Province (which encompasses the Los Angeles basin as well as Catalina and San Clemente islands) is dominated by block-fault structures trending north and south and extending southward into Baja California. With steep eastern slopes and with their gentler western flanks terraced by ancient shorelines, they are the most densely populated of California landforms. Despite its earthquakes, brush fires, air pollution, floods, and water shortages, the region continues to attract new residents from all over the world.

Other Geomorphic Regions

Five additional landforms make up slightly less than half of California's surface area. Cutting across the northeastern corner of the state, where it extends from Oregon and into Nevada, is the Modoc Plateau. With an average elevation of over 4,000 feet, this area contains basalt lava flows interspersed with some higher relief. Rocky and unproductive, it shares its volcanic origins with the Cascade Range.

The Basin and Range country lies east of both the Modoc Plateau and the Sierra Nevada. Its topography is characteristic of and extends across the state of Nevada. It is composed mostly of faulted north and south trending blocks with a jumbled pattern of elevation, some blocks having moved up and others having moved down. Death Valley, at its lowest point, is 282 feet below sea level. It lies in the rain-shadow of the Sierra; as a consequence, its desert erosion patterns have produced intriguing formations—dry lakes, dead-end canyons, and alluvial fans. The region also contains rich mineral deposits, which include boron, borax, and gold.

The Mojave Desert lies in the southeast corner of the state. It contains a series of broad basins, interspersed with heavily eroded mountain ranges. The nearly treeless basins vary in elevation from as high as 2,800 feet in the western area to as low as 500 feet in the southeast corner. The cinder cones and lava flows that dot the area

7

Mt. Shasta, a towering volcanic peak of the Cascade Range, reflected in a mill pond. *(Union Pacfic Railroad)*

Mojave Desert scene with yucca plants in bloom.
(From Dr. Rolle's collection)

9

give evidence of recent volcanic activity. Although the Mojave is extremely arid, there is native vegetation, including the Joshua tree and wild flowers of many colors.

The Colorado Desert is lower and hotter than the Mojave and extends southward across the border to the Gulf of California. It was once a freshwater lake. As much as 245 feet below sea level at its lowest point, it contains the Coachella and Imperial valleys as well as the Salton Sea. Irrigated with water brought from the Colorado River, this region has over a half-million acres of productive farmland.

The Central Valley of California lies between the Coast Ranges and the Sierra Nevada and is drained by the Sacramento River in the north and by the San Joaquin in the south. The area was under water during prehistoric times, covered by the Pacific Ocean, and later, by huge freshwater lakes created by melting Sierra glaciers. Composed of deep and fertile sediments, the Central Valley is the largest agricultural region west of the Rocky Mountains. By water being diverted from its flooded northern and eastern sections to the arid regions in the south and west, almost all of its land has become productive. The variety and quantity of its crops are remarkable.

One geographical landform does not occupy any of California's present surface. This is because it is made up of the offshore continental shelf. Extremely variable in width and depth, this important region includes several submarine canyons and a number of deep structural troughs. Only recently explored in detail, it contains rich fisheries, valuable oil deposits, and an extremely complicated ecology.

Earthquakes and Their Measurement

Earthquake tremors large enough to be felt occur almost daily somewhere in the state. Seismographs located in various scientific centers record the magnitude and location of each disturbance. The intensity is measured on the logarithmic Richter Scale. It is possible to estimate the size of quakes that occurred in earlier times by comparing physical evidence such as displacement along faults and damage to structures. Although the average movement along the San Andreas Fault has been 2½ inches per year, it moved 20 feet in some places during the San Francisco quake.

The largest quakes in California's recorded history included tremors at San Juan Capistrano in 1812 (intensity unknown), Fort Tejón (8.0) in 1857, San Francisco (8.3) in 1906, Santa Barbara (6.3)

10

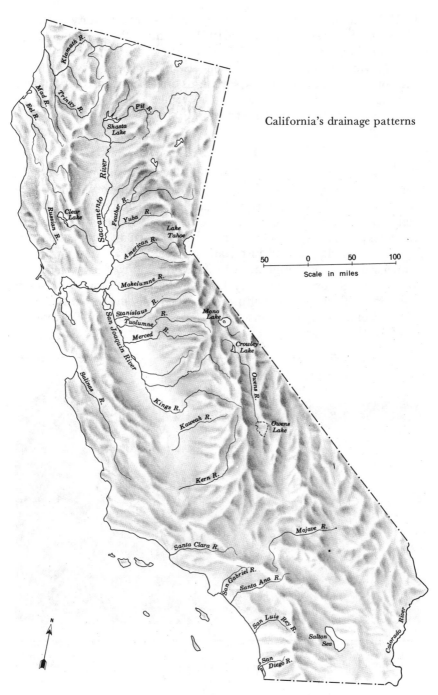

California's drainage patterns

50   0   50   100
Scale in miles

11

in 1925, Long Beach (6.3) in 1933, Arvin—Kern County—(7.7) in 1952, and San Fernando (6.6) in 1971. Of these, the best known are the San Francisco quake, which is discussed later, the Long Beach quake, which destroyed several school buildings and led to the passage of a law that placed new standards on school construction, and the San Fernando quake, which destroyed two hospitals—one of them supposedly earthquake-resistant.

THE ORIGINAL CALIFORNIANS

The prehistoric background of the native American Indians of California is uncertain. They must have lived in California from a very distant age, so remote that their beginnings had literally been forgotten. On the basis of carbon-dated human bone fragments, some authorities place the date of their arrival in California over 20,000 years ago. Anthropologists and historians generally agree that all of the Indians of America originated in Asia and came eastward via the Bering Straits or a temporary land bridge that connected North America with the Asian continent. Artifacts discovered at the time of the building of the Trans-Alaska pipeline (in the 1970s) tend to confirm this theory.

The Hunter—Lake Pomo, 1924. *(Photo by Edward Sheriff Curtis, courtesy of Southwest Museum)*

The California Indians, like other minority groups, have been portrayed in an unfortunate manner. It was once believed that these Indians could not be measured favorably against other tribal groups in North America. As compared to the land they inhabited, rich in natural products and attractive in physical beauty, these first inhabitants did represent something of a contrast. Despite the mild climate and the abundance of wild plant and animal foods, the first Californians did not advance very far toward developing a "civilized" way of life. They should not be measured, however, only against Caucasian standards. From ancient times, these Indians arrived at an adjustment to their environment which they considered workable. Though their general culture was simple, the native Americans of California acknowledged no peers in certain specialized activities. Among these were their well-developed, even complex, cult religions, their intricate basket designs, their clever acorn-leaching operations, and their skill in flint chipping. Their dependence upon acorns as a basic food possibly discouraged interest in organized agriculture. Similarly, their excellent and serviceable basketry work may have accounted for their neglect of pottery. Like other North American Indians, these first Californians did not understand the principle of the wheel, had no real system of writing, and in general led a Stone Age level of existence.

Usually happy and peaceful in outlook, they lived in tune with their environment. A few tribes, among them the Hupa and the Yurok, showed some highly developed culture traits. It is difficult to generalize about so many different tribal groupings, but the basic fact about the California Indians is that, relatively isolated from other North American Indian cultures by mountain barriers and deserts, they developed a society suited to their own geographic needs. Theirs was a style of living built around food gathering and fishing rather than sowing, planting, or harvesting. Instead of describing that way of life in terms of a culture lag, it is more accurate and contemporary to speak of the California Indian culture as uncomplicated but effective in providing the people with a livelihood. Their social system remained essentially intact for thousands of years, until historic times.

That these natives were not dull-witted is shown by the facility with which they acquired use of the Spanish language. They soon learned to speak it clearly and correctly. The Spaniards also taught them to read music and to sing church chorals. Since California's aborigines were without formal education, such accomplishments as they acquired in a very few years of mission instruction seem remark-

13

Hupa girl in ceremonial dress. *(Courtesy of Southwest Museum)*

Baskets made by California Indians.
(Title Insurance and Trust Company, Los Angeles)

able. Their ability to learn mechanical arts is illustrated in the remains of California missions, erected almost entirely by Indian workmen under the direction of friars. In the industrial schools of the missions, Indians became fairly skillful carpenters, weavers, and farmers. There were no better cattle herders, although the Indians had never seen domesticated animals, including horses, before the coming of the Spaniards.

Native Dwellings

Native dwellings varied in accordance with local climate. In the northwest and also in central California, they were sometimes partly excavated, with sides and roof of heavy wood slabs; center posts held up the roofs of larger structures. These "houses," half above and half below ground, kept the Indians warm in cold weather, but the damp atmosphere of their interiors would be considered unendurable today. The dwellings of the Klamath River tribes, built above the surface, were rectangular, with walls and roof constructed of redwood planks. The Yurok and Hupa built frame houses. Mountain Indians usually preferred bark or wood-slab buildings. Among the Chumash, along the Santa Barbara coast, houses of "half-orange" shape were built of poles drawn together and tied at the top. Thatched grass, foliage, or wet earth covered these dwellings, whose light construction was suited to the mild climate of the area. Cohabitation was also practiced by various Sierra Indians, but in the warmer parts of California the natives were satisfied with a thatch or brush shelter, piled up heavily on its windy side. Whatever the style, however, in one respect these structures were alike: they were generally kept in a state of filth. When the collection of bones and other refuse strewn on the floor became too offensive, and the fleas and vermin too numerous, an Indian family sometimes set fire to their "house" and built a new one elsewhere.

Food

The first sound usually heard on approaching a native village was likely to be the pounding of pestles in mortars. The major food staple of the California Indians was the acorn. Acorns constituted, with dried salmon and nuts, the basic provisions stored by most natives for winter. Before acorns could be eaten, they had to be hulled, parched, and pulverized, and the tannic acid had to be leached out. This last operation was done in a basket or in a sand basin. Next, the Indians boiled the sweetened ground acorn meal. The Shastas roasted moist-

16

ened meal, while the Pomo and other groups mixed red earth with their meal, sometimes baking it; the mixture that resulted was eaten or stored. The Indians also ate, after boiling them, the green leaves of many plants. Although they possessed no intoxicating drinks, they did smoke wild tobacco.

California's native Americans ate the flesh of animals whenever they could obtain it. Weapons were few in number and poor in quality—usually small bows and arrows and flint-tipped lances. When hunting large game, the Indians made up for lack of efficient weapons by strategy. Wonderfully deft and skilled in stalking game, they contrived disguises with the head and upper part of the skins of animals. They also set out decoys to attract birds within arrowshot. Game drives were organized, with the animals chased past hidden hunters. Less common was the technique of running down a deer by human relays until it fell from exhaustion. Pits and traps were used to catch larger game, except the grizzly bear. The Indians held this animal in such fear and respect that they let it alone, believing the bear possessed of a demon. Wood rats, squirrels, coyotes, crows, rabbits, lizards, field mice, and snakes were all, however, fair game. Cactus apples and berries were a special treat. The Indians were not fastidious in their tastes, and they did not disdain to eat snails, caterpillars, minnows, crickets, grubs found in decayed trees, slugs, fly larvae gathered from the tops of bushes in swamps (these had a texture rather like tapioca pudding), horned toads, earthworms (used in soup), grasshoppers (roasted and powdered), and skunks (killed and dressed with due caution). Fish, especially salmon and shellfish, formed an important part of the diet of coastal Indians. These people were often excellent fishermen who jealously guarded their "salmon waters." Incursions by intruders upon salmon fishing areas along northern rivers resulted in bloody conflicts.

Food, whether animal or vegetable, was almost wholly provided by nature. Although the Colorado River Indians were settled agricultural tribes, most of the other natives of California followed no form of agriculture, except the occasional scattering of seeds of wild tobacco. Indeed, after the coming of the padres, male Indians frequently opposed such radical notions as organized crop cultivation, involving backbreaking labor in the fields.

Social Customs and Organization

The women and children performed much of the drudgery among the California tribes, while the men engaged in hunting and fishing. The women hunted small animals, gathered acorns, caught fish,

17

scraped animal skins, fashioned robes, hauled water and firewood, wove baskets, barbecued meat, and constructed some dwellings. Creation of a male paradise on earth seems to have been the Indians' objective. Yet it is incorrect to label the males as lazy. They specialized in certain occupations. Among the Hupa, for example, these included making bows, arrows, nets, and pipes; dressing hides; and preparing ceremonial fire-sticks from cottonwood roots.

California's natives were different in their behavior from the eastern Indians of James Fenimore Cooper's Leatherstocking tradition. The California Indians impressed visitors as a joyous race, among the happiest and most gregarious of all American aborigines. Far from resenting the coming of most white men, they gave them a friendly welcome. Indeed, a major complaint of numerous Spaniards was that the singing and dancing of the Indians was so continual, day and night, that they had little opportunity for sleep.

The Indians were fond of dancing, in which they engaged not only for amusement, but also in celebration of every important event, public or private. The northwest tribes for example, had the salmon dance; special dances for the newborn child, for the black bear, for the new clover, for the white deer; the dance of welcome for visiting Indians; the dance of peace; and, of course, war dances. Along with dancing, singing and chanting also played an important part in the lives of the Indians.

A special source of pride for the Indians was their watercraft, which they handled with dexterity and skill. One of the most common types was the tule balsa, a sort of raft made out of river rushes; this craft, used for fishing, was usually poled or paddled on inland waters. They also made much use of wooden plank canoes, which they burned or chopped out of large trees.

The native Americans were fond of athletics, in which they displayed unusual talent. In various ball games and in leaping, jumping, and similar contests, they generally accepted defeat with the same sportsmanship as they did victory; there was, nevertheless, a certain amount of familial and local pride in achievement.

Each family was a law unto itself, and there was no fully systematic punishment for crime. Yet atonement for injury was not unknown. Sometimes serious offenses could be excused for "money." A murderer could even buy himself off by paying the family of the deceased in skins or shells, after which friendship might be restored between him and the aggrieved.

In pre-Columbian California, a strict political or tribal system cannot easily be discerned. Except for a minority of well-defined tribes or tribelets, including the Yumas and some of the Indians of

Members of the Diegueno tribe, Mesa Grande, 1906.
(Museum of the American Indian)

California's northwest coast, the basic political unit was the village community settlement. *Rancherias* (more properly *ranchorillas*), as the Spanish called these separate village units, were loosely knit groupings of several hundred aborigines. A *ranchorilla* typically had a leader whose authority was generally limited to giving advice. The term "chief" can be applied to him only with considerable qualification. Sons of chieftains inherited the father's power only if they were potentially of similar capacity. Wealth played a part in chieftainship,

19

but personal ability to inspire confidence had to be demonstrated anew by each generation.

California's native Americans were not generally nomadic. Boundaries were defined, and to pass beyond a local boundary sometimes meant death to the trespasser. This led mothers to teach children the landmarks of their own family or tribal limits. These lessons were imparted in a singsong enumeration of the stones, boulders, mountains, high trees, and other objects on the landscape beyond which it was dangerous to wander. Women and children, of course, depended upon husbands and fathers for protection against enemies. Controversies between different villages sometimes led to "wars." Rock and arrow fights took place around acorn groves or salmon streams.

Because the California Indians seemed less warlike than many tribes in the East, their comparative mildness of character led early writers to speak of them as cowardly. Actually, the Spaniards had many sharp encounters with them before they were finally subjugated. Americans, later finding them already subdued by the Spaniards, failed to realize how much "frontier work" had been accomplished before their arrival.

An institution the Californians had in common with most other American Indians was that of the sorcerer or "medicine man," and they had profound faith in his ability to cure illness. His treatment consisted mainly of reciting incantations, after which he placed one end of a hollow tube, a basic tool of the trade, against the body of the patient. He then pretended to suck out the cause of the disease, which might be a sliver of bone, a sharp-edged flint flake, or a dead lizard or other small animal, which he had previously hidden in his mouth. His success, in fact, depended partly upon his ability to fabricate incredible stories. Notwithstanding the pretenses of these practitioners, they had some knowledge of the medicinal properties of herbs and roots and other natural remedies and often used it to benefit their patients. Even the Spanish sometimes consulted Indian medicine men when all other means failed to cure them. Until the coming of the Spaniards, the Indian seems not to have suffered from such white man's diseases as smallpox, influenza, and measles. Tuberculosis was unknown to them, and the common cold was rare.

Religion

Religion seemed quite primitive in the pre-Columbian era. There were various cults based on distinct ideas about the creation of the world and about the primeval flood. Each family believed that the creation took place at a spot within their local territory. A general tradition held that at a remote time in the past a billowing sea rolled up onto the plains to fill the valleys until it covered the mountains. Nearly all living beings were destroyed in this deluge, except a few who had gone to the high peaks. There was some vague notion among the Indians of a supreme being, known by various names among the different groups. They also held a concept of immortality: in eternity good Indians would go to a happy land beyond the water, where food would be plentiful and available without effort and there would be nothing to do but eat, sleep, and dance. When the coming of the new moon was celebrated, an old man would dance in a circle, saying, "As the moon dieth and cometh to life again, so we also, having to die, will live again." California Indian mythology was extensive and complex, including countless Aesopian fables dealing with lion, coyote, raven, snake, and so on.

Languages

California's native Americans possessed a wide variety of languages. Within the present boundaries of California, there were twenty-two linguistic families and no less than 135 regional dialects. This confusion of tongues was one of the principal difficulties with which missionaries had to contend. Many Indian groups could not understand each other's speech, though separated in distance sometimes by only the width of a stream.

The natives of California left behind little of greater permanance than the place names taken from their various dialects. The meaning and origin of most of these place names remains cloaked in mystery because they had been forgotten before the white men grew inquisitive enough to study them. We must be content with the historic interest that the sound of these names, sometimes pleasing, sometimes harsh, gives to California.

DECIMATION OF THE NATIVE INDIAN POPULATION

As compared with most regions of North American, California had a dense native population, doubtless as a result of the mild climate and relatively ample food supply. An early estimate placed the number of natives at the time of the European discovery of California at 100,000 to 150,000 or one-eighth the entire native American popula-

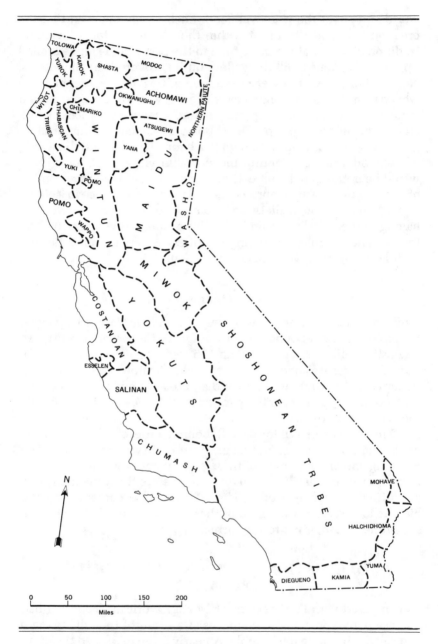

Major Indian linguistic groups in California. *Adapted from A. L. Kroeber,*
Handbook of the Indians of California
(Bureau of American Ethnology Bulletin 78, Washington, 1925, Plate I)

tion in the area now covered by the United States, although the territory these Indians occupied was only one-twentieth of that total land area. With the Spaniards came previously unknown diseases, such as measles, smallpox, and diphtheria. Whole tribes were wiped out, and the Indians' overall population was drastically reduced.

Following the decline of the missions in California's Mexican period, the condition of the natives deteriorated further. Goldmining operations destroyed their food sources. Northern "salmon waters" were so roiled up that fish no longer swam up some of California's streams to spawn. Miners cut down acorn groves for firewood. The whites also seized valuable land, the loss of which was a prime cause of the destruction of the native culture. Induced to sign treaties that they did not understand, the natives were, still later, moved off fertile lands into rocky deserts.

Crushing the Natives

Starvation, disease, and liquor conspired with bullet and knife against the Indians. Some Gringos, or Americans, commonly paid no more attention to Indians on "government lands" then if they were so

INDIAN POPULATION TABLE*

Pre-1542	300,000**
1769–1822	100,000
1870	30,000
1880	16,277
1890	16,624
1900	15,377
1910	16,371
1920	17,360
1930	19,212
1940	18,675
1950	19,947
1960	39,014
1970	91,018
1978	70,000***

*Population census statistics are muddled by changing criteria. Indians were not included in census data before 1890. Early data are approximate. Later figures include in-migration from other areas.
**Only 133,000 to 150,000 according to A. L. Kroeber. The larger figure is based upon Sherburn F. Cook's estimate of 310,000.
***Includes the Yumas, who also live in Arizona. The figure is also confused by Chicanos being numbered as Indians.

23

many coyotes. Pioneers who had been shot at by Indian warriors while crossing the Plains were scarcely in a friendly mood. To some settlers an Indian was a kind of animal, and well-armed whites usually had their way in the struggle over land.

Driven from their homes and from the land of their fathers, the natives, for the most part, fled to inaccessible and desolate spots. In spite of their mistreatment, the majority were peaceable, in contrast to the Plains Indians.

Reservations

After the Gold Rush of 1849, Indian raids on outlying ranches increased demands by ranchers and settlers that they be controlled. Travelers in California also demanded protection. Some sort of reservation system seemed necessary, and, as a result, the federal government authorized the negotiation of treaties with Indian tribes, by which they were to vacate their traditional hunting grounds in favor of life on reservations.

The Treaty of Guadalupe Hidalgo (1848), which transferred sovereignty over California from Mexico to the United States, contained provisions designed to protect the interests of the Indians. Among these was a guarantee to repay Indians for lands that had been taken from them. In accordance with this agreement, United States commissioners concluded eighteen treaties with the leaders of 139 native bands, representing practically the total native population of the state. The Indians agreed to recognize the sovereignty of the United States, to keep the peace, and to refrain from acts of retaliation. They accepted eighteen reservations and promised at the same time to cede old land rights to the government. In 1852, these California treaties were transmitted by President Millard Fillmore to the United States Senate, but the Senate failed to ratify them. The Indians claimed they had promptly complied with the terms imposed, but the compensatory acreages promised them had, for the most part, not been forthcoming.

The management of California's Indian reservations, from their inception in 1853 until relatively recent times, is hardly a matter for pride. During the 1850s and 1860s, many of the officials placed in charge of Indian affairs were unfit for their posts. Too often, whenever a reservation contained valuable land, selfish whites were permitted to swoop in, and the Indians were driven onto rocky or sandy terrain. Some Indians voluntarily left the reservations to become unskilled laborers on ranches and farms, but these were often considered a shiftless and irresponsible element to be exploited by the whites.

The federal policy of dealing with the natives was as unsuccessful in California as elsewhere—with one notable exception. In 1853, Edward F. Beale became the first superintendent of Indian affairs within the state. At Fort Tejón, south of the Tehachapi Mountains, Beale attempted to convert a wild, mountainous region into a model preserve for Indians. He believed that a relatively small group of natives could become self-sufficient and that such an experiment might be influential throughout the West. Work at Tejón proceeded so well that Beale gave his Indian wards a voice in their own affairs —an almost unheard-of innovation in Indian relations. Fort Tejón was later whittled down to 25,000 acres, and its federal appropriation was cut in half. Finally, in 1863, Tejón was abandoned. Mismanagement of Indian affairs had occurred partly because two agencies of the federal government, the War Department and the Department of the Interior, quarrelled over how to handle the Indian. When he escaped from inhospitable reservations, the War Department chased him back. The army insisted that, unless given complete control of the Indian, it could not shoulder responsibility for the safety of whites. Whenever the lives of Caucasians were at stake, the army usually got its way.

It is remarkable that the Indians displayed so little hostility toward the settlers. In the south there was only one significant uprising. However, skirmishing took place frequently in northern California. In one case an expedition against retreating Indians led to the discovery of one of the world's most beautiful valleys, the Yosemite.

The Modoc War

The most dramatic, and the last, of California's Indian conflicts was the Modoc War. The first bloodshed had occurred in 1852, when the Indians attacked an immigrant train en route to California. Nearby miners formulated a plan for exterminating the Indians. Throwing the Modocs off their guard by proposing a peaceful settlement of differences, the Americans then massacred the Indians. The surviving Modocs never forgot the treachery of the white man. After years of sporadic fighting, the Modocs were finally chased into the safety of caves guarded by jagged rocks and ledges of the lava beds. Though cut off from food supplies, the Indians could subsist by eating field mice and bats found in the caves, and by drinking water from underground springs. The army was determined to force the Modocs back

25

onto the reservation. The cost of dislodging the small band of natives, secure in their lava fortress and supplied with old muzzle-loading rifles and other antique arms, was to prove high.

On January 17, 1873, the army advanced on the Modocs. Volley after volley of cannon was fired into the lava, but the attack had little effect upon the Indians. Concealed behind the rocks, they returned a deadly fire against the charging soldiers. The army retreated.

With 1,000 men surrounding the Modocs, General E. R. S. Canby moved his camp to the edge of the lava beds, 1-1/2 miles from the Modoc stronghold, and pitched a council tent between the opposing camps. A fatal peace conference was held on Good Friday, April 11, 1873. Both Indian and white emissaries had agreed to be unarmed. Actually, not only did the Modocs bring along concealed pistols and knives, but several young warriors lay hidden in the nearby bushes, armed with rifles. Captain Jack, the Modoc chief, gave the signal for attack, then himself shot General Canby, thus fulfilling the treacherous promise he had made to his fellow tribesmen at the Indian war council.

Canby's troops determined to punish the killer of their commander. There could be but one end to the unequal struggle between the Modoc Indians and the United States Army. When Captain Jack's warriors finally could hold out no longer, they escaped from their caves and fought on until Captain Jack was captured. He and two other Indians were tried by court martial and hanged. The Modoc War cost the United States government a half-million dollars, in addition to the lives of a general and about seventy-five men. This might have been avoided if the Modocs had been allowed to remain occupants of a few remote lava beds and some poor grazing land.

BEFRIENDING THE NATIVE AMERICANS

The swift disappearance of the California Indians, especially in the latter half of the nineteenth century, is both tragic and pathetic. It seems incredible that between the beginning of the American period and the opening of the twentieth century their number declined from 100,000 to 15,500. In these few decades a proud people were utterly broken in health and morale. The California Indian had a few champions. One of these was Helen Hunt Jackson, whose two influential books, *A Century of Dishonor* (1881) and *Ramona* (1884), focusing upon California, called attention to the mistreatment of the Indian.

The Indians finally came to be viewed as wards of the federal government rather than as "nations" with which to sign treaties. Under the Dawes Act of 1887, by which the government finally acknowledged responsibility for the care of Indians, they were given many of the privileges of white citizens, including the right of each family to own 160 acres of land. This land was, however, to be held in trust for twenty-five years, after which time the Indians were to receive full ownership of their holdings and full American citizenship.

Most of today's California Indians have been assimilated into the general population, though some linger on in the confining atmosphere of reservations. Of these, the largest is the Hoopa Valley Reservation in Humboldt County and the most recently (1970) established is an eighty-acre tract set aside for the Washoe tribe. Most reservations lack rich soil and a sufficient water supply with which to carry on agriculture.

Efforts to Right Old Wrongs

In the 1930s the State of California tried to obtain federal money to compensate the Indians for the land they had ceded in the never ratified 1852 Indian treaties. After years of litigation, the Indians were awarded less than one-third of their original claim which had placed the value of the land at only $1.25 an acre. In the 1950s, using both the courts and the Congress, the seventy-one surviving members of the Agua Caliente band of the Cahuilla Indians regained ownership of over 30,000 acres of desert land, including much of the popular resort town of Palm Springs. Following extensive hearings in the 1950s and 1960s, a federal Indian Claims Commission ruled that California's Indians held an aboriginal title to 64 million acres of land, for which they were awarded $29 million. These legal victories came rather late in the history of the Indian and have scarcely proved useful in salvaging his tribal integrity. Instead, the Indian had to make a difficult adjustment to the society which succeeded in overwhelming his own way of life.

The Indian Rights Movement

Late in entering the civil rights protest picture, the American Indian Movement (AIM) has succeeded in calling attention to the plight of native Americans in today's world. Several "media events" have been staged. Among these was the 1969–1971 occupation of the abandoned federal prison on Alcatraz, a rocky twelve-acre island in San Francisco Bay. Another widely publicized event occurred at the 1973 academy awards ceremony when an Indian woman dressed in native costume accepted actor Marlon Brando's Oscar award but then proceeded to read a statement criticizing the film industry for its negative stereotyping of American Indians. Militant activities, including marches, occupations, and protests, keep Indian grievances before the public, but land rights, water rights, and—most importantly—the rights to a culturally different heritage continue to be threatened.

STUDY SUGGESTIONS

To understand the chapter you should know (1) the meaning and importance of key phrases and terms, (2) the contributions to California history of major personalities, and (3) the location and significance of geographic place names.

1. *Key phrases and terms*

   acorns
   Alcatraz
   American Indian
       Movement
   Dawes Act
   geomorphic regions
   Indian Claims Commission
   lava beds
   leaching
   medicine man

   Modoc War
   mortars and pestles
   nomadic
   rain-shadow
   ranchorilla (sometimes
       ranchoria)
   reservation
   salmon waters
   San Andreas Fault
   Treaty of Guadalupe Hidalgo

2. *Major personalities*

   Edward F. Beale
   General E. R. S. Canby

   Captain Jack
   Helen Hunt Jackson

3. *Important geographic place names*

   Bering Straits
   Carmel
   Cascade Range
   Colorado Desert

   Death Valley
   Klamath Range
   Modoc Plateau
   Mojave Desert

28

Mount Lassen	San Joaquin River
Mount Shasta	Sierra Nevada
Mount Whitney	Tejón Pass
Sacramento River	Yosemite

FOR ADDITIONAL STUDY

Warren A. Beck and Ynez D. Haase, *Historical Atlas of California.* Norman, Okla., 1973.

Dee Brown, *Bury My Heart at Wounded Knee.* New York, 1970.

Charles L. Camp, *Earth Song: A Prologue to History.* Palo Alto, 1970.

John W. and Laree Caughey (Eds.), *California Heritage.* Los Angeles, 1962.

Harold E. Driver, *Indians of North America.* Chicago, 1961.

Robert W. Durrenberger, *Patterns on the Land.* Palo Alto, 1965.

Robert F. Heizer (Ed.), *California. Handbook of North American Indians,* Vol. 8. Washington, D. C., 1978.

Mary Hill, *Geology of the Sierra Nevada.* Berkeley, 1975.

Robert Iacopi, *Earthquake Country.* Menlo Park, 1964.

Helen Hunt Jackson, *A Century of Dishonor.* Edited by A. F. Rolle. New York, 1965.

Alfred L. Kroeber, *Handbook of the Indians of California.* Bureau of American Ethnology Bulletin 78. Washington, D. C., 1925.

Theodora Kroeber, *Ishi in Two Worlds.* Berkeley, 1961.

John Muir, *The Mountains of California.* New York, 1894.

Scott O'Dell, *Island of the Blue Dolphins.* New York, 1960.

*Andrew F. Rolle, *California, A History.* 3rd ed. Arlington Heights, Ill., 1978.

———, *California: A Students' Guide to Localized History.* New York, 1965.

Edith B. Webb, *Indian Life at the Old Missions.* Los Angeles, 1951.

J. Tuzo Wilson, Ed., *Continents Adrift and Continents Aground.* San Francisco, 1976.

Charles Wollenberg, Ed., *Ethnic Conflict in California History.* Los Angeles, 1970.

*General history

•2•

EUROPEAN DISCOVERY, EXPLORATION, AND COLONIZATION

EUROPEAN DISCOVERY AND EXPLORATION

California's name was derived from a fifteenth-century Spanish romance, *Las Sergas de Esplandían (The Exploits of Esplandían)*, written by Garcí Ordóñez de Montalvo. In this second-rate novel of chivalry, the word *California* appears as the name of a wonderful island inhabited by Amazons and ruled by a pagan queen, Calafía. The description of the island went as follows:

> Know ye that at the right hand of the Indies there is an island named California, very close to that part of the Terrestrial Paradise, which was inhabited by black women, without a single man among them, and they lived in the manner of Amazons. The island itself is one of the wildest in the world on account of the bold and craggy rocks. Their weapons were all made of gold. The island everywhere abounds with gold and precious stones, and upon it no other metal was found.

How did the name of this mythical island reach America and become attached to a region on its western shore? The novel was at its height of popularity when Hernando Cortés was conducting his explorations in America, and the likelihood is great that he and his men were familiar with it. The fact that he asked for the prohibition of such romances of chivalry in the American colonies probably indicates that the craze had affected the discipline of his soldiers. Following the conquest of New Spain, or Mexico, in 1519–1521, Cortés

31

himself wrote to the Spanish King about a rumored "island of Amazons or women only, abounding in pearls and gold, lying ten days' journey from Colima." The Spaniards still believed the peninsula of Lower California to be an island, an impression possibly gained from the Colima Indians of Mexico, who told them of land lying across the Gulf of California.

The Pacific Explorations of Cortés

Once Cortés had completed his conquest of Mexico, he turned toward the newly discovered western sea. He had been commissioned by the king of Spain, Charles V, to engage in the search for the legendary northern Strait of Anián or Northwest Passage, and it seemed to him that the best plan was to launch exploratory voyages from the western coast of Mexico. In the years from 1527–1539, Cortés was to sponsor numerous discouraging expeditions into the Pacific.

Cortés had another reason for undertaking explorations in the Pacific. Spain became increasingly interested in establishing a maritime trade between America and the Philippines, which Magellan had recently discovered and claimed for Spain. Cortés established a shipbuilding station on the western shore of Mexico and ordered the carpenters and shipwrights to build four stout vessels. The construction of these primitive ships in colonial Mexico was a remarkable feat, all of their iron work and rigging having to be laboriously brought from the Atlantic port of Vera Cruz on the backs of Indians and animals. However, the ships were built, and exploration was begun.

One of the expeditions landed, probably early in 1534, in the Bay of La Paz above the southern tip of the gulf shore of Lower California. Rumor had it that pearls were located there. This place was inhabited by savage Indians. When the Spaniards, twenty-one in number, went ashore to get water, they were attacked and all were killed but two sailors, who had been left on the ship. These men made their way back to Cortés on the mainland. In spite of the disastrous outcome of the voyage, it had succeeded in touching for the first time the peninsula (believed to be an island) of Lower California; and thus it contributed to the discovery of what is now the State of California. Furthermore, the two survivors brought back rumors of pearl beds just off the Lower California cape, which stimulated later exploration.

After this expedition, Cortés determined to send no more captains into the Pacific, but to go himself. On May 3, 1535, he entered

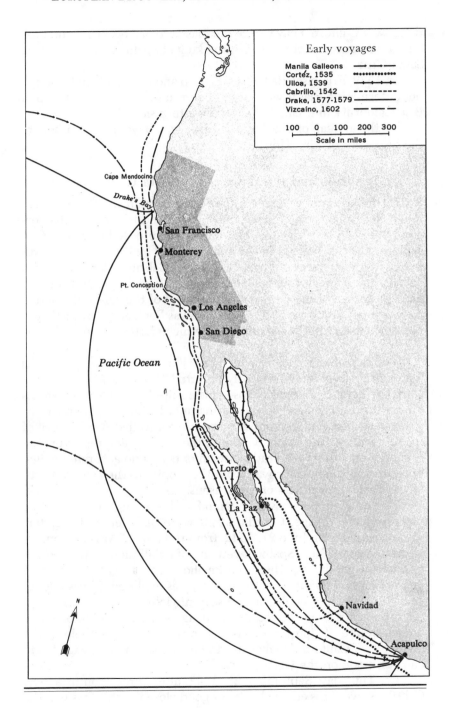

Early voyages

Manila Galleons
Cortéz, 1535
Ulloa, 1539
Cabrillo, 1542
Drake, 1577-1579
Vizcaíno, 1602

100   0   100   200   300
Scale in miles

Cape Mendocino

Drake's Bay

San Francisco

Monterey

Pt. Conception

Los Angeles

San Diego

Pacific Ocean

Loreto

La Paz

Navidad

Acapulco

the Lower California bay where the massacre had occurred and took formal possession in the name of the king of Spain, calling the place Santa Cruz.

In 1539, Francisco de Ulloa sailed up and down the gulf, though not determining that it was a gulf, then rounded the southern tip of Baja California, and sailed along the western side of the "island." So started the first lap of a series of voyages which would lead others to the discovery of Alta (Upper) California.

Cabrillo and the Discovery of Alta California

In a further attempt to discover the Strait of Anián and the treasures to which it might lead, Spain's officials decided to send another exploratory party north by sea. This one would proceed with orders to explore the coast beyond the latitude reached by Ulloa. A leader was found in the person of Juan Rodríguez Cabrillo, described as a "navigator of great courage and honor and a thorough seaman." Little is known of the personal background of this sailor, the actual discoverer of California, except that he was Portuguese by birth and had participated in the expedition in which Cortés conquered Mexico.

The two small vessels to which Cabrillo entrusted the lives of his men were poorly built and badly outfitted. Their anchors and ironwork had been carried, like those of the ships built by Cortés, across Mexico to the Pacific. They were manned by conscripts and were sparsely provisioned; the crews were subject to that deadly peril of the sea, scurvy. One can only admire the courage and perseverance of such men, who, with crude instruments and no accurate navigational maps, fought their way from the tropics to the remote north of the Pacific, regardless of the seasons.

The usual prayers having been offered to Almighty God for the success of the voyage, Cabrillo's sails were unfurled and the start made at midday on June 27, 1542, from the port of Navidad, on the western coast of New Spain. Seven and one-half months were spent in this voyage, during which the Pacific Coast, at least as far as 41 degrees and 30 minutes north latitude, was explored. It was folly to start the expedition so late in the season; violent winter storms battered the ships and protracted the voyage so that it had to be abandoned before its purpose was accomplished. Nevertheless, the discovery of California makes this the most important voyage Spain had yet made on the western coast.

On Thursday, September 28, 1542, after three months at sea, Cabrillo's two ships entered a "very good closed port." This was the

34

(Title Insurance and Trust Company, Los Angeles)

JUAN RODRIGUEZ CABRILLO.

future harbor of San Diego. Their entrance into this bay formally marked the discovery of California—or Alta (Upper) California, as it was called in distinction to the peninsula of Baja (Lower) California. When Cabrillo's party landed, they found Indians, who exhibited great fear. In fact, almost all of the natives fled. To those that remained, Cabrillo gave gifts of beads and other trifles and endeavored by his kindness to win their confidence. In contrast to the early history of Mexico and Latin America, that of California was not marked by the widespread shedding of Indian blood.

At Santa Catalina Island, the Spanish visitors encountered other astonished but passive natives. Along the shoreline opposite Santa Monica, Cabrillo noted an indentation on the mainland, which he called "the Bay of Smokes." Even in those days before smog, Indian campfires covered the bay near today's Los Angeles with spirals of smoke. Cabrillo's party found the Santa Barbara Channel above Ventura teeming with a dense Indian population, whose seaworthy boats presented a marked contrast to the primitive rafts the Spaniards had seen on the Lower California coast.

Upon rounding Point Conception, just above today's Santa Barbara, the voyagers encountered a heavy northwest wind which forced them out to sea. There they came in sight of the islands now known as San Miguel and Santa Rosa. Seeking refuge from the wind, they landed on San Miguel Island. This island, too, was populated by Indians. They lived by fishing and traded beads, manufactured from fish bones, with the Indians on the mainland. In their long hair were intertwined cords into which were thrust daggers of flint, bone, and wood. They wore no clothing and painted their faces in squares, like a checkerboard. Cabrillo spent a week on this island, in the course of which he suffered a fall, breaking his arm.

Ragged stretch along the northern coast of California first explored by Cabrillo.
(*Redwood Empire Association*)

Despite this painful accident and severe winter storms, the commander gave orders to continue the search for the Strait of Anián. The vague Spanish quest for a great river or strait kept luring them onward. Despite the severe winter storms, the Spaniards proceeded to beat their way northward, having skirted such landmarks as Monterey Bay and the Golden Gate without seeing them.

On the return voyage they were glad to reenter their snug harbor at San Miguel Island. Almost continuous storms and high winds over the next two months compelled them to winter on the islands of the Santa Barbara Channel, chiefly at San Miguel. Here the expedition sustained a grave misfortune. On January 3, 1543, Cabrillo died, probably as a result of his earlier fall and the exposure of the hard northern voyage. After his men laid their commander to rest, they renamed the island La Isla de Juan Rodríguez. Drifting sand and cliffs, which have since fallen into the sea, long ago obliterated his last resting place; not even the name of the island has been retained to commemorate his achievement. That Cabrillo was beloved of his men is implicit in a statement found in the expedition's records: "They returned to Navidad sorrowful for having lost their commander."

As he lay dying, Cabrillo had charged his men to resume their quest and to explore the coast as far northward as possible. After his death, his pilot, Bartolomé Ferrer, took command, and the expedition set sail again in obedience to Cabrillo's wishes. Scudding northward before a storm, on March 1 Ferrer reached the northern limit of his voyage, possibly at the Rogue River in Oregon, but at least as far north as the Eel River of California. At this point the crews, in an almost crazed condition from scurvy, forced Ferrer to turn back. He returned to the harbor of Navidad in New Spain on April 14, 1543.

This first "true voyage" to California had failed to find the Strait of Anián. Cabrillo had seen no cities with gold and silver walls—indeed, no advanced Indian civilization with treasure lying in its streets, no "other" lands so rich as the Aztec and Inca empires to the south.

The Philippine Trade

Recalling Cortés' interest in the Philippines, the Spanish in 1565 began a significant trade from the west coast of North America that lasted until 1815. For almost 250 years the Manila galleons, largest and richest ships of their age, carried to New Spain the fabulous luxuries of the Orient. They returned to the Philippines laden with

37

silver ingots from Mexican mines. Almost every English and Dutch privateer sought to capture these cumbersome vessels as they drifted awkwardly down the west coast toward Acapulco, home port of the galleons. These ships were often at sea for months. Upper California was originally to have been a waystation for the galleons, where they could obtain sorely needed wood, water, and fresh food. Although this objective was never accomplished, the quest for such ports made the Manila galleons important for the subsequent settlement of California.

Drake

By the late sixteenth century, when the English achieved access into the "Spanish lake" known as the Pacific, news of Spain's rich Pacific galleons had spread around the world. English privateers, little more than licensed pirates, then began to brave passage through the Strait

Sir Francis Drake.
(Title Insurance and Trust Company
Los Angeles)

of Magellan in order to reach the western coast of the Americas. There they could lie in wait for galleons returning from Manila.

In 1577, the magnificent sea dog, Francis Drake, bearing a secret commission from Queen Elizabeth to "annoy the King of Spain in his Indies," set sail from Plymouth in England on a voyage that would last several years. In his famous vessel the *Golden Hind,* he made his way through the Magellan passage and swooped down upon unsuspecting Spanish outposts on the Pacific like a hawk among barnyard fowl. Boldly attacking both coastal settlements and Spanish vessels, Drake captured ship after ship, sending them to run before the wind with all sails flying after taking off their treasure and crews. He stopped in the ports of Lima—in present-day Peru—and Guatulco—today in the Mexican province of Oaxaca—long enough to sack these towns before the terror-stricken populace of either could collect their wits sufficiently to make any defense. He was a courtly robber and in his operations on the western coast of the New World never killed a man; instead, he treated his prisoners like honored guests, even giving them money and clothing after he set them free.

With the *Golden Hind* loaded almost to the sinking point with treasure, and in constant danger of capture, Drake finally set sail for England by way of California and the northern Pacific. Fearing that Spanish ships would be lying in wait for him back at the Strait of Magellan, Drake wanted to find a passage through the Arctic if possible. According to some accounts, this was a major purpose of his voyage. In any case, Drake sailed north along a route that took him to the Upper California coast. On June 17, 1579, his lookout sighted a "convenient and fit harborough," at 38 degrees and 30 minutes latitude on the California shoreline. Into this sandy bay he entered for the purpose of repairing his ship. However, the exact location of Drake's anchorage in California is uncertain and has long been a matter of controversy.

During his stay on the California coast, Drake maintained friendly relations with the Indians, exchanged gifts with them, and went through ceremonials that the English later chose to regard as acceptance by the natives of England's sovereignty. These symbolic acts probably corresponded to the smoking of a "peace pipe." After completing repairs on their ship, Drake's party held religious services, during which—the documents of the expedition solemnly assert—the natives made loud responses, possibly incantations similar to those of their own medicine men.

Before he departed from California, Drake claimed title to the country for his queen by leaving behind a plate of brasse, fast nailed to a great and firm poste, whereon is engraven her grace's name and the day and year of our arrivall there, and of the free giving up of the province and kingdome, both by the king and people, into her Majestie's hands; together with her highnesse picture and armes in a piese of sixpence currant English monie shewing itself by a hole made of purpose through the plate; underneath was likewise engraven the name of our General.

In 1934, such a plate of brass was allegedly found near the Laguna Ranch on Drake's Bay; after being thrown away, it was "rediscovered" in 1936 under circumstances that led skeptics to question its authenticity. For more than forty years, however, most historians foolishly considered this artifact genuine. Professor Herbert Bolton of the University of California, Berkeley, pronounced it "one of the world's long-lost historical treasures."

Only in 1977 did metallurgists carefully reexamine the plate, pronouncing it a modern forgery. It contained too much zinc and too little copper or lead to be genuine sixteenth-century brass. A few historians, furthermore, had been suspicious about the quality of the lettering, believing that Drake's gunsmiths could have done a far more elegant job; the plate was obviously cut by modern machine tools. It now seems incredible that Bolton could have become a victim of his own enthusiasm.

Vizcaíno at Monterey

Sebastián Vizcaíno's "fleet" of three tiny vessels passed out of the harbor of Acapulco on May 5, 1602. The party proceeded up the coast, stopping at many of the points visited by Cabrillo and renaming them. To the Vizcaíno expedition we owe many familiar place names—San Diego, Santa Catalina Island, Santa Barbara, Point Conception, Monterey, and Carmel. At 36 degrees latitude, Vizcaíno, on December 16, 1602, sailed into Monterey Bay. This became the principal event of Vizcaíno's voyage, and he named the place after the viceroy who sponsored his expedition. Under an oak tree which stood so close to the shore that its branches were wet by the incoming tide, the explorers took part in a religious ceremony:

The mass of the Holy Ghost was held so that God might give light to the general and those of his council, in order that they might decide what would be most conducive to the service of the Lord and of his Majesty.

40

As Vizcaíno looked about him at the ring of hills, dark with the growth of pines covering them from base to summit, he became so enamored of the place that he wrote a glowing description of it to the viceroy. His praise of a harbor defended from all winds was so misleading that the Spaniards, who next saw Monterey in 1769, failed to recognize it. Vizcaíno, continuing the voyage to the north, passed Cape Mendocino; he then decided, due to the miserable condition of his crews, to turn about and make for Acapulco.

On the way down the coast, Vizcaíno's men were unable to land. The number of able-bodied men was so reduced that they dared not let go of their anchors lest they not be able to raise them again. Crew members died from scurvy and starvation. Because of their sore mouths and loss of teeth, Vizcaíno's men could not eat the coarse food they had on board. At Cedros Island most of them were able only to crawl ashore on their hands and knees; by a supreme effort, they somehow managed to take on wood and water. Forty-five men, probably half the crew members, died on the voyage, which lasted eleven months. Yet they had made a detailed exploration of the coast as far north as Monterey, and they had visited the fine harbor of San Diego. For more than a century and a half, little was added to the knowledge produced by Vizcaíno's voyage.

HISPANIC COLONIZATION

Nearly a century before the first English colonists landed at Jamestown, on the eastern shores of North America, Spanish soldiers and priests went to New Spain to spread their civilization northward from Mexico City. In small bands—and sometimes individually— these representatives of king and church sought treasure for Spain and converts for the church, while bringing order to the frontier. For the padres, the principal object was the wealth of men's souls: but Spain's government was astute enough to realize the value of missionaries also in subduing wild peoples with a minimum of expense and bloodshed, and hence in securing the material riches that would hopefully flow from colonization. In the Spanish colonial system the Cross marched side by side with the Sword.

During the period between the Vizcaíno expedition of 1602 and the permanent settlement of California in 1769, New Spain's northern border extended in a sort of arc, from a series of garrisons located along the Red River in present-day Louisiana to a remote chain of Jesuit missions spread throughout northern Mexico and Lower California. Along this colonial frontier were established increasing numbers of missions, mining camps, cattle ranches, and crude adobe *presidios,* or forts. Most of the colonization took place below the present border of California, but it laid the groundwork for later advances toward the north and thus was important to the history of that province.

The foremost historical figure of the frontier was a Jesuit priest, Eusebio Francesco Kino. As explorer, cartographer, and mission builder, Kino was responsible, in the years 1687–1712, for the founding of numerous missions on New Spain's northern frontiers. In 1702, Kino's explorations and maps proved that California was not an island. He and other priests gave a solid foundation to the frontier establishments from which later military and clerical officials would move toward Upper California.

By the middle of the eighteenth century, representatives of the king of Spain had pushed the frontier up to the Gila and Colorado rivers. It would only be a matter of time before the coastline of Upper California, past which Spain's galleons had so long been sailing, would be fully explored and settled by Europeans.

In spite of the success achieved by her colonizers, Spain was still beset by fears of competition from other nations. At the end of the Seven Years' War between France and England, in 1763, the British

SEBASTIAN VISCAINO.

(Title Insurance and Trust Company,
Los Angeles)

Point Lobos, part of the rugged coastline near Monterey, explored by Viscaino. *(Union Pacific Railroad)*

took over most of North America from the French. As a result, Spain came to share a common frontier with England in the Mississippi Valley. Might this advance of the British encourage them to attempt colonization further west, perhaps from ports in California? Or might the Russians, probing across the northern Pacific in search of furs, decide to enter California waters?

43

Gálvez

In 1765, Charles III appointed José de Gálvez *visitador-general,* or inspector general, of New Spain. Gálvez' chief mission was to increase the royal revenues, but as an enthusiastic expansionist, he was also deeply interested in fortifying New Spain's northern frontier. Gálvez sailed to Lower California from the port of San Blas on the west coast of New Spain; his personal inspection of the peninsula lasted almost a year. During this tour he reorganized missions and also developed preliminary plans for a further land expedition to Upper California.

While Gálvez was in Lower California in the spring of 1768, an order came from King Charles expelling the Jesuits from the Spanish colonies—partly because he feared and distrusted the political power they might wield on behalf of various European monarchs. They were replaced in Lower California by a determined group of fourteen gray-robed Franciscan friars under the leadership of fifty-five-year-old Junípero Serra, who arrived at La Paz to continue the work begun earlier by Kino. As mission builders and instructors of the Indians, these men would serve a useful colonizing purpose for Gálvez, a leader of colossal ego who became absorbed with plans to mount an assault upon Upper California. The Russians provided him with his best excuse for this projected expansion.

Russian encroachments from the north upon Spain's Pacific preserves—particularly the voyages to the American Northwest led by Vitus Bering and Alexei Chirikof in 1741—disturbed the Spanish lethargy that had prevailed since Vizcaíno's voyage to Monterey in 1602. As Russian otter-hunting ships extended their cruises farther southward each year, these threats added decisively to those of the increasing English entrenchment in the lower Ohio Valley and of the Dutch and English corsairs lurking off the coast of Lower California. Gálvez became convinced that he must safeguard Spain's future on her northern frontiers and that he must occupy Upper California to achieve this purpose.

Without personally setting foot on the soil of Upper California, Inspector General Gálvez planned an expedition to occupy and settle the ports of San Diego and Monterey. Two divisions were to go by sea and two by land; if one party should fail, another might succeed. The four groups would meet at San Diego and then press onward to Monterey. Religious supervision of the expedition was entrusted to the Franciscan order, which had recently yielded control of Lower California to the Dominicans. This trust was almost joyfully accepted by the Franciscans; in fact, when these missionaries heard they were to turn over the peninsula to the Dominicans and move on to Upper California, they celebrated the news by ringing bells and holding a thanksgiving mass. Ever since Cabrillo and Vizcaíno had reported the existence of a large population of docile and friendly natives in California, an ardent desire to convert them had possessed the Franciscan friars.

Serra and Portolá, Torchbearers

Officials in New Spain took great care to select the right man to lead the Franciscans into the new land; never was better judgment used than when they chose Fray Junípero Serra for the purpose. The selection of Don Gaspar de Portolá to lead the military branch of the expedition was equally wise. Instead of a Cortés or a Pizarro, Serra the idealist and Portolá the dutiful soldier were the first colonizers to have a hand in shaping the development of California.

Serra had first come to America with a party of missionaries in 1749; he gave up prestige and a brilliant future to labor among the savages of the New World. In the inception and carrying out of a plan for the occupation of California, Serra was the right hand of Gálvez; his zeal brushed aside obstacles that would have stopped lesser men. One of the worst of these was his own frail health, aggravated by a lame leg, from which he suffered nearly all of his life. When he set out on the 1769 expedition to Upper California, he was so weak that it was necessary for two men to lift him into the saddle of his mule.

Serra's military companion, Portolá, was a member of a noble family of Catalonia, Spain and had served in various European campaigns as a captain of dragoons. A steadfast soldier, he was sent to Lower California as its first governor at the time of the expulsion of the Jesuits. On hearing of Gálvez' plan, he volunteered to lead the expedition to occupy and colonize the unknown north.

The First Colonizing Expedition

In addition to occupying the ports of San Diego and Monterey, Portolá and Serra hoped in 1769 to establish five missions in Upper California. Church ornaments and sacred vessels did not constitute all of Serra's cargo, however; the seeds of flowers and vegetables from both the Old World and the New were transported to California to become the basis of future mission gardens. It was also arranged for the two land expeditions to take a herd of 200 cattle from the north-

ernmost mission of the peninsula. From these few animals were
descended the herds which in time roamed the hills and valleys of
Upper California—the chief source of her wealth for several generations during the pastoral era of the province. The Baja California
missions were called upon to contribute all of the horses, mules, dried
meat, grain, flour, cornmeal, and dry biscuits they could spare.

Two small vessels, the *San Carlos* and *San Antonio,* were made
available for the sea expedition. On January 9, 1769, the *San Carlos*
was ready to start at La Paz in Lower California. Added to her crew
were twenty-five volunteers, primarily in order to have a military
party that could overcome any native resistance in landing. After a
solemn mass and an address by Gálvez, in which he exhorted all to
do their duty in the sacred and historic mission on which they were
embarking, the little ship, with a total of sixty-two men aboard, unfurled its sails, rounded the Lower California cape, and was off. The
San Antonio was not ready until February 15, when, after another
exhortation from Gálvez and a last shout of *buen viaje* from those
who remained ashore, she also shook out her sails for California. The
first stop for both vessels was to be San Diego, far to the north.

Meanwhile, preparations for the two land expeditions were ac-
tively under way in Lower California. By the latter part of March, the
first division, strengthened by twenty-five leather-jacketed soldiers
from Loreto in Lower California and forty-two Christian Indians, was
ready to start from the northern frontier. This division was accompanied by an intimate associate of Serra, Fray Juan Crespi, a missionary, pathfinder, and provincial record keeper whose name was also
to become prominent in the later story of California. He eventually
accompanied Portolá all the way to San Francisco and left a journal
of the entire march. Crespi's careful account, which records much of
the early history of California, is valued as a major source concerning
the expeditions of 1769. On March 22, 1769, this small army, made
up of veterans seasoned in frontier life, set off northward into the
desert; it became the first overland party to reach California. The
other land contingent, under Portolá, accompanied by the father-
president of the missions, Serra, started last of the four groups bound
for California. This second overland party, with Portolá, bronzed and
bearded, riding at its head, set out on its march to San Diego on May
15, 1769.

San Diego was, of course, also the objective of the two sea expeditions which had gone in advance. Contrary to expectations, the *San
Antonio,* which started a month later than the *San Carlos,* was the
first to arrive, on April 11. On April 29, to the joy of those on the

San Antonio, the long-delayed sister ship sailed alongside and dropped anchor. When no boat was lowered from the *San Carlos,* however, they became apprehensive. A visit, in one of the *San Antonio's* boats, revealed a frightful state of affairs. The long voyage—110 days from the cape—had caused such ravages from scurvy on the *San Carlos* that there were no men aboard able to lower a shore boat. Twenty-four crew members were dead.

All thought of continuing the voyage to Monterey was temporarily abandoned. Every moment and every man were occupied in caring for the sick and burying the dead. The expedition's two vessels remained anchored offshore, near what later became New Town in San Diego. A third ship, the *San José,* apparently a supply vessel, had also been dispatched by Gálvez; she failed to appear at San Diego, apparently having been lost at sea.

The Settlement of San Diego

On May 14, 1769, the gloom was greatly lightened by the appearance of the first overland party, with its band of leather-jackets, muleteers, and native bearers from Lower California. To get a better water supply, the camp was moved nearer the river. There the party built a stockade, Upper California's first military fortification. The sick were moved into a handful of rude huts, and for six weeks the officers and priests cared for them completely unloading the *San Antonio* while they awaited the arrival of Governor Portolá and Father Serra with the last overland party. At the end of June, the camp was thrown into confusion by the sound of musket shots, announcing the approach of Portolá, the military commander and governor. Portolá's men had experienced an easier land trip and arrived in good condition. As previously noted, they had not left Lower California until May 15, a day after the arrival of the first land party at San Diego.

More than a third of the 300 men who had set out for Upper California, both by land and by sea, had failed to survive the trip. Half of those still alive were physically disabled. Portolá and his sea and land commanders now held a consultation, during which they decided that the loss of so many men, mostly sailors, made a change in plans absolutely necessary. They also decided to send the *San Antonio* back to the peninsula for supplies; then they would leave the friars with a guard of soldiers in care of the sick at San Diego, while Portolá pressed on to Monterey with the main force.

47

The outlook was bleak for the new colonists. Deaths were still occurring; most of the men were seriously weakened by hunger, dysentery, and scurvy, and no relief was in sight. But Portolá, a dedicated soldier, set to work at once to prepare for the advance to Monterey. Serra, equally determined and remembering the thousands of natives living in heathenism, declared that if necessary he would remain in Upper California alone to carry on his labors among them. Portolá wrote a friend about his preparations for the journey to Monterey:

> Leaving the sick under a hut of poles which I had erected, I gathered the small portion of food which had not been spoiled in the ships and went on by land with that small company of persons, or rather skeletons, who had been spared by scurvy, hunger, and thirst.

Portolá's party of sixty-four men left San Diego on July 14, 1769.

The Failure to Recognize Monterey

The Indians were friendly, and they furnished the party with food. Portolá pressed on until he reached the shallow Salinas River. He then marched along its banks to the sea near Monterey Bay. There he stood upon a hill and saw an open *ensenada* or gulf spread out before him. Although it was in the latitude of Monterey, it did not fit the descriptions of Monterey Bay given by early navigators, including Vizcaíno, as "a fine harbor sheltered from all winds." The bay of Monterey, though beautiful, cannot be called a well-protected port. Mystified, the little company gazed over the expanse of dark blue water that lay before them. The sand of the long curving beach glistened in the sun. But where was the grand landlocked harbor Vizcaíno had described? Great swells from the ocean rolled in without obstruction, and there was no safety from the wind except in the small hook of the horseshoe where the town of Monterey now stands. The party, in effect, had failed to recognize the bay of Monterey.

After holding a solemn mass at the mouth of the Salinas River, Portolá's group concluded that their only hope of finding Monterey was by continuing the journey to the north. The party pushed on up the coast, with eleven of the men so ill that they had to be carried in litters swung between mules. They had their first sight of the "Big Trees," which Portolá named *palo colorado,* or redwood, because of the color of their wood. At one stopping place, they saw a giant tree of this species which they called *Palo Alto* (high tree). The town located there still bears that name.

48

The Discovery of San Francisco Bay

Weak and confused, Portolá's men passed northward over land never before trodden upon except by Indians. Their path was hindered by numerous *arroyos,* or gulches, over which bridges had to be built to permit the animals to pass. After exploring in the direction of Point Reyes, an advance party excitedly reported to Portolá their discovery of a "great arm of the sea, extending to the southeast farther than the eye could reach." This, of course, was San Francisco Bay, whose magnificent panorama the whole party viewed for the first time on October 11, 1769. Astonished by the sight of so vast a body of water, the explorers concluded correctly that Monterey Bay must now be behind them and that this was yet another large estuary. For decades ships had passed by the opening of the bay of San Francisco. Yet it remained for a land expedition to discover the greatest harbor on the Pacific Coast.

After a feast of mussels, wild ducks, and geese, which abounded in the region, the group decided to return southward to Point Pinos near Monterey, taking nearly the same route by which they had come. When Portolá and his men reached Carmel Bay, they set up a large cross near the shore, with a letter buried at its base; if future ships should come into the vicinity, they would thus be informed that Portolá's expedition had been there. His men then crossed Cypress Point, and very near the bay which they still did not recognize as that of Monterey, they erected another wooden cross. On its arms they carved these words with a knife: "The land expedition is returning to San Diego for lack of provisions, today, December 9, 1769."

The Return to San Diego

Retracing their route, Portolá's men found themselves in dire need of food. Winter was coming on, and snow already covered the Santa Lucia Mountains, which they had to cross. In their plight the party welcomed any sort of food. For posterity Portolá wrote: "We shut our eyes and fell to on a scaly mule (what misery) like hungry lions. We ate twelve in as many days, obtaining from them perforce all our sustenance, all our appetite, all our delectation." As their mules disappeared, the party, upon approaching San Luis Obispo, obtained fish from the Indians. "Smelling frightfully of mules," they finally returned, on January 24, 1770, to the makeshift wood and adobe walls of their San Diego palisade. With foreboding they approached the camp, not knowing whether they would find the place a mortuary. Their fears were exaggerated, however; and when they fired their muskets as a salute, those who were still alive rushed out to exchange embraces and greetings.

The accomplishments of this expedition, sent out by Gálvez a year before, were already significant. The first mission in Upper California had been founded, July 16, 1769, and named San Diego de Alcala. A good part of the coast to the north had been explored. On the other hand, trouble clearly lay ahead. The Indians had quickly lost their awe of white men, and they began to steal even the bed sheets from under the sick. One sharp encounter had taken place in which a boy belonging to the garrison had been killed and several men wounded by arrows. Death continued its ravages, and provisions grew alarmingly short. Now Portolá became disheartened. Earlier he had sent the ship *San Antonio* back to San Blas on the Mexican west coast for supplies. It had not yet returned. On February 10, 1770, Portolá sent a small party of the strongest men back to Lower California by land to seek supplies. Rather than expose his men to starvation, he reluctantly decided to abandon the enterprise and return to the peninsula himself if no relief ship should arrive by March 20.

It may seem odd that men should starve in a country like California, but little could be obtained from the Indians, who lived precariously off the countryside, raising nothing. As for wild game, ammunition was too precious for defense against possible attack to be spared for such purposes. Around San Francisco Bay wild geese were so abundant and tame that they could be knocked down with a stick, but this was not possible elsewhere.

The decision to depart was a disappointment to Serra and his friars, for they knew that if the party withdrew from Upper California, it would probably be years before another attempt would be made at exploration and colonization. The rest of the company clamored for departure, and the whole camp waited tensely to see if new supplies would arrive by the appointed time. Each day the missionaries knelt in supplication for the coming of a supply ship and began a nine-day prayer or novena to San José, patron saint of the expedition. On the afternoon of the last day of grace, March 19, 1770, as twilight began to obscure the horizon, a loud cry of "The ship! The ship!" rang through the camp. For a moment a sail was dimly seen; then it disappeared. The *San Antonio* had run on northward, probably through a mistake in reckoning. In four days it mercifully sailed back into the harbor and dropped anchor.

The Rediscovery of Monterey

Their hunger and despair relieved by a large feast, the Spaniards again started preparations for a new expedition to find Monterey. Sending the *San Antonio* ahead by sea, Portolá led a land party over the same route as before and finally reached the spot where they had set up the second cross, near Monterey Bay, the previous winter. They found the cross still standing, but now it was surrounded with a circle of feathered arrows thrust in the ground, as well as some sticks on which were hung sardines. This they accepted as an offering of friendship on the part of local Indians.

This time Portolá recognized the bay of Monterey. The *San Antonio* arrived a week later. On June 3, 1770, beneath the very oak tree under which the Vizcaíno expedition had held services in 1602, Father Serra conducted a solemn mass amid the ringing of bells and salvos of artillery. Here was founded the second mission in Upper California, dedicated to San Carlos Borroméo. For convenience in obtaining wood and water, the mission was later moved to the little bay of Carmel, about four miles from Monterey. From Carmel, which became Serra's headquarters, Serra wrote his friend Father Palóu, "If you will come, I shall be content to live and die in this spot." A second presidio was established overlooking Monterey Bay. This site, later occupied by the United States Army, is still called the Presidio of Monterey.

On July 9, 1770, Portolá turned the military command over to Pedro Fages and sailed away on the *San Antonio;* California heard no more of him. In its history he must always be a prominent figure, as the first of its governors, the leader of the first expedition over the 1,000-mile trail from the peninsula, and the discoverer of San Francisco Bay.

EXPLORATIONS ALONG THE NORTHWEST COAST

The Spanish explorers along the California coast pursued their aims so energetically that much of the geography of that area had been mapped before other Europeans made a significant appearance there. The charting of the northwest coast in particular, the later opening of the interior valleys, and the pacification of many of the natives—each one an effect of Spanish occupation—proved to be major contributions to the opening up of California to further development.

In 1770 and 1772, Pedro Fages led two expeditions to San Francisco Bay. Serra then suggested that other explorations be undertaken on the coast north of San Francisco. Captain Juan Pérez was appointed the leader of a new expedition to investigate both Russian and English activity above California as well as to chart the northwest coastline.

When, late in August 1774, Pérez' frigate dropped anchor in Monterey Bay, he had surveyed a large part of the coastlines of British Columbia, Washington, and Oregon, in addition to that of northern California. Pérez was deprived of his just renown because of Spain's policy of keeping such voyages secret. Thus, even the names Pérez gave to points on the northwest coast were eventually discarded in favor of place names left by other explorers. In 1775, expeditions under Heceta and Bodega explored the northwest coast, discovering the Columbia River and proceeding as far north as Vancouver Island.

For the first sixteen years of the history of Upper California as a Spanish province, its isolation was almost complete. Their geographic separation from Spain's other colonies, as well as the rigid mercantilist trade policy that restricted them from trading with countries other than Spain, forced the Californians to lead calm, even dull, lives. They knew the name of their king and that of the pope but very little more about events abroad. They did, however, realize that visiting ships flying the flags of other nations could bring the sorely needed goods which the decrepit Spanish supply system failed to provide.

Gradually, foreign vessels, as it happened, began to appear in California waters as a result of the great fur trade that began to develop on the Pacific northwest coast.

"THE BRITISH ARE COMING!"

On November 14, 1792, George Vancouver entered San Francisco Bay in the British warship *Discovery*. He had orders to explore the entire coast, to examine the extent of Spanish possessions, and to seize unclaimed territory. Despite strained relations between Spain and England, Vancouver was given a cordial reception by both the padres and the military officials, who wined and dined him and sent meat and vegetables aboard his ship.

Vancouver's party visited Mission Santa Clara—the first foreigners to penetrate so far into the interior—and were struck by the physical beauty of California's northern valleys. From Santa Clara they returned to San Francisco, where they gave the Spaniards presents of English culinary and table utensils, bar-iron, and a few ornaments for the church. Then they sailed out of the bay, which members of the party declared to be "as fine a port as the world affords."

Further south at the capital of Monterey, Vancouver was received as hospitably as he had been in San Francisco Bay. Despite this cordiality, Vancouver was in Pacific waters primarily to advance British interests, and these were in conflict with those of Spain. Vancouver remarked in his report on this trip to California: "The only defenses against foreign attack are a few poor cannon, inconveniently placed, at San Francisco, Monterey, and San Diego." This lack of preparation for defense was to have marked consequences for California's future.

STUDY SUGGESTIONS

To understand the chapter you should know (1) the meaning and importance of key phrases and terms, (2) the contributions to California history of major personalities, and (3) the location and significance of geographic place names.

1. *Key phrases and terms*

Bay of Smokes
Discovery
Franciscans
Golden Hind
Jesuits

latitude
Manila galleons
privateer
San Antonio

2. *Major personalities*

Calafía
Hernando Cortés
Fray Juan Crespi
Sir Francis Drake
José de Gálvez
Fray Eusebio Kino

Don Gaspar de Portolá
Juan Rodríguez Cabrillo
Fray Junípero Serra
George Vancouver
Sebastián Vizcaíno

53

3. *Important geographic place names*

Drake's Bay
Gulf of California
Lower California
Monterey Bay
New Spain
Salinas River

San Diego
San Francisco Bay
San Miguel Island
Santa Catalina
Strait of Anián

FOR ADDITIONAL STUDY

*Robert G. Cleland, *From Wilderness to Empire* (New York, 1944).

Maynard J. Geiger, *Life and Times of Fray Junipero Serra* (Washington, D.C., 1959).

Samuel Eliot Morison, *The European Discovery of America, The Southern Voyages, 1492–1616* (New York, 1974).

Philip W. Powell, *Soldiers, Indians and Silver: The Northward Advance of New Spain, 1550–1600* (Berkeley, 1952).

Andrew F. Rolle, *California: A History* 3rd ed., (Arlington Heights, Ill, 1978).

Henry R. Wagner, *Juan Rodríguez Cabrillo, Discoverer of the Coast of California* (San Francisco, 1941).

*General history

·3·

HISPANIC CALIFORNIA

THE MISSIONS

Among the four institutions used by Spain to colonize Upper California—the mission, the presidio, the pueblo, and the rancho—the mission was most important. Spain expected the missions to accomplish two purposes: first, to save the souls of Indians and, second, to win their allegiance to Spain. In accordance with these goals, it was necessary to civilize and train the Indians in many things beyond religion and politics.

California was one of Spain's last colonies. Though the mission system operated practically the same as elsewhere in the Spanish empire, the circumstances of its founding in California were somewhat different. From the time of Kino, it was considered foolhardy for individual missionaries to face the dangers of the frontier alone. Those priests who went to the Upper California mission stations were accompanied by guards and supplied with provisions until the missions could gather Indian colonies around them and become self-supporting. A total of twenty-one missions was established in California, forming a chain from San Diego to Sonoma. They were separated by about a day's travel on horseback—some thirty miles apart. The King's Highway, *El Camino Real,* was then scarcely more than a dusty path, the only road from mission to mission and from presidio to presidio.

Three prime requisites determined the choice of a mission site —arable soil for crops, a convenient water supply, and a large local Indian population. Observation of their sites even today indicates the good judgment of the missionaries. By the time the twenty-one missions were established, the friars had in their possession much of the choicest land in the province, a fact that led to later resentment.

The first mission buildings were of the rudest thatch construction, mere huts of sticks, plastered with mud or clay and roofed with tule. Mission chapels, too, were made of these materials and were distinguished only by an altar and other crude wooden church furniture. The permanent adobe-brick or cut-stone buildings, with which tourists are familiar, still appear dignified though they are in partial ruin. These missions were slowly built with Indian labor, for the most part after the era of the pioneer missionaries. Today's stone walls at Carmel Mission were never seen by Father Serra, though he died there.

Architecturally, the missions of Upper California are distinctive, differing in many particulars from those in other parts of America. The California padres, in their isolation, evolved a plan of their own. "California mission architecture" is characterized by open courts, long colonnades, and numerous arches and corridors. The typical red-tiled roofs were adopted as one solution to bitter experiences with fire. Similarly, the destruction of many of the earlier buildings by earthquakes led to the use of thick walls, sometimes reinforced with heavy buttresses. These give mission buildings their massive, imposing appearance.

Mission San Luis Rey, from Robinson's *Life in California before the Conquest,*
1846. *(C. C. Pierce Collection, courtesy of the Huntington Library)*

56

The missionaries assumed a paternal attitude toward the Indians and treated them as wards. Usually two friars occupied an establishment, the elder of whom had charge of interior matters and religious instruction, while the younger attended to agricultural and other outside work. Each of the mission administrators was subject to the authority of a father-president for all of California. Except in the punishment of capital crimes, the friars had full control of the destinies of their Indian charges, and these padres became virtual rulers of their mission domains. Floggings and other forms of corporal punishment were occasionally administered to the Indians for various offenses. The missionaries defended their discipline on the ground that it was the only effective means of controlling the childlike natives.

The missions were not devoted entirely to religious instruction. Each was also a sort of industrial school, in which the natives learned the formal meaning of work for the first time and where they were taught various trades. Native strength was harnassed with missionary inventive genius and mechanical skill to produce remarkable results, for example, irrigation works. The Franciscans, indeed, were the pioneers of California's future water system, and some of the mission

Fray Junipero Serra.
(Title Insurance and Trust Company, Los Angeles)

Retrato del Rev. Padre Fray Junipero Serra Apos la Alta California, tomado del original que se conserva Convento de la Santa Cruz de Querétaro.

Arches at Mission San Juan Capistrano, photographed in 1890.
(Title Insurance and Trust Company, Los Angeles)

dams and canals whose construction they directed are still in a good state of preservation.

The friars, by the nature of the task confronting them, served as teachers, musicians, weavers, carpenters, masons, architects, and

58

physicians of both soul and body. In addition, sometimes putting their own hands to the plow, they raised enough food for mission use and occasionally a surplus of meal, wine, oil, hemp, hides, or tallow. This was shipped down the coast to New Spain; at Acapulco, principally, these products were exchanged for articles needed in the new Alta California colony—clothing, furniture, implements, and tools. At mission farms and orchards the missionaries tried to adapt various crops to the climate and soil. Semitropical fruits, such as oranges, lemons, figs, dates, and olives, flourished in the mission gardens. Even cotton was grown at some missions, in quantities sufficient to prove the feasibility of raising it in that environment.

At the time of Serra's death, in 1784, he and his followers had been in California for sixteen years; out of a primitive native culture they had fashioned the beginnings of civilization in the province. The nine flourishing missions they had founded claimed a total of 5,800 converts. The flocks and herds of these establishments ranged over thousands of acres, and in their busy workshops the Indians labored at spinning, weaving, carpentry, and masonry besides raising crops for food. It was from Mission San Gabriel that the wheat which was traded to the Russians came, and at Mission San José the padres planted a large tract of wheat.

The missions also played a part in the maintenance of law and order. With their extensive activities and control of society, the padres did much to stabilize California's provincial life. Baptisms, confirmations, marriages, and other vital ceremonies were, of course, performed at the missions. Even wedding dinners were held there. The missions also served as an inn for wayfarers, who could always count on a night's lodging. Mission accommodations were of the barest sort—usually consisting of a bed of rawhide, scratchy flaxen sheets—and the meals, cooked by Indian servants, were simple in the extreme. The warmth of greeting, however, often made up for the discomforts, and on a windy night, as the wind whipped across mission tile roofs, travelers were thankful for the warmth of the fragrant pine logs burning in their fireplace grates.

Decline of the Missions

Soon after Mexico won its independence from Spain in 1821, the role of the missions began to wane. There were two reasons for this: first, the Mexicans were displeased because most church leaders had opposed independence; second, there was mounting sentiment for freeing the Indians from church control. Another reason, which was

Mission San Carlos Borromeo at Carmel. *(Union Pacific Railroad)*

not usually mentioned, was the desire to take away the rich church properties, not the least of which were the missions. Under the Secularization Law of 1833 the missions were stripped of their lands and converted into parish churches. Half of the land and livestock was distributed among the Indians; the other half went to the government. The Indians did not accept their new freedom joyfully. Rather, they lingered about the missions, reluctant to leave the places that had been the only homes they had known, in some cases for as long as sixty years. Deprived of their major source of income, most of the missions collapsed altogether. A few were successful as parish churches, and some were sold and converted to other uses. Others were abandoned and allowed to decay; their roofs caved in and their thick adobe walls literally melted away. In recent years the missions have become tourist attractions, and many have been restored to their former beauty.

PRESIDIOS AND MILITARY TOWNS

California's presidios, or frontier fortresses, were originally built to protect the missions from hostile Indians and to guard Spanish claims to the area against foreign aggression. These presidios were located at strategic positions, generally at the entrances of the best ports. Small groups of houses, inhabited principally by settlers, traders, and the families of soldiers, grew up around the presidios, and such "military towns" developed into colonial centers. These presidio towns— San Diego, Monterey, San Francisco, and Santa Barbara—were at first under military rule, but each eventually acquired its own civil government. An early presidio typically consisted of a square enclosure surrounded by a ditch and rampart of earth or brick, within which were located a small church, quarters for officers and soldiers, civilian houses, storehouses, workshops, wells, and cisterns. Outside were grouped a few dwellings, and at a little distance were fields of crops and pasturage for the horses and mules of the garrison.

In addition to strictly military pursuits, such as exploring, hunting, capturing runaway mission Indians, and carrying the mails, the duties of the soldiers who manned the presidios included construction of buildings, the care of herds and flocks, and cultivation of the soil. These occupations were not always to their liking, and they soon learned to employ Indians for many services. For their labor, the Indians received such pay as a string of beads, a dish of porridge, shoes, or a bit of cloth.

The soldiers of the early presidios were poorly outfitted, wearing a uniform that consisted of a long leather jacket over their leather armor, as in medieval times. With a few bronze cannon mounted on ramparts and often without powder for them, these men were equipped to resist attack only by still more poorly armed Indians. Not one of the presidios could have stood up against a well-equipped ship of war. Indeed, they were maintained more as a warning against possible enemies than with any expectation of making a fight. In time the cannon rusted, and the presidios took on an air of dilapidation. Even the officers, the aristocracy of the presidios, lived under primitive conditions that awakened the pity of foreign visitors. Like exiles in a strange land, they waited for the day when they might return to more comfortable homes.

Juan Bautista de Anza, who founded the San Francisco presidio, was, like Portolá, a military man and one of the significant trail breakers and tough Indian fighters of the West. He learned his vocation from his father and grandfather, also frontier captains. Anza had long planned to explore a route northwestward from Sonora to the ocean, believing that such a land passage would avoid the delay and perils of the sea voyage on which California still relied for major contact with the outside world. The Mexican viceroy, convinced of the importance of strengthening the California settlements, saw in Anza's proposal an opportunity not only to open a new land route, but also to send additional colonists under the protection of a thoroughly capable leader. Women settlers, provisions, and domestic animals were in particularly great demand in California. In January 1774, with the priest Father Francisco Garcés as his guide and a band of thirty-four men, Anza set out westward from northern Mexico. Theirs was the first sizable crossing by white men into southern California from the Colorado basin through the San Jacinto Mountains. On March 22, 1774, Anza's party reached Mission San Gabriel in California, where they were received with enthusiasm by the padres. Anza and his men then moved on to Monterey, returning later that year on the Sonora frontier. An overland route to California some 2,200 miles long had now been opened. Except for the lack of water across the sand dunes of the Colorado, it was a fairly practical route.

In 1775, preparations were made to send Anza with another party of colonists, recruited throughout Sinaloa and Sonora and so impoverished that they had to be given clothing and pay in advance. On October 23, Anza left at the head of this second company, consisting of 240 men, women, and children. He led them and a herd of 200 cattle beyond the Colorado River once more to Mission San Gabriel and on to Monterey. A few colonists then accompanied him to the site of the future San Francisco. Not only did Anza make this second trip from Sonora without the loss of a single life, but eight more persons had been added to his party by births along the way. Though Anza selected sites for a presidio and a mission, he did not remain long in California.

On September 17, 1776, the presidio of San Francisco de Asís was formally dedicated, and on October 9 the mission was founded. Though a mission and presidio now existed at the future site of San Francisco, the community was not yet a real pueblo. Its potential, however, was well understood by the Spanish officials, who sponsored other expeditions into the area in addition to those led by Anza.

THE PUEBLOS

The civil pueblos, usually considered the first real municipalities of California, were established and administered according to a plan formulated by California's Governor Felipe de Neve in his code of laws, or *Reglamento,* issued in June 1779. Neve's regulations granted each pueblo four square leagues of land, laid out according to the topography of the country. First a plaza was marked out—in inland towns a rectangular space in the center, but often on the waterfront in the case of a town or a river or bay. Facing upon the plaza were such public buildings as the council house, the church, storerooms, and the jail, the remaining frontage being occupied by settlers' houses. The life of the community revolved around these central squares; even bullfights took place in them.

Brief descriptions of California's first three civic pueblos will illustrate the pattern of their development. The earliest of these was San José, founded November 29, 1777, when a few mud huts were erected on the banks of the Guadalupe River and occupied by soldiers and their families. Not until 1786 did the residents receive formal legal possession of their lands. The growth of the town was slow; for years it consisted of a few scattered houses of settlers who barely eked out a living.

Further south, the second civic pueblo, Nuestra Señora la Reina de los Angeles de Porciúncula, abbreviated today to Los Angeles, was founded at sundown on September 4, 1781, by eleven couples and their families. Recruited in Sinaloa, Mexico, they had trudged northward to San Gabriel Mission. From there, under the authorization of Governor de Neve, they had moved on a few more miles to settle

63

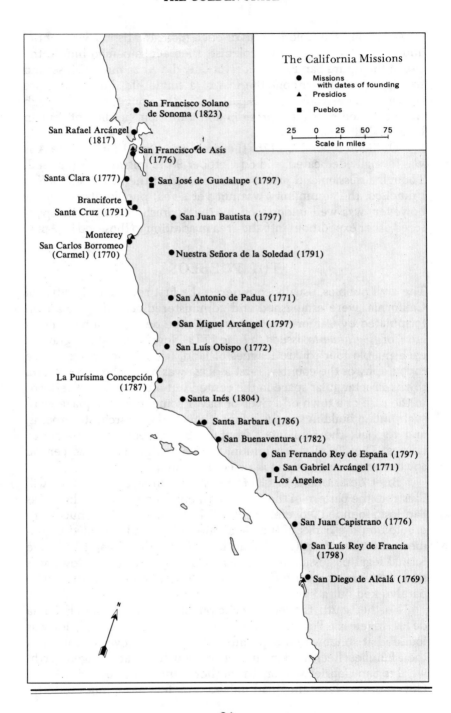

The California Missions

● Missions
  with dates of founding
▲ Presidios
■ Pueblos

25   0   25   50   75
Scale in miles

San Francisco Solano de Sonoma (1823)

San Rafael Arcángel (1817)

San Francisco de Asís (1776)

Santa Clara (1777)

San José de Guadalupe (1797)

Branciforte
Santa Cruz (1791)

San Juan Bautista (1797)

Monterey
San Carlos Borromeo (Carmel) (1770)

Nuestra Señora de la Soledad (1791)

San Antonio de Padua (1771)

San Miguel Arcángel (1797)

San Luís Obispo (1772)

La Purísima Concepción (1787)

Santa Inés (1804)

Santa Barbara (1786)

San Buenaventura (1782)

San Fernando Rey de España (1797)

San Gabriel Arcángel (1771)
Los Angeles

San Juan Capistrano (1776)

San Luís Rey de Francia (1798)

San Diego de Alcalá (1769)

N

"The Pueblo of Our Lady, the Queen of the Angels." Nothing could be more humble than the beginnings of this city. Its first citizens were mainly Indians and blacks with only a moderate admixture of Spanish. It was difficult to induce Spain's Mexican colonials of standing to accept a measure of exile to such a distant wilderness as California. Yet, by 1784 this motley band of colonists had replaced their first rude huts with adobe houses and laid the foundations for a church and other public buildings. Two years afterward, when land titles were finally issued them, each Angeleno affixed his cross to these documents; apparently not one of Los Angeles' first citizens could write his name. Later the town assumed increased importance from its overland trade with New Mexico—over what came to be known as The Old Spanish Trail.

California's third civic community, Branciforte, named after a viceroy of that name and designed for defense as well as for colonization, was founded in 1797 near the present city of Santa Cruz. It was a failure almost from the beginning and soon passed out of existence. Its demise is usually connected to the type of colonists who founded it: these were partly convicts sent by Spanish officials in Mexico to serve out sentences of banishment in California.

Valuable inducements were offered to settlers who would make their homes in pueblos. Each was entitled to a lot on which to build a house, stock and implements, an allowance in clothing and supplies, the use of government land as common pasture, and, finally, exemption from taxes for five years. In return for this aid, the settler was required to sell his surplus agricultural products to the presidios and to hold himself, his horse, and his musket in readiness for military service in any emergency. He was also required to build houses, dig irrigating ditches, cultivate the land, keep his implements in repair, and maintain a specified number of animals. Each pueblo was expected to construct its own dams, canals, roads and streets, church, and other town buildings and to help till the public lands. From the town's agricultural production, municipal expenses were theoretically to be paid.

These arrangements were provisional for the first five years, at the end of which settlers were to receive permanent title to their lands. As a safeguard against the carelessness of improvident persons, no one had the right to sell or mortgage his land. This measure was intended to protect people from their own folly, but it was sometimes evaded.

Municipal officers—consisting of an *alcalde* (similar to a mayor), and a board of councilmen (*ayuntamiento*)—were at first appointed by the governor, but were afterward elected by the people. The powers of an alcalde were almost unlimited in his own domain, and generally these officials were honest in their administration of justice. The alcalde was in effect the "little father" of a town, to whom all carried their troubles, public and private. There was no pay attached to the office, the honor of holding public office compensating the holders for their labors.

Pueblo Life

The entire white population of the province as late as 1848 was an estimated 14,000, divided nearly equally between Californians and foreigners. By "Californian" is meant a person of Spanish birth or background who settled in the province as a resident during either the Spanish or Mexican eras. (The Mexican era is generally considered as beginning in 1821 when Mexico declared its independence.) In addition, a small percentage of the Indians, between 3,000 and 4,000, lived in or near the sleepy pueblos; so did perhaps 40 percent of the white population. Although mere hamlets, Los Angeles and Monterey were social centers of the province. Yerba Buena, as San Francisco was called during its early years, was even smaller. The wealthier rancheros owned pueblo dwellings in addition to their ranchos and divided their time between them.

In the towns bull-and-bear fights, a form of entertainment somewhat varied from that of old Spain, were popular. These blood-curdling events were generally conducted in an improvised arena in the public plaza, sometimes in front of the local church. A trapped bear was tied by one foot to a bull, after which the two beasts fought it out until one or the other was killed. The people gambled on the outcome.

Despite the efforts of various governors to encourage education, provincial schools were limited in number and quality. School was sometimes held in empty granaries or in barracks. Among the teachers were soldiers, whose only qualification was some knowledge of reading, writing, and "figuring." Their chief instructional assistant was the *disciplina,* a sort of cat-o'-nine-tails, which was liberally applied to youngsters. Despite the discouraging conditions in public schools, ambitious young men managed to acquire some additional education through private instruction from priests, military officers, and especially foreigners.

A surgeon, usually a graduate of a Spanish medical school, was in residence at the presidio of the capital, but California boasted few other doctors. Nevertheless, the health of the people was remarkably good, and astounding longevity was sometimes recorded. At a time when medicine was still in a relatively primitive state, even in Europe, California probably would not have benefited greatly from the arrival of more doctors.

Theft, murder, and other crimes were relatively rare in provincial California. Foreign sea captains would sometimes sell goods to rancheros along the coast on credit and return months later to receive their pay in hides and tallow. Banditry, except by Indians, was reputedly unknown until after the beginning of American occupation.

THE RANCHOS

Conditions in California during the colonial period seemed favorable to only one means of livelihood—the ancient one of the shepherd or rancher. The sparseness of the frontier population severely limited the markets available for both agricultural production and potential manufacturing. Ranching conditions, however, were almost perfect in California: abundant pastureland and water existed in addition to a large supply of Indian labor. The climate was mild enough to permit animals to live throughout the year with little shelter, and there was no necessity to fence in stock. Ranching, moreover, was popular in the Spanish motherland, and it suited the natural disposition of the Spanish Californians, who liked outdoor life on horseback. The small band of 200 cattle brought to California by the Portolá expedition, and the few that survived the overland trip with Anza's party, provided the stock from which most of the California herds developed. These herds yielded hides and tallow in abundance for export.

In order to raise cattle, settlers had to have land. No phase of California history has produced more far-reaching consequences than the disposition of the large private land grants during the Spanish and Mexican eras. California land titles today are grounded upon these original grants, which the Californians regarded as the very origin of their wealth. In Spanish California, land was for the most part granted only for pueblos, less than thirty-five grants being ceded to private persons in the entire Spanish period. The missionaries enjoyed only temporary rights to land, and they sought to preserve it intact from ownership by private persons because they feared that the Indians might be morally contaminated by settlers. On the other hand, the government was concerned with the impossibility of protecting outlying and scattered ranches from unpredictable native attacks. Consequently, settlers were generally required to live "in the pueblos, and not dispersed." In time, however, the private rancho became a needed institution. The first land grant was made in 1775. The colonial governors were empowered to make private grants, not to exceed three square leagues, each beyond the limits of the existing pueblos and not conflicting with the property of missions or Indian villages. The grantee had to agree to build a storehouse and to stock his holdings with at least 2,000 head of cattle.

Most of the land grants were made during the Mexican regime. A colonization law of 1824 promised security of both person and property to landowners, as well as freedom from taxes for five years. Any Mexican of good character or any foreigner willing to become naturalized and to accept the Catholic faith might petition for eleven square leagues of land. Nevertheless, Mexican citizens were preferred to foreign settlers, who could not ordinarily obtain grants within ten leagues of the sea coast.

The square leagues by which the grants were measured comprised a little more than 4,438 acres each, and a rancho of four or five leagues was considered small. Boundaries were loosely defined by well-known landmarks, such as a chain of hills, a clump of cacti, or the center of a stream bed; in other cases the whitened skull of a steer might be placed so as to mark the limits of a grant. Beginning at a point marked by a pile of stones, called a *mojonera,* a horseman measured the tract by galloping at full speed with a fifty-foot-long *reata,* or rope, trailing behind him. The quantity of land was roughly guessed at, the convenient phrase *poco mas ó menos* (a little more or less) being used to cover any deficiency or excess. This vagueness of description inevitably led to disputes when rancho properties later fell into the hands of American occupants.

Cattle and Horse Raising

In 1790, there were only nineteen private ranches in California; by 1830, there were some fifty in existence. Many of the holdings were at first stocked with horses and cattle borrowed from the missions. As their endeavors proved profitable, some Californians came to own several ranchos, each with herds of cattles and horses. Many family fortunes were founded on the success of the ranchos, especially after the beginning of the extensive trade with English and American vessels in search of hides and tallow.

Cattle were the mainstay of the California economy, and beef, the principal item of food. Leather hides provided harnesses, saddles, soles for shoes, even door hinges; the long horns of cattle were used as added protection on top of adobe walls or fences in towns, as well as for shoe buttons. Tallow went into the molding of candles.

Hides and tallow also became the main items of exchange. Although trading accounts were kept in *pesos* and *reales,* little cash was exchanged. The Californians increasingly obtained their wearing apparel and other manufactured necessities by bartering with foreign trading vessels. The term "California bank note" came to be used widely for a dried steer hide, which had a value of approximately one dollar.

The term *rancho* usually described land devoted to stock raising. Few crops were planted on ranchos. (In Mexico, farms raising crops were called *haciendas.*) Some ranchos employed over a hundred Indian laborers. In fact, without Indians the ranchos could hardly have carried on. Despite their previous lack of experience with stock animals, Indians seemed to take almost naturally to handling both horses and cattle. They generally considered it an honor to work among the cattle or in a domestic capacity. Only Christianized Indians were so employed; the more lowly tasks of planting and plowing were left to other less adaptable natives.

Also indispensable in the care of cattle herds were the rancho's horses. During the rancho era they sold for a trifle: a passably good horse could be bought for three dollars—less than the cost of his saddle and bridle. Capable of great speed and endurance, the California horses acquired skill in rounding up and handling cattle hardly less extraordinary than that of their riders.

These cowboys, or *vaqueros,* were required in large numbers because of the absence of fences. Free-running stock became so wild and fierce that it was unsafe to go among such herds on foot or unarmed; any man who rode the range was as likely to need to defend himself against savage bulls as against ferocious grizzlies, which were often encountered near the mountains.

The lack of fences also led to the institution known as the *rodéo,* or roundup, devised to separate and brand stock belonging to different owners. Every rancher had his own distinctive brand, and each was registered. No one could adopt or change a brand without permission of the governor. At intervals the rancheros held bloody *matanzas,* or cattle slaughterings. Men rode at full speed through the herds and killed the animals with one cut of a knife directed at a vital part of the neck. Next skinners stripped off the hides, and butchers cut the meat into strips for drying. The tallow was melted and poured into bags made of hides, to be delivered to offshore trading ships, often by floating these bags out to the vessels. Most of the carcasses,

*The Vaquero. (Title Insurance and Trust Company,
Los Angeles. Painting by James Walker.)*

for which there was no market, were left on the field to be disposed
of by the Indians and wild animals or to rot.

California's colonials never held sheep in the same esteem as
they did cattle; nevertheless, each mission establishment and most of
the private ranchos raised small flocks of sheep for their mutton and
wool. The wool was coarse and wiry, but strong, and was woven by
the Indians on handmade looms into clothes and blankets.

Life on the Ranchos

Life on the ranchos was simple. The rancho family was a self-sustaining economic and social unit. The *ranchero,* the unquestioned mas-

70

The hide and tallow trade. *(Automobile Club of Southern California)*

ter of his estate, was implicitly obeyed by both his family and Indian retainers. Yet he did not generally abuse his authority, for he was, ideally, a born gentleman—kindhearted and mild-tempered.

Probably no society ever existed in which a stronger bond linked the members of a family, particularly parents and children. Families numbered from fifteen to twenty members or even more, to which were added in-laws and orphans. To undertake the care of an orphaned child was considered a privilege rather than a burden. In

71

spite of its intensely affectionate ties, the family observed strict discipline; fathers could administer corporal punishment to sons even sixty years of age, and no son dared smoke in his father's presence. Children even asked permission to sit down. Dances were begun by elders, while young people stood by and awaited their turn. Even where no family relationship existed, older people could inflict physical punishment upon young people when they saw fit.

Rancho life was a blend of abundance—principally in the things each rancho could produce for itself—and barrenness. Ordinarily, insufficient supplies of clothing, furniture, and other manufactured articles existed in California. The ranchero and his family, too, inherited a certain austerity from their Spanish ancestors. If anyone needed meat or corn, he was encouraged to ask a richer neighbor for it and it was freely given, often without mention of price or indebtedness.

Food on the rancho was plain but nourishing and plentiful, beef forming the principal dish. Wine was used in moderation. This meat and drink, as well as grain, a little fruit, and certain of the more ordinary vegetables, were all produced by the rancho. Though beef, wheat, barley, and corn were sometimes supplemented by fish and wild game, it is accurate to say that each rancho supplied the basic needs of the people who lived and worked on it.

Housing and Clothing

The houses on the ranchos and in the towns were generally square or oblong structures of adobe, as unadorned on the inside as on the outside. The fact that lumber was not used widely as a building material, in a country so rich in fine timber, is best explained by the absence of sawmills and woodworking tools. Adobe, however, offered advantages in addition to its availability; the dwellings made of it, with their thick walls and spacious rooms, were warm in winter and cool in summer. At first, homes were built on high spots, bare of surrounding tree or bushes, for defense against attacks by the Indians. As this fear receded, the rancheros planted gardens and fruit orchards around the rancho buildings. Interior furnishings, except among the richest persons, were usually confined to the most necessary articles. Those who could afford it, however, bought mahogany furniture made in South America or the Philippines and brought to California by trading ships.

The well-to-do ranchero was sometimes outfitted in elaborate gold or silver embroidered clothes. Ordinarily, ranch dress was much less costly and elaborate. As a matter of fact, fancy attire was not often seen, and fashions varied but little in a culture where clothing remained scarce. It was literally true that a man might wear his grandfather's hat or coat.

Amusements

Of the various forms of entertainment, hunting grizzly bear, elk, and other game was one of the most popular. Hunters met a grizzly on foot and in single combat, armed only with a long knife and an oxhide shield. The large California elk, extinct today, was also a dangerous animal, and when brought to bay, it required all of the skill and alertness that a man possessed.

There were also entertainments of a milder sort, especially picnics, in which entire communities joined. Young people rode their best horses, while the older ladies and the children were satisfied to climb into clumsy, creaking two-wheeled carts, or *carretas,* to jog along to some grassy picnic place behind the slow oxen with much chatter and laughter. After barbecued beef, roast chicken, turkeys, *enchiladas,* and *tamales* were disposed of, the rest of the afternoon might be spent in singing and dancing to the music of guitars.

Every event, public or private, from the birth of a child to the arrival of a new governor, was celebrated with dancing. Even in the absence of a special event, it was a rare evening when there were no guests at a ranch house to join the family, old and young, in the *fandango* or any of the numerous other dances.

MORAGA AND THE OPENING OF THE CENTRAL VALLEY

The area of California occupied by the Spaniards was generally limited to the coastal region extending from San Francisco to San Diego. Soledad was the farthest inland settlement in the province, some thirty miles from the sea. The vast interior valley lying between the Coast Range and the Sierra Nevada was explored last and never settled by the Spanish and Mexicans.

By the beginning of the nineteenth century, a few of California's most exposed settlements were occasionally threatened by warlike tribes from the interior which were bolder and more aggressive than the mission Indians. Gabriel Moraga organized military campaigns against these Indians and penetrated into the foothills of the Sierra Nevada during a number of these forays, which began in 1806.

Moraga, as a result of his pioneering leadership, is entitled to the credit for the opening of California's Central Valley. A robust ex-

73

plorer, he could be ruthless when occasion demanded, and he has been called the best soldier of his time. After his death, Moraga's forays into an unpromising interior of tule swamps and hot sands were continued by others. Later, during the Mexican period, similar parties went inland to recover stolen animals and to suppress Indian uprisings. Neither the Spanish nor the Mexican governments, however, established towns or missions in the interior. The region remained of secondary importance until the arrival of the Yankees.

THE RUSSIAN INTERLUDE

The Russians came into California not with sword in hand, threatening violence, but as uninvited traders who gradually won governmental tolerance if not an official welcome. Since the 1740s, when Vitus Bering had prepared the groundwork upon which Alexander Baranov in 1799 established the monopolistic Russian-American Fur Company in Alaska, the Russians had slowly expanded their sphere of influence. They accumulated valuable caches of furs at their trading station in Sitka. However, they were frequently on the verge of starvation in the midst of their riches; the harsh climate and barrenness of the country made agriculture virtually impossible. Cold, forlorn, and eager to purchase supplies from the Yankee sea captains, who were also seeking sea-otter and seal furs in the North Pacific, the Russians listened carefully to the Americans' report on the abundance of wheat and other cereals in California.

In 1803, the American captain Joseph O'Cain, after selling Baranov goods worth 10,000 rubles, suggested that the Russian send a company of Aleuts, natives of the Aleutian Islands, to California. With their *bidarkas* (skin canoes), they would hunt otter "on shares." Baranov agreed to this proposal with reluctance, foreseeing danger as a result of Spain's aversion to foreigners in California waters, but he had heard of the abundance of otter to the south and was anxious to secure information about Spanish California. The venture turned out to be profitable, and the Russians were eager to repeat it. This marked the beginning of the contract system by which, in partnership, Russians and Americans hunted land and sea otter on the southern coasts for a decade or more. The furs were secured partly by skilled Aleut hunters and partly by contraband trade with the Californians for goods. Notwithstanding the large number of skins they obtained in this manner, the Russians came to realize that it would have been wiser to keep the fur trade in their own hands and pay cash for such goods as they needed. The Russian-American Fur Company later sent its own hunters south toward California until they penetrated the bay of San Francisco; the Californians, who had not even a boat available to repel such operations, were suitably exasperated. Soon the Spaniards would complain that Russian hunters were infesting the coast.

Rezanov

In 1805, Nikolai Petrovich Rezanov, chamberlain of the czar, was sent out to inspect the condition of the Russian colonies in the North Pacific. At Sitka, he found the settlers reduced to eating crows and devilfish—almost anything that could be swallowed. Russian supply ships had faltered badly in caring for the needs of the colony. In this emergency, Rezanov decided to go to California in search of supplies, and on March 8, 1806, he sailed from Sitka aboard the former American ship *Juno.*

Rezanov's party was courteously received at San Francisco, but Governor Arrillaga feared that furnishing such foreigners with supplies would be considered an act of disloyalty by his government. He thus balked at doing so. A novel element was, however, injected into the negotiations between the Russians and the Spaniards. The Russian envoy suddenly fell in love with the vivacious and beautiful seventeen-year-old daughter of the *comandante* of the port. Rezanov's private correspondence with his government suggests that in wooing this girl, Concepción Argüello, diplomacy as well as romance entered into his behavior; but there is no reason to suspect that his affections were not also genuinely involved. The betrothal of the couple required the permission of the girl's parents, Governor Arrillaga, and the friars; all of them consented, and thus Rezanov was placed in a new position. As a future member of the *comandante's* family, he had no trouble in persuading the governor to furnish supplies for the starving Russian colony at Sitka.

The *Juno* was laden with wheat, barley, peas, beans, tallow, and dried meat, and on May 8, 1806, Rezanov sailed away while the Argüellos waved farewell from the fort. The understanding when Rezanov left was that immediately upon his return to St. Petersburg he would go to Madrid as an envoy from the Imperial Russian Court, in order to smooth over misunderstandings between Spain and Russia in the Pacific. Thence he would return, via New Spain, to San Francisco to claim his bride and settle those matters relative to the commerce Russia wished to promote. But the departing Russian never returned to California; after years of waiting for news of him,

Señorita Argüello, who had finally taken the vows of a religious order, learned of Rezanov's death in Siberia on his way home from California.

Fort Ross

Although the immediate objective of Rezanov's voyage was to obtain supplies to relieve the Russian food scarcity at Sitka, he hoped in time also to extend Russian power southward. The Russians held that Spain's claim to the coast above San Francisco was slight.

In 1809, an officer of the Russian-American Fur Company, Ivan Kuskov, was sent to California from Alaska to select a favorable site for a southern outpost. He landed at Bodega Bay, which he reported to be a good harbor and a fine building site, possessing tillable lands, a mild climate, and an abundance of fish and fur-bearing animals. In 1812, Kuskov returned, this time with equipment for a trading station and with a number of Aleut Indians to fish for the community. Kuskov made no pretense of consulting Spanish officials; he simply chose a strategic shoreline site, eighteen miles north of Bodega on a plateau rising seventy-five to one hundred feet above high tide. A rectangular fort, painted blue and surrounded by a strong palisade with bastions at the corners pierced for cannon, was built and mounted with ten pieces of artillery. Inside the stockade a wooden house of six or eight rooms, furnished with carpets and a piano, and boasting even glass windows, was built for the officers. In one corner of the enclosure was a chapel, which had a round dome and a belfry with chimes. Granaries, workshops, and redwood huts for the Aleuts were constructed outside the stockade, and on the beach the Russians erected a wharf, a tannery, and a bath house. The stockade and fort were practically impregnable to attacks by Indians or Spaniards.

This place was given the name Ross, a derivation from the word Russia. Because of its fortifications, it became generally known as Fort Ross. It lacked a good anchorage, and consequently the Russian ships wintered and made repairs at Bodega, where warehouses were built for the storage of goods. Attempts at raising vegetables were only moderately successful, and the Russians never did well with wheat cultivation; they were forced to rely upon the Spanish Californians for their grain.

While Kuskov was building Fort Ross, the Spanish officer Gabriel Moraga was sent to investigate Russian activity north of San Francisco. The Russians allowed the emissary to inspect the fort, and, after pointing out their deficiencies in wheat, indicated that they would like to improve trade relations with their California neighbors to the south. Moraga, on his return to San Francisco, reported to the officials of the province that the Russians seriously needed food. In January 1813, he returned with three horses, twenty head of cattle, several *fanegas* (a Spanish unit of measure) of wheat, and limited permission from Governor Arrillaga to carry on trade with Fort Ross. The Spaniards thereby courteously allowed the Russians to evade their restrictions against foreign ships in California ports.

The trade established by Moraga was continued, though with growing reluctance on the part of the California government, throughout the Russian stay on the coast. Formal permission was never given the Russians to settle in the country or to trade directly with the people of California. In fact, as soon as the viceroy at Mexico City received word from Arrillaga of the Russians' arrival, he sent instructions to the governor to notify Kuskov that his occupation of California territory was in clear violation of a treaty between Russia and Spain. Through Arrillaga the viceroy requested Kuskov to remove his settlement immediately. But the Russians knew that Governor Arrillaga's weak garrisons were in no position to enforce the viceroy's offer.

Discipline at Fort Ross was strict, and temptations few, but the Russian colonists surely preferred life there to the privations farther north. The population of the post was never large, ranging from about 100 to 400 persons, including Aleuts and their Indian wives, with whom the Russians mixed socially. With the Aleuts as hunters, the Russians pursued the sea otters so assiduously that before long these animals were cleared out of the coast between Trinidad and San Francisco Bay.

The Russian establishment at Fort Ross became a heavy financial burden. In its last four years of operation, the fort had lost 45,000 rubles for its owners. They finally withdrew from California in 1842. The news was received with great joy at Monterey. Before their departure the Russians carefully disposed of both property and equipment. In the autumn of 1841, the Russians concluded a sale with Johann Augustus Sutter, who was to play a prominent role in California's later development, that solved this problem. Although the Swiss was heavily in debt, he arranged to purchase all movable property at Fort Ross. So ended thirty years of Russian occupancy of their outpost in California.

INTERNATIONAL COMPLICATIONS

In the early nineteenth century, the United States, Great Britain, Russia, and Spain claimed overlapping portions of the coastline of

Russian Church (reconstructed) at Fort Ross. *(Beaches and Parks Division, Department of Natural Resources, State of California)*

North America. In 1818, the British and Americans agreed to joint occupation of the Oregon country, then a vast ill-defined region between Spanish Alta California and Russian Alaska. In 1819, Spain gave up its historic claims north of the 42nd parallel and thereby established the northern boundary of California. Uncertain Russian intentions in the region were alluded to in President James Monroe's annual message to Congress in 1823:

> ... instructions have been transmitted to the minister of the United States at St. Petersburg to arrange by amicable negotiations the respective rights and interests of the two nations on the northeast coast of this continent. ... In the discussions to which this interest have given rise and in the arrangements by which they may terminate, the occasion has

been judged proper for asserting, as a principle in which the rights and interests of the United States are involved, that the American continents, by the free and independent condition which they have assumed and maintain, are henceforth not to be considered as subjects for future colonization by any European powers.

This statement, along with several other declarations contained in the same message, have come to be known as the Monroe Doctrine. In 1824, the czar agreed to give up any claims below 54° 40' north latitude. The remaining Oregon country continued under joint occupation of the United States and Britain until 1846 when it was divided at the 49th parallel.

MEXICAN CALIFORNIA

After three centuries of dominance by the motherland, the Spanish colonies in the New World grew steadily more restive under what they considered to be an unjust system of economic, governmental, and social discrimination. Discontent kindled the flame of revolution, which spread from province to province in the years between 1808 and the middle 1820s. Almost to the last, Alta California, one of the most isolated of all Spain's provinces, remained loyal. This was partly because little news reached provincial California of revolutionary activities in Mexico and elsewhere in Latin America.

When news of Mexican independence reached California in 1821, it was at first received with disbelief. The various revolutions that followed within Mexico altered but little the political beliefs of Californians. They remained more aloof than most other provincials within the former Spanish empire and continued to distrust foreigners, remembering with affection the Spanish pioneers from Cabrillo to Serra who had first planted the flag of Castile on California soil.

The change of the province's status was followed by the usual aftermath of revolution—a long period of unrest. California was fortunate in having been so far from the center of the struggle and lucky also to have received independence from Spain without the bloodletting that drenched Mexico's soil for many years. Yet the province did not entirely escape the political turbulence and personal rivalries that afflicted the other Spanish colonies following their separation from the homeland. Scarcely a California governor during the Mexican period served his term unharassed by conspiratorial outbreaks against him. The bonds that connected California with Mexico were even looser than those with Spain had been, and no very violent jolts were required to break them. The distance and the difficulty of communication, feelings of resentment against Mexican power, and strong local pride all encouraged the growth of sectionalism; Californians identified themselves with California, not Mexico.

Mexico's most distant new province now found itself without adequate funds to carry on its government. The demands for money seemed endless: the pueblos had to be supervised, a *diputado* (deputy) had to be sent to Mexico City, roads had to be repaired, schools needed to be supported, troops needed to be fed, and the Indians had to be controlled. Accordingly, local crops as well as branded cattle were to be taxed as never before, and the missions were expected to share the burden. When the padres learned of the plans to tax the missions, they vigorously protested that these historic establishments, founded to care for the Indians, in fact belonged to the natives and were therefore untaxable. However, because the missions held much of the best land in the province, to exempt them would have deprived the new government of a major means of support.

INCREASED FOREIGN ACTIVITY

During the Mexican period, increasingly large numbers of foreigners arrived in California. This especially pleased the rancheros, for they were no longer dependent upon the uncertain arrival of government supply vessels. Ship captains also found the new system financially advantageous, because they could now load and unload their vessels at central collecting points, rather than at numerous secret landfalls scattered up and down the coast.

One large American firm maintained a chain of ships plying the sea lanes between Boston, California, Hawaii, and China. It carried probably a half-million hides from California to New England's shoe industry. During this period—from the middle 1820s to the outbreak of the Mexican War in 1846—California added numerous Yankee traders to its population. These traders reaped rich rewards from the marketing of their all-year stock of goods. Almost everyone, in fact, profited from their activities—except, occasionally, the Mexican customs collectors whose regulations the traders were expert at avoiding. They quickly acquired a thorough knowledge of the province, established the friendliest relations with its people, and made themselves indispensable in the exchange of the necessities and luxuries of life.

INTERPRETATION AND REINTERPRETATION

Among the writers who glorified the Hispanic heritage of California was the New Englander Charles Fletcher Lummis, whose *The Land of Poco Tiempo* (1893) and *The Spanish Pioneers* (1893) set the trend for other nostalgic books about the Spanish period in California. Lummis eccentrically wore a green corduroy suit, with a Spanish sombrero on his head and a red sash wrapped around his middle. He lived out his own interpretation of Spanish colonial life in *El Alisal*, the house which he constructed from boulders on the edge of Los Angeles' Arroyo Seco. Nearby, Lummis founded the Southwest Museum, which houses a world-famous collection of native American Indian artifacts; he also dedicated himself to the restoration of the missions and the saving of Indian-Spanish folk traditions.

Critics of the romantic interpretation of the Spanish era point out that the exaggeration and distortion of past glories and the failure to report more recent events and current frustrations, lead to a false and demeaning view of Mexican-Americans and their culture. Writing in *El Grito, A Journal of Contemporary Mexican-American Thought*, Chicano spokesman Octavio Romano in 1968 deplored historians who wrote

> about the glorious and romantic Conquistadors; about dedicated priests and colorful missions, about gracious and noble Spanish grandees, all of whom were dashing builders of empires and savers of souls. They wrote about rolling California hills, vast and colorful haciendas, guitars and señoritas, missions and galleons, and everything else that was dead in the past, if ever, indeed, it had actually lived.

Romano also complained that too many historians have "cleanly, antiseptically, amputated from the history of the Southwest" the Mexican-Americans' long struggle for economic, social, and political justice. Unfortunately, a review of most textbooks provides substantial evidence to support his accusations.

STUDY SUGGESTIONS

To understand the chapter you should know (1) the meaning and importance of key phrases and terms, (2) the contributions to California history of major personalities, and (3) the location and significance of geographic place names.

1. *Key phrases and terms*

alcalde
Aleuts
California bank note
El Alisal
El Camino Real
El Grito
Fort Ross
hide and tallow trade
Juno
land grant
Mexican independence

mission
Old Spanish Trail
plaza
pueblo
rancho
rodeo
Russian-American Fur
 Company
Secularization Law of 1883
Southwest Museum
vaqueros

2. *Major personalities*

Juan Bautista de Anza
Concepción Argüello
Alexander Baranov
Felipe de Neve
Ivan Kuskov

Charles Fletcher Lummis
Gabriel Moraga
Nikolai Rezanov
Octavio Romano

3. *Important geographic place names*

Arroyo Seco
Bodega Bay
Central Valley
Los Angeles

San Gabriel
San Jacinto Mountains
San Jose

FOR ADDITIONAL STUDY

*John W. Caughey, *California.* New York, 1953.

Charles E. Chapman, *A History of California: The Spanish Period* New York, 1921.

Richard Henry Dana, *Two Years Before the Mast.* New York, 1840.

Omer Englebert, *The Last of the Conquistadores: Junipero Serra, 1713–1784.* New York, 1956.

Paul C. Johnson, (Ed.), *The California Missions: A Pictorial History.* Menlo Park, 1964.

W. W. Robinson, *Los Angeles from the Days of the Pueblo.* San Francisco, 1959.

*Andrew F. Rolle, *California: A History,* 3rd ed., Arlington Heights, Ill., 1978.

*General history

• 4 •

THE AMERICANIZING OF CALIFORNIA

UNITED STATES SEA TRADERS AND WHALERS

In 1796, the first United States ship actually to anchor in a California port, the *Otter* of Boston, took on wood and water near Monterey. After that time, United States vessels in California waters were a frequent occurrence. During the years between 1808 and 1821, when Spain's New World colonies outside California were in rebellion, her supply ships bound for California were stopped by the revolutionists. This afforded rare commercial opportunities for American traders, who grew steadily bolder. Despite regulations against contact between foreign vessels and the Californians, a contraband business sprang up. Local officials gave only limited interference. They were powerless to prevent the trade with the "Boston ships." Furthermore, their own wants were nearly as dire as those of any other resident.

The arrival in California of increasing numbers of foreign ships roused the viceroy at Mexico City to issue stricter orders against trading with them. Since, however, he had no means of carrying out such *pronunciamentos,* the Yankee poachers continued to operate—although at peril to themselves and their ships. The American traders became an important factor in breaking down the restrictions imposed upon California by the Spanish crown, and accordingly they sometimes suffered severe consequences when caught.

Illegal trafficking, by which New England wares or Chinese luxuries were exchanged for sea otter furs, steer hides, tallow, and cow horns (to be made into buttons), continued to be most dangerous. Yet

83

the rewards were great. In the first few decades of the nineteenth century, the price of prime otter pelts at Canton, China, was from $50 to $100. As many as 18,000 skins were delivered to the China market from California in a single season. In the hands of visiting New England traders, therefore, this traffic became a significant branch of the great American China trade. Out of it grew the fortunes of many prominent New England families.

One further economic link connected New England with California. In the later Mexican period of California's history, a new approach to trade was established by Yankee whalers. These seamen stayed away from their home ports as long as four years. Battered and bruised by the gales of the North Pacific, they were grateful to find in California protected ports of call in which they could repair their ships and spirits. Fresh meat, fruit, grains, and other provisions for the long homeward voyage around the Horn were readily obtainable there. These ships carried small stocks of manufactured goods to exchange for gold and silver coins or for local products. Out of their sea chests came needles, stockings, jewelry, thread, bolts of cloth, and other comparatively luxurious commodities. On the eve of reoutfitting their vessels for New England, the whalers undercut the prices of other traders and thereby came to be especially popular among the native Californians. This trade conducted by the whalers served as the forerunner of the more systematic commerce that developed later during the hide- and tallow-trading era. At Monterey, one of their favorite retreats, these men of Nantucket and New Bedford left behind a permanent souvenir of their stay—a whalebone sidewalk— as a token of their appreciation for the shelter the town had afforded them. Whalers, furthermore, carried home glowing accounts of pastoral California, which helped popularize the province.

JEDEDIAH SMITH, FIRST OVERLAND AMERICAN

The unrest that had led to revolution in many of Spain's former colonies was in part due to discontent caused by contact with foreigners. In California such contact came first by sea but also eventually by way of the seemingly impenetrable wilderness of desert and mountains that, for all practical purposes, had once sealed the remote province off from the East. California might have remained dormant and tranquil behind this barrier for perhaps another generation had it not been for a hardy band of American fur trappers.

Jedediah Smith was a young trapper of New England parentage, who blazed a trail from the United States to southern California. Smith, at the head of a small group of fur traders, was in search of beaver and other fur-bearing animals. His southwestward trek, undertaken twenty-odd years after Lewis and Clark penetrated the American Northwest, has kindled the imagination of historians. Smith has become almost a legendary figure, a brave and adventurous Knight in Buckskin. He earned this reputation through his indomitable personal courage and capacity for withstanding the perils of the wilderness. On one occasion a ferocious grizzly bear attacked him, taking his head between its jaws and leaving an ear and part of the scalp hanging from his bleeding skull. One of Smith's men stitched up the lacerated trapper with needle and thread, and he was presently on his way again.

In the late summer of 1823, Smith undertook the first of many trips west. His route made him one of the earliest white men to cross the continental divide via South Pass, along what later became the Oregon Trail. In 1826, he led a trapping expedition of from fifteen to twenty men and fifty horses out of today's northern Utah. This departure signaled the beginning of an extensive penetration of the region between the Great Salt Lake and the Pacific shoreline, via the unexplored deserts of present-day Nevada and Arizona. Smith's party was composed of rough adventurers, capable of almost inconceivable endurance.

At the age of twenty-eight, Smith became the first white person to reach California overland, traveling through many hundred miles of wilderness and undergoing Indian attack and severe shortages of food and water. Once he entered that remote area, Smith's adversaries were no longer the blistering white heat of the desert by day and the chilling winds that blew by night. With these he knew how to cope. Quite another matter were the inquisitive Mexicans he was about to face, who were at once polite and supremely suspicious.

Guided by two runaway Indians from San Gabriel Mission, Smith's party moved across the desert area between the Colorado River and the California pueblos. On November 27, 1826, he and his remaining group of bedraggled men reached San Gabriel. (The Indians, of course, did not accompany them that far.) The astonished priests at the mission received the uncouth-looking strangers warmly. In a singular exchange for the food, wine, and lodging extended them, the trappers provided the friars with bear traps to be used to catch Indians who poached oranges from mission groves.

Jedediah Smith at Mission San Gabriel, as painted by Carl Oscar Borg.
(Automobile Club of Southern California)

When Smith sought permission to trap in California, he was jailed as a spy and freed only following a strong appeal by visiting Boston shipmasters. After his humiliating imprisonment, the trapper was allowed to return to San Gabriel. There he picked up his men, upon condition that he leave California, never to return. Via the Cajon Pass, Smith recrossed the mountain range by which he had come, then slowly moved northward along the eastern foothills of those mountains into the San Joaquin Valley. In order to trap along the Stanislaus and Kings rivers, as well as other streams, the party established camp in California's Central Valley. In the spring of 1827, Smith and two companions made the first crossing of the Sierra.

California, however, had not seen the last of Jedediah Smith. On July 13, 1827, after spending only ten days at the rendezvous with his fellow trappers, he began the trek back to rejoin the men he had left west of the Sierra. In spite of attacks by unfriendly Indians and another jail term, Smith rejoined his men and led them north, blazing a trail into Oregon, only to have all but two of his men killed in an Indian massacre. The overland movement to California pioneered by Jedediah Smith was soon joined by other American trappers.

THE PATTIES

Prominent among these "mountain men" was James Ohio Pattie, who in 1824 set out with his father, Sylvester, on a trapping expedition southwestward from the Missouri River frontier. For several years the Patties trapped for beaver along muddy and unattractive streams which no white men had even seen before. They were the first Americans to trap along the California and Arizona frontier. As they made their way throughout the uncharted Southwest, they took many furs. The expedition's prospects seemed excellent, but they were soon attacked by marauding Indians, their pack animals were stolen, and their furs were lost. When, early in 1828, the Patties reached the junction of the Gila and Colorado rivers, they built canoes and floated down the Colorado, setting traps along the banks as they went. As the party approached the Gulf of California, they abandoned their small handmade canoes and set out farther westward across Baja California. They came finally to the mission of Santa Catalina and were promptly thrown into jail, where the elder Pattie died.

When a smallpox epidemic began to rage in the upper part of the province and casualties multiplied alarmingly, the governor promised Pattie a passport for a year if he would vaccinate the people with the scarce vaccine he had brought along. The governor agreed to pay him for the service and to grant him his liberty. Pattie accepted and vaccinated some 10,000 Indians and other California residents.

Upon completion of his task, Pattie was thunderstruck when confronted with the demand that he become a Catholic before receiving the favors promised him by the governor. He refused to change his religion and early in 1830 left California by sea. Pattie was significant not only because he pioneered the Gila River route to California, but also because he left for posterity an exciting record of Western adventure, his fascinating but often unreliable *Personal Narrative.*

SUTTER'S NEW HELVETIA

Johann Sutter left Switzerland for America in 1834 to escape a debtor's prison and an angry wife. Called "a dreamer with a gifted tongue," Sutter achieved a distinctive place in California's history. He brought with him to California Hawaiian laborers, hoping to build a self-sustaining colony and fort in the Sacramento Valley. In 1839, he obtained permission from Governor Alvarado to occupy a virtually unexplored 50,000-acre tract of land near the junction of the

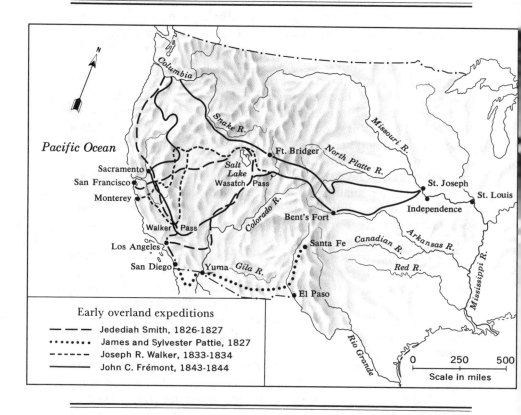

Early overland expeditions

— — — Jedediah Smith, 1826-1827
• • • • • • • James and Sylvester Pattie, 1827
- - - - - Joseph R. Walker, 1833-1834
——— John C. Frémont, 1843-1844

Sacramento and American rivers which was to become the future site of Sacramento. The governor also promised Sutter Mexican citizenship. Fearful of Indians, Sutter took two pieces of artillery with him into the wilderness. When, after eight days, the company reached their destination, they found 700 to 800 Indians awaiting them. Sutter prepared his party to resist attack, but the Indians were more curious than hostile.

Sutter began construction in 1840 of a defense outpost although the work was not completed on it until several years later. His fort, when finished, featured an adobe wall eighteen feet high by three feet thick. Sutter named his colony New Helvetia in honor of his homeland.

Once naturalized as a Mexican citizen, Sutter took steps to prevent robberies, to repress Indian hostilities, and to check illegal trapping and fishing. However, his friendliness for Americans coming into California over the Sierra passes naturally irritated California leaders. Within a short time, Sutter, in effect, established a barony at New Helvetia, consisting of Indian workers who tended thousands of sheep, cattle, horses, and hogs that roamed at will over his principality. He developed a profitable trade in beaver skins and other agricultural products and acted the role of lord of all he surveyed.

Because New Helvetia was located on the main line of overland immigration, it came to be recognized not only as a logical trade center, but also as a rendezvous for newcomers winding down the trails from the heart of the Sierra Nevada. The name of Captain Sutter became commonplace to these immigrants, to whom it stood for generosity and goodness of heart. Later, by a strange fate, the gold discovery which enriched others proved to be the undoing of Sutter. His laborers were lured away by the glamor and higher wages that were associated with gold. His land titles under American law were questioned, and finally Sutter was reduced from his former position of wealth and power to a position of bankruptcy.

BIDWELL AND THE FIRST OVERLAND MIGRANTS

In 1840, Antoine Robideaux, upon his return from a trapping expedition to California, started a campaign of publicity which aroused a fever of excitement in the little frontier town of Weston, Missouri. The trapper claimed he had found "a perfect paradise, a perpetual spring" out West. During that year almost every inhabitant of Weston and the surrounding countryside planned to migrate to California; hundreds banded together into a Western Emigration Society.

Local businessmen threw cold water upon the plan, circulating unfavorable news concerning California, and before spring, zeal for the great migration had cooled. The Western Emigration Society collapsed. One spirited member, however, a twenty-year-old school teacher named John Bidwell, was set on the idea of seeing the great West and California. Accordingly, he helped to ready a migration party though he "had barely means to buy a wagon, a gun, and provisions." By May 1, 1841, Bidwell's company was organized, consisting of forty-seven emigrants, three trappers, a group of Catholic missionaries and their wagons (eleven in all), a lone Methodist minister, and various adventurers. Fifteen women and children were in the party. Thomas Fitzpatrick ("Broken Hand"), who had trapped in the Rocky Mountains and was headed for that area again, was the only person familiar with the country to be traversed.

On May 19, 1841, the caravan, known popularly as "the first emigrant train to California," started on its dusty way from Sapling Grove, Missouri. First came the missionaries, with four carts and one wagon. Next in line of march were eight wagons drawn by horses and mules. Then came the last unit, consisting of five wagons drawn by seventeen yoke of oxen. As clerk, Bidwell kept a journal, especially valuable for its account of daily life in a wagon train. After two months on the trail, the party divided, with one group going to Oregon and the other proceeding on to California.

Staggering through the alkali flats near the Great Salt Lake, with constant mirages ahead, the travelers threw away more and more of their heaviest possessions, including furniture, washpans, butter churns, baggage, and even cumbersome wagons. Inexperienced and trail-weary, the group wandered for days through Nevada with most of their provisions gone.

After slaughtering their remaining oxen and drying the meat for the trip ahead, the group began the ascent of the high Sierra. As they traveled through deep snows, they carefully kept together. Bidwell's diary reports, of the twenty-eighth of October: "We ate the last of our beef this evening and killed a mule to finish our supper. Distance six miles." Two days later, to their great relief, the travelers "beheld a wide valley," and on the last day of the month they killed two antelope and some wild fowl. They had come to the edge of the Sacramento Valley. Their journey had taken almost six months. John Bidwell quickly found employment under Sutter at New Helvetia,

90

and, in time, he was to become closely identified with the development of California.

During the early 1840s, hundreds of Americans entered California by various overland routes; many came in small parties from Missouri and Arkansas, with Independence, Missouri, being the most usual gathering point for the caravans. By word of mouth and through newspapers, magazines, and pamphlets, an effective though uncoordinated publicity campaign developed, coaxing immigrants from all parts of the United States over the western trails by the hundreds. Frequently small parties, meeting on the plains, joined forces to travel in long trains together for weeks on end. Once in California they could count on Sutter to protect them from hostile California authorities.

THE DONNER PARTY

In the spring of 1846, James F. Reed of Springfield, Illinois, with two friends, George and Jacob Donner, formed one of many emigrant companies to depart for California that year. Their party was doomed to play a fateful, indeed tragic, role in the history of the American West. Bad luck as well as bad judgment plagued the whole enterprise although some of its participants displayed notable heroism in the midst of disaster. Included in the party were well-to-do farmers and poor families, persons of learning and ignorant folk, native Americans and Irish and German emigrants. Upon trying a "shortcut" south of Salt Lake, they met many problems and delays. Because of lack of water, they left thirty-six head of cattle on the desert. A mirage, revealing the waters of a lake, turned disappointment into anguish. Return was impossible; there was no alternative but to continue desperately onward.

The situation grew more tense after an argument that resulted when one member of the party was murdered by the husband of a woman he had accidentally struck with a bullwhip. The murderer was banished to make his way alone.

As they slowly moved toward the Sierra, the Donner leaders made another mistake. Winter was coming on fast. Instead of pressing forward, the party spent four days for a badly needed rest. Clouds high on the mountain crest gave a clear indication of approaching winter, and there was a nip in the air. The wagons could not be dragged through the early snows that fell in the Sierra that year. One wagon broke its axle and tipped over onto little Eliza Donner, three years old, and Georgia, age four; the children were almost crushed by the avalanche of household goods that fell upon them. There was further delay as the party repacked the cumbersome oxen.

Winter descended upon the Donners almost a month ahead of time in the vicinity of upper Alder Creek. The snow became so deep that the train was snowbound at an elevation of 7,150 feet. The party was forced to wait thus for the four months until early spring, inadequately sheltered by the snow-covered pines on one of the Sierra's windiest and coldest passes, since called the Donner Pass in memory of the brave party. The snow that winter eventually reached a depth of twenty-two feet. No one knows the full extent of the harrowing experiences endured during the battle against freezing and starvation. It is probable that desperate conditions caused most of the marooned pioneers who survived to eat the flesh of dead companions.

During the winter, the group made repeated efforts to get out of the mountains. They improvised snowshoes out of oxbows and strips of rawhide. In mid-December, 1846, a party known as The Fifteen left the rest. After weeks of severe suffering, dazed and stumbling about in the snow, seven survivors emerged from the Sierra via Emigrant Gap onto a California rancho. On February 19, 1847, the emigrants back up on the Sierra crest were startled by shouts. The strongest of them, climbing to the top of a huge snow bank, witnessed the "most welcome sight of their lives"—a reconnaissance party of seven men, which had been provisioned by Sutter, composed of some of the formerly snowed-in survivors. Each man bore a pack of provisions. Even the murderer who had been banished earlier from the party arrived with a second relief party to save some of the very men who had cast him out. He was overjoyed to find his wife and four children still alive, despite their privations. A third rescue group also appeared to offer help to the emigrants. George Donner, however, leader of the train, was now too weak and sick to travel. His wife, though able to make the journey, refused to leave her husband, allowing her little daughters to be taken from her to safety. When the fourth and last relief party arrived in the spring, they found that Mrs. Donner too had died. Forty-five out of the seventy-nine persons in the Donner party had survived.

MANIFEST DESTINY

American sentiment for the acquisition of California had deep roots. Even before the appearance of the first trappers, traders, and homeseekers in the western province, the United States had expressed

The Sierra Country—Twin Lakes near Bridgeport, California.
(Union Pacific Railroad)

official interest in purchasing it. In 1829, President Andrew Jackson had sent an envoy into Mexico to attempt to buy extensive territory in the American Southwest. One United States diplomat pointed out the particular advantages of possessing San Francisco Bay, calling it "capacious enough to receive the navies of all the world." He contended: "It will be worth a war of twenty years to prevent England from acquiring it."

In 1842, the Stars and Stripes had momentarily supplanted the Mexican eagle in California; Commodore Thomas Ap Catesby Jones had, under the mistaken impression that war between the United States and Mexico had been declared, made a hurried run from Peruvian waters to raise the flag of the United States prematurely at Monterey. Convinced of his great error within only a few hours, Jones restored the Mexican flag and the difficulty was composed, for the moment, in a friendly manner. This was a great embarrassment to Jones, to the navy, and to the United States government. Although Secretary of State Daniel Webster tendered the Mexican government a formal apology, the episode revealed that the United States did not intend to be caught unprepared in any race between the great powers to acquire California. California officials were understandably antagonized and remained on their guard against future American designs.

President Polk was elected in 1844 on a platform favoring the annexation of Texas and settlement of the Oregon boundary with England. Also implicit in the platform was strong interest in California. Polk sent Thomas O. Larkin to Monterey to report in detail on conditions there and to prepare the groundwork for peaceful American penetration. Even before Americans in large numbers settled in California, it had been clear that the province could not long remain under Mexican rule. Mexico was too weak administratively to cope with the foreign challenge.

Polk first hoped to attempt the purchase of California. If he should fail, there were three other possibilities: (1) a revolt instigated by leading Californians against Mexico which would be aided by American residents who could be expected to seek admission into the Union; (2) patient delay while the province was occupied by more Americans who would inevitably seek their independence; and (3) forcible seizure in a war with Mexico. Polk's undeniably aggressive policy involved the appointment of John Slidell as his representative in Mexico, partly to explore the possibility of purchasing or annexing Texas and obtaining California and New Mexico. United States failure in negotiations for the southwestern territories was due

John C. Frémont, about 1850.
*(C. C. Pierce collection, courtesy
of the Huntington Library)*

as much to disturbed internal Mexican political conditions as to Mexico's unwillingness to sell, although the Mexicans did regard the very suggestion of giving up these territories to Yankees as insulting. After the American annexation of Texas in 1845, Mexican-American relations went from bad to worse. Mexico resented this "seizure" of one of its provinces although, since 1836, the Texans had proclaimed themselves independent. As a result of this annexation, the United States got involved in a dispute over the boundary between Texas and Mexico. By 1846, two hostile armies faced each other in the contested area.

JOHN C. FRÉMONT

By 1842, the days of the mountain men had begun to wane. As many independent trappers settled down to a life of trading, an era of exploration by government survey parties began. The year 1843–1844 saw the arrival in California of John C. Frémont, naturalist-explorer-scientist, on his second expedition to the Far West.

With Kit Carson as his guide, late in 1843 Frémont moved boldly through northwestern Nevada, continuing to the Truckee and Carson rivers. He originally had no plans to cross the Sierra Nevada into California, but on reaching the mountains rashly decided to take his weary men over them. While ascending the eastern slope of the Sierra, on January 28, 1844, he found it necessary to discard a twelve-pound brass cannon which his party, supposedly a scientific venture, had lugged along.

After an icy crossing of the Sierra, Frémont rested for several weeks at Sutter's New Helvetia, then moved southward along the San Joaquin Valley to the Kings River. He next crossed Tehachapi Pass toward the Great Salt Lake and returned to Saint Louis. Although Frémont's entry into California was almost accidental, it was important for later events: by mapping, surveying, and charting the trails of the trappers, he publicized their routes and thus helped to attract more overland travelers to the West.

Frémont, well aware that war with Mexico over the annexation of Texas and other territorial conflicts in the Southwest was possible, left Saint Louis in May 1845, with his third western expedition. Its professed purpose, further exploration of the Great Basin and of the Pacific Coast, was not likely to relieve the tension between the two countries. Frémont again crossed the Sierra to Sutter's Fort, reaching California in December 1845. This time he traveled as far south as Monterey, where he held a conference with Consul Larkin. José Castro, who commanded the garrison at the capital city, was suspicious of the motives which had brought Frémont there. Frémont explained that his expedition was purely scientific and peaceful and that he had come to Monterey only to purchase needed supplies.

Accepting this explanation, Castro reluctantly granted him permission to spend the winter in California. As Frémont's party was marching out of California the following spring, it was overtaken by a messenger with instructions from the United States government. The precise content of these orders is not clear, but their effect was to turn Frémont back into California. His decision to return to the Sacramento Valley, an act which he later declared to have been "the first step in the conquest of California," transformed him from an explorer into a soldier. American settlers, disturbed and excited by rumors of approaching war between the United States and Mexico, flocked to his camp north of Sutter's Fort. As their fears mounted, these men organized what became known as the Bear Flag Revolt. Although Frémont was not their official leader at this time, his refusal to interfere with their activities encouraged them.

THE BEAR FLAG REVOLT

Early in June 1846, several Mexican officials were driving a band of horses from Sonoma to the Santa Clara Valley by way of Sutter's Fort. A group of adventurous though unruly Americans stole the horses and took them to Frémont's camp. A few days later the Americans, led by William B. Ide, captured General Vallejo's headquarters in northern California, Sonoma. This event, occurring before news of the loss of the horses had reached Vallejo, was surprising because he was known to be a strong supporter of Americans in California. In fact, Larkin had counted upon Vallejo's prestige to help in smoothing the possible annexation of California to the United States. At dawn on June 14, several Americans burst into Vallejo's home and routed the general from his bed, forcing the embarrassed Vallejo to surrender and placing him under arrest.

As a result of his boldness at Sonoma, Ide emerged as the leader of the American revolt. His followers had already provided themselves a flag with which to dignify their movement. They would have liked to use the American Stars and Stripes, but Frémont would not authorize them to do so. Therefore, Ide and his men had improvised a red and white flag, on which a grizzly bear faced a red star. They selected the bear because the grizzly was the strongest animal in California. The flag bore the following statement, "A bear stands his ground always, and as long as the stars shine we stand for the cause." On the day they captured Sonoma, the Bear Flaggers raised their standard over the plaza. They spoke of themselves thereafter as representatives of the California Republic, and made Sonoma their headquarters. Ide issued a proclamation establishing the goals of the republic. On June 24, they engaged in a relatively bloodless skirmish with the Californians between the pueblos of San Rafael and Sonoma. Neither they nor the Californians whom they fought had yet heard that an official state of war existed between Mexico and the United States.

To what lengths this revolution might have gone will, however, never be known. The Bear Flag movement came to a sudden halt when Ide's men heard of the capture of Monterey on July 7, 1846, by the naval forces of Commodore John Sloat. As commander of United States naval forces in Pacific waters, Sloat had been instructed to seize Monterey in the event of war with Mexico. He had heard of the outbreak of war early in June while anchored at Mazatlán on the west coast of Mexico and had quietly slipped out of that harbor and proceeded to California.

97

Provincial pride and historical romanticism have created the legend that the Bear Flag Revolt produced an independent California, which then became a part of the United States. Actually, the Bear Flag uprising was of limited importance in the acquisition of California. It reflected the attitude of only a few disgruntled settlers and it accomplished little. The conquest of California would have occurred without it.

THE MEXICAN WAR IN CALIFORNIA

Sloat's men had marched into Monterey without any opposition. They raised the American flag over the customs house, fired a twenty-one gun salute, and Sloat read a proclamation. It referred to the state of war between the two nations but announced:

> "I declare to the inhabitants of California that, although I come in arms with a powerful force, I do not come among them as an enemy of California; on the contrary, I come as their best friend, as henceforward California will be a portion of the United States and its peaceful inhabitants will enjoy the same rights and privileges as the citizens of any portion of that territory. . . ."

On July 15, 1846, Commodore Robert Stockton arrived at Monterey to replace Sloat and immediately announced his plans to take vigorous action "against those boasting and abusive chiefs" of the interior and southern districts. The Bear Flaggers, now taking orders from Frémont, offered to help Stockton. Frémont was promoted to the rank of major, and he joined Stockton in a spectacular capture of most of California. "We simply marched all over California, from Sonoma to San Diego," wrote John Bidwell afterward, "and raised the American flag without protest. We tried to find an enemy, but could not." This early success was possible because the Californians had no army worthy of the name.

Revolt at Los Angeles

On the afternoon of August 13, 1846, American forces entered Los Angeles and raised their flag without opposition. Stockton issued several more proclamations and concluded what may be called the conquest of California. A captain, Archibald H. Gillespie, was left in command of Los Angeles with a garrison of only fifty men.

Resentment at Gillespie's arbitrary actions and his threats of punishment stirred up the Angelenos. On September 23, Gillespie's small garrison was attacked and surrounded by several hundred an-

98

gry citizens. Besieged and short of water, Gillespie was in a perilous situation. Under cover of darkness, he sent a courier on the long journey northward for aid from Commodore Stockton. The daring ride of Juan Flaco has become almost legendary. "Lean John," the Paul Revere of California history, covered the more than 500 miles between Los Angeles and San Francisco in about four and one-half days. The dispatch he carried was written on cigarette papers and concealed in his long hair. He was pursued for miles by unfriendly California horsemen, but kept riding. Despite lack of sleep and difficulty in securing fresh horses, he finally delivered Gillespie's message of distress to Commodore Stockton.

Gillespie had been allowed to retreat with his men under a flag of truce to San Pedro, with the provision that the Americans would depart by sea when they reached that port. Gillespie, however, promptly set aside the hasty agreement with the Californians when he saw the 350 men Stockton had sent to rescue him.

There followed an engagement, known as the Battle of the Old Woman's Gun. In this conflict the Californians fought under the command of José Antonio Carrillo. They were mounted on horses

Commodore Robert Stockton.
*(Title Insurance and Trust
Company, Los Angeles)*

and armed with sharp willow lances and smoothbore carbines; their most damaging weapon, however, was a four-pound cannon, an antique firearm that had been hidden by an old woman during the first American assault of Los Angeles. The Californians used the cannon so effectively that the Americans were forced to retreat to their ships, having suffered five killed and a number wounded.

With this success, anti-American opposition spread, and for a brief time the territory from Santa Barbara to San Diego was again in the hands of the Californians. A skirmish took place on November 14, 1846, in the Salinas Valley—the only actual engagement fought by American forces north of Los Angeles during this phase of the hostilities. Known as the Battle of Natividad, this conflict resulted in four Americans killed and as many more wounded, the Californians sustaining a similar loss.

Stockton proceeded south to occupy San Diego and began planning an attack on the "horse-covered" hills toward the north. Suddenly an important message arrived which changed not only his plans, but also the entire course of events in California. This was a desperate dispatch from General Stephen W. Kearny. In June 1846, the War Department had ordered Kearny, a veteran of the War of 1812 and an experienced army officer, to proceed overland with an "Army of the West" from Fort Leavenworth, Kansas. He was to seize Sante Fe in the province of New Mexico, then to move toward California.

En route, General Kearny met the celebrated scout Kit Carson, who was taking official dispatches from Stockton to President Polk. Carson had left before the renewed fighting in southern California broke out, and hence did not know of it. He told Kearny that the American flag was flying from every important position in California, that the war had ended, and that Mexican control of that province was over. Kearny therefore decided to send a large share of his force back to Santa Fe while he continued on toward California with about 200 men and two small cannon.

The Battle of San Pascual

On December 5, 1846, northeast of San Diego, General Kearny ran into an unexpected hornet's nest of opposition. More than 150 armed Californians, under Andrés Pico, were encamped at the Indian village of San Pascual (near present-day Escondido). Kearny rashly ordered an attack before dawn in a cold rain. At first the Californians

100

seemed to retreat from the field. Suddenly, however, they wheeled about and charged Kearny's scattered, water-soaked forces with muskets and long, sharp willow lances. The Americans, their carbine ammunition wet, tried to beat off the onslaught by hand-to-hand combat, but they were at a marked disadvantage in the melee. Eighteen Americans lay dead in the mud before Kearny's rear guard could bring up howitzers to repel the attackers. Nineteen other soldiers were wounded and one was missing. Most of the fatalities resulted from lance thrusts rather than from gun wounds. The total number of Americans who ultimately died was twenty-two. General Kearny himself was wounded. The Californians suffered only minor injuries.

Kearny composed a message to Stockton urgently pleading for help; he described how the battle had been fought with valor against

Kit Carson, 1867. (*Title Insurance and Trust Company, Los Angeles*)

101

heavy odds, how his cumbersome, tired, and bony mules were no match for the quick California ponies, and how his short sabers offered practically no defense against the long lances of his mounted opponents. After receiving reinforcements, Kearny resumed his march, reaching San Diego on December 12, 1846. The Battle of San Pascual, despite the relatively small number of casualties it involved, had taken its place in history as the largest armed conflict ever to occur within the boundaries of California.

The Reconquest of Los Angeles and War's End

Shortly after arriving in San Diego, Kearny let it be known that the army was taking over, but Stockton understandably declined to give up full command of his land forces and his position as military governor. In spite of their quarrels, the two combined their resources into a force numbering about 600 men and left San Diego on December 29 to attack Los Angeles. Frémont, now a lieutenant colonel, was also about to approach Los Angeles from the north. He moved southward from Monterey with 400 men and, after a week's delay to obtain supplies at Santa Barbara, entered the San Fernando Valley near Los Angeles on January 11, 1847.

In their march on Los Angeles from the south, Kearny and Stockton met no real opposition until they reached the banks of the San Gabriel River. Near the present town of Montebello, they encamped on January 7. Two days later, the forces under Kearny and Stockton fought the final conflict of the war in California. Known as the Battle of La Mesa, this was of slight importance as a military contest, but it did permit the actual reoccupation of Los Angeles. This was, in effect, the end of resistance to the invading Americans, whose army and navy had triumphed together. On January 10, 1847, American troops entered the City of the Angels and marched to its plaza, where Gillespie hoisted the flag he had been compelled to haul down the previous September.

It was, however, Frémont, arriving on the scene from the north, who received the surrender of the last armed forces in California. Andrés Pico may have feared that Kearny and Stockton would place him before a firing squad; apparently he preferred to surrender to Frémont and did so on January 13, 1847, in the outskirts of Los Angeles. Frémont, fully confident as to his own authority to conduct official negotiations, now entered into a truce with Andrés Pico and

102

Los Angeles, 1857 (contemporary print).
(Courtesy of the Huntington Library)

other local leaders. The peace treaty he concluded with them, known as the Cahuenga Capitulation, was in fact a generous document.

The war between the United States and Mexico formally came to an end with the signing of the Treaty of Guadalupe Hidalgo on February 2, 1848. A new southwestern boundary now gave the United States all of Upper California as well as New Mexico and Texas.

GOLD

James Wilson Marshall's discovery of gold on January 24, 1848, was one of those major events that influenced United States history as well as California's. This was not the first discovery of California gold. Minor finds had been made long before 1848, principally by mission Indians who brought the metal to the padres; but the friars reputedly cautioned the natives not to divulge the location of the gold, lest the province be inundated by money-mad foreigners. One of these ear-lier discoveries was made by Francisco Lopez, a ranchero, in 1842. Lopez had been searching for some stray horses in a canyon near modern-day Newhall in southern California. Stopping to rest, he dug up some wild onions to eat and noticed some bright flakes and nug-gets clinging to their roots. Excitedly, he uprooted more of the plants. The quantity of gold was small, however, and the discovery attracted little attention.

Marshall's discovery focused the attention of the entire world on a new El Dorado. Equipped with a modest education, a flintlock rifle, and his father's trade as a coach and wagon builder, Marshall had come to California from his native New Jersey by emigrant train in 1844. First he had gone to work for Sutter, subsequently buying two leagues of land nearby on Little Butte Creek where he built and repaired spinning wheels, plows, ox yokes, and carts—in short, he was self-employed as a general utility man around Sutter's Fort. In 1846, he joined the Bear Flag group and then enlisted in Frémont's California Battalion, continuing in military service until after the American conquest. Marshall then returned to Sutter's Fort, "bare-footed and in a very sorry plight," to find that nearly all his livestock had strayed from his ranch or had been stolen. Like many another California combatant, Marshall had received no pay for his volunteer war services. He was glad to find employment again with Sutter.

Sutter sent him to search for good accessible timber and a suit-able location for a mill. The site chosen was on the south fork of the American River some forty-five miles northeast of Sutter's Fort. It was here that Marshall accidently detected particles of shining metal along the mill race.

Sutter, at first incredulous about the flakes and grains of gold, many the size of wheat grains, tried to keep the find secret. It would have been better for him if he could have done so. After the discov-ery of gold on his property, the baron of the Sacramento River began to undergo a whole series of misfortunes. His diary tells how in early March a party of Mormons working for him "left for washing and digging Gold and very soon all followed, and left me only sick and lame behind." He complains that many other workmen thereafter left his service, hurting every branch of his interconnected business operations. Even the Indians, wrote Sutter, were "impatient to run" to the gold streams, and he was compelled to leave a year's wheat crop ungathered in the fields around New Helvetia. Moreover, he had spent large sums on the Coloma sawmill and on a flour mill at Brighton, which he could find no one to operate.

The Gold Rush

Marshall's and Sutter's secret proved too great to keep. Not long after the discovery, Sam Brannan galloped down from Sutter's Fort to San Francisco with dust and nuggets from the new gold fields. As he rode along its streets, he shouted "Gold! Gold! Gold from the American River!" swinging his hat wildly with one hand and in the other waving a medicine bottle full of bright dust. Soon a stampede started as people, singly and in bands, deserted their homes for the icy streams of the Sierra in quest of riches.

Labor costs in towns near the coast rose rapidly. Almost all business, except the most urgent, stopped. Seamen deserted ships in San Francisco Bay, soldiers departed from barracks, and servants left their masters, forfeiting accumulated wages in a frenzy of excitement. Threats, punishment, and money were equally powerless to stem this human tide. Forgetting to collect debts or to pay their bills, gold seekers rode, walked, and even hobbled on crutches toward the Sierra. Amidst the hysteria, San Francisco's early newspaper, the *Californian,* suspended publication on May 29, 1848, announcing:

> The majority of our subscribers and many of our advertisers have closed their doors and places of business and left town. . . . The whole country, from San Francisco to Los Angeles and from the seashore to the base of the Sierra Nevada, resounds with the sordid cry of 'gold! Gold!! GOLD!!!' while the field is left half planted, the house half built, and everything neglected but the manufacture of shovels and pickaxes. . . .

Thomas O. Larkin bitterly lamented the depopulation of his beloved Monterey, where buildings fell into disrepair and stores closed. He wrote of the local scarcity of supplies: "Every bowl, tray, and warming pan has gone to the mines. Everything in short that has a scoop in it and will hold sand and water." "The gold mines," wrote Walter Colton, "have upset all social and domestic arrangements in Monterey; the master has become his own servant, and the servant his own lord. The millionaire is obliged to groom his own horse, and roll his wheelbarrow."

Within a few months, news of California gold had found its way to every part of the globe. Exaggeration of the riches was so prevalent that one writer remarked: "A grain of gold taken from the mine became a pennyweight at Panama, an ounce in New York and Boston, and a pound nugget at London." Marshall's discovery occurred almost at the moment of the signing of the Treaty of Guadalupe

Hidalgo between the United States and Mexico. By May 1848, gold had been found at distances of thirty miles surrounding Sutter's Mill. By the first of June, 2,000 men were already digging for gold, and in another month that number doubled. Before the end of the year, California's gold yield had reached $10 million. The gold hunters of 1848, however, constituted but the vanguard of a human avalanche soon to descend upon California.

After President Polk mentioned the discovery of gold in his presidential message of December 5, 1848, even wider publicity was given the event. At the beginning of 1849, there were, exclusive of Indians, only some 26,000 persons in California. Before midsummer, the number had reached 50,000. By the end of the year, it was probably 115,000, notwithstanding the official but inaccurate census report of 92,597 for the year 1850. Possibly four-fifths of the population were Americans and most were men. San Francisco became the most rapidly growing city in the world. From only 812 persons in March 1848, it came to contain upward of 5,000 by early summer of 1849, and by 1850 it was a boom town of 25,000 people. Those who flocked to California in search of gold became known as the forty-niners, and to this day tales of them live on in American folklore and music.

The Argonauts or Gold Seekers

Some immigrants moved into California southward from Oregon; others made their way northwest over the Sonora Trail from Mexico; numbers of them came via Hawaii. The overwhelming majority of Americans who reached California during those hectic days, however, selected one or another of three main routes—around the Horn, by way of the Isthmus, and across the plains.

The route around Cape Horn to San Francisco required six to nine months of travel. The actual passage through or around Cape Horn was particularly disagreeable and hazardous. It might take a vessel many days to break through the choppy Strait of Magellan, which was usually enveloped by strong currents and dense fogs. Yet thousands made it to California in this way, via what became known as the "white-collar route" because lack of exercise softened up most passengers after they had spent several seasick weeks on shipboard.

Even more Americans reached California via the Isthmus of Panama during the late forties and early fifties. Under favorable conditions, the Isthmus route was the shortest and quickest way to California. The voyage from New York to the Panama Coast was

106

Miner panning for gold in the Colorado River, about 1890.
(C. C. Pierce collection, courtesy of the Huntington Library)

2,500 miles, and the trip across the Isthmus 60 miles more; from Panama to San Francisco, it was 3,500 miles. Travel conditions were seldom favorable; passengers were crowded into vessels like sardines.

Fully as dangerous as the occasional shipboard epidemics was the necessity of crossing the Isthmus of Panama. Malarial fever and other tropical diseases were common. Especially at the beginning of the rush, the gold seeker faced a long and sweaty delay before a ship to California might appear. Then came the hazardous journey to San Francisco.

The covered wagon, or prairie schooner, symbolizes the vast population movement during the Gold Rush as much as does the clipper ship or steamer. Fortunately the principal routes across the Great Plains were marked out before the rush. With luck, the 2,000 miles to the gold fields over these routes could be covered in 100 days. Many circumstances, however, could cause delay. Rivers had to be forded, food supplies conserved, and trains guarded against Indian attack. Not infrequently, wagons had to be unloaded and reloaded several times in a single day due to the difficulty of crossing rough terrain or streams. The larger overland companies had to subdivide when more grass was required for the livestock than could be found in any one place. A few of the miners, for example, the William Lewis Manly party, had the misfortune of trying to go through Death Valley. Their horrible experiences led to the name for this hot, dry desert just east of the Sierras.

Boom or Bust

Once the gold seekers reached California, they were confronted with a new set of problems. Mining was hard work, and living conditions were rugged. Most "claims" were along stream beds where thousands of persons, using every imaginable tool and method, tried to strike "pay dirt." There was little sinking of shafts until later years.

At first, miners had little experience or knowledge that would help them find gold. Of all the instruments for washing gold ore, the pan was the simplest. Other miners utilized the washing rocker or "cradle"; this was essentially a machine that extracted loose particles of gold from gravel by a washing operation. The relatively heavier gold sand remained in the bottom of whatever vessel was being used. Lighter gravel was washed away by the action of the water.

The lonely prospector, equipped with gold pan, with canvas-covered supplies loaded haphazardly on the back of his surefooted

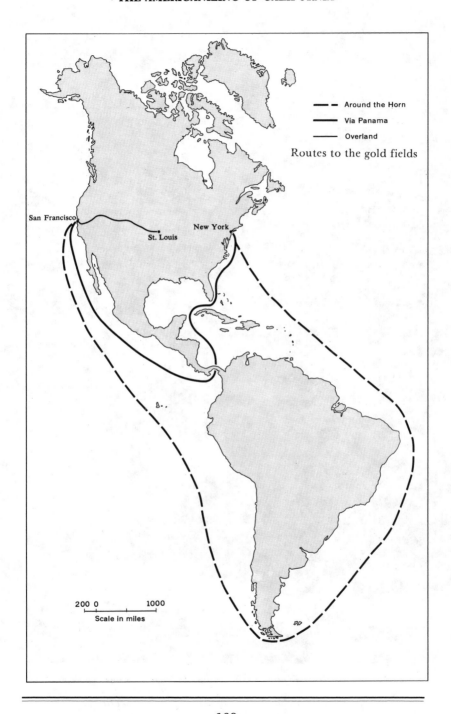

Around the Horn
Via Panama
Overland

Routes to the gold fields

San Francisco
St. Louis
New York

200 0   1000
Scale in miles

Floor of Death Valley. *(From Dr. Rolle's collection)*

mule, became the symbol of the Gold Rush era and of the thousands who moved from place to place in search of the precious metal. The remarkable vein which the miners worked was known as the Mother Lode.

A number of picturesque place names came to be applied to the towns that mushroomed in the mining regions. These included Git-Up-and-Git, Lazy Man's Canyon, Skunk Gulch, Gospel Swamp, Shinbone Peak, Humpback Slide, Bogus Thunder, Poker Flat, Ground Hog Glory, and Delirium Tremens. Placerville was first named Hangtown because of an 1849 hanging there by lynch law.

Despite the generally rowdy environment, genuine fellowship and hospitality were found in the tents and dugouts of the miners. On Sunday, observed by most gold seekers as a day of rest, the men did their week's washing, baking, or mending, and, remembering wives and children back home, wrote letters. Sunday afternoons and evenings were enlivened by horse racing, yarn swapping, or gambling.

As they churned up the ground, looking for nuggets, the majority of gold seekers averaged earnings of about $100 per month. Gold was selling for $16 per ounce. One lucky fellow scooped up two and a half pounds in fifteen minutes. This was a notable exception, however, and many miners quickly used up their savings, instead of being able to show a profit for their efforts.

Prices charged for luxuries and even essential supplies were fantastic, especially in an age when money in the eastern United States had several times the purchasing power of today. Copies of eastern newspapers were grabbed up at $1 apiece. A loaf of bread, which cost 4 or 5 cents on the Atlantic seaboard, sold for 50 or 75 cents at San Francisco. Apples sold for $1 to $5, eggs for $50 a dozen (one boiled egg in a restaurant cost as much as $5), and coffee $5 a pound. Sacramento merchants sold butcher knives for $30 each, blankets for $40, boots for $100 a pair, and tacks to nail flapping canvas tents for as much as $192 a pound. Medicine cost $10 a pill or $1 a drop, and certain hotel accommodations $1,000 per month.

After much of the loose ore had been panned out of California's stream beds in the late 1840s, relatively pure gold became more and more difficult to discover. The days of pick, shovel, pan, and burro were over. Along with the numerous technological changes in California mining, there occurred a decline in gold productivity. By 1854, the "easy pickings" of placer mining had practically disappeared and miners looked elsewhere for new diggings.

111

GOOD NEWS

FOR

MINERS.

NEW GOODS,

PROVISIONS, TOOLS,

CLOTHING, &c. &c.

GREAT BARGAINS!

JUST RECEIVED BY THE SUBSCRIBERS, AT THE LARGE TENT ON THE HILL,

A superior Lot of New, Valuable and most DESIRABLE GOODS for Miners and for residents also. Among them are the following:

STAPLE PROVISIONS AND STORES.

Pork, Flour, Bread, Beef, Hams, Mackerel, Sugar, Molasses, Coffee, Teas, Butter & Cheese, Pickles, Beans, Peas, Rice, Chocolate, Spices, Salt, Soap, Vinegar, &c.

EXTRA PROVISIONS AND STORES.

Every variety of Preserved Meats and Vegetables and Fruits, [more than eighty different kinds] Tongues and Sounds; Smoked Halibut; Dry Cod Fish; Eggs fresh and fine; Figs, Raisins, Almonds and Nuts; China Preserves; China Bread and Cakes; Butter Crackers, Boston Crackers, and many other very desirable and *choice bits.*

DESIRABLE GOODS FOR COMFORT, AND HEALTH.

Patent Cot Bedsteads, Mattresses and Pillows, Blankets and Comforters. Also, in Clothing—Overcoats, Jackets, Miner's heavy Velvet Coats and Pantaloons, Woolen Pants, Guernsey Frocks, Flannel Shirts and Drawers, Stockings and Socks, Boots, Shoes; Rubber Waders, Coats, Blankets, &c.

MINING TOOLS, &c.; BUILDING MATERIALS, &c.

Cradles, Shovels, Spades, Hoes, Picks, Axes, Hatchets, Hammers; every variety of Workman's Tools, Nails, Screws, Brads, &c.

SUPERIOR GOLD SCALES.   MEDICINE CHESTS, &c.

Superior Medicine Chests, well assorted, together with the principal Important Medicines for Dysentery, Fever and Fever and Ague, Scurvy, &c.

N.B.—Important Express Arrangement for Miners.

The Subscribers will run an EXPRESS to and from every Steamer, carrying and returning Letters for the Post Office and Expresses to the States. Also, conveying "GOLD DUST" or Parcels, to and from the Mines to the Banking Houses, or the several Expresses for the States, insuring their safety.——The various NEWSPAPERS from the Eastern, Western and Southern States, will also be found on sale at our stores, together with a large stock of BOOKS and PAMPHLETS constantly on hand.

Excelsior Tent, Mormon Island, | **WARREN & CO.**
January 1, 1850. | ALTA CALIFORNIA PRESS

Broadside advertisement of the Mormon Island Emporium, in the California mines, 1848–1849. *(Courtesy of the Huntington Library)*

Once the gold bonanza drew to a close, prices declined rapidly. Merchants found it difficult to sell the expensive "Long Nine" Havana cigars that had once commanded high prices. Shopkeepers threw sacks of spoiled flour into the streets of Sacramento and San Francisco to help fill muddy holes; unsalable cast-iron cookstoves were dismantled and used as sidewalks. Discouraged miners, returning empty-handed from the diggings, left ghost towns behind them as they flocked back into the cities, anxious to find any sort of work. Others moved into the countryside. Some wisely bought farm lands after the rush and lived to amass the fortunes they had not found in the placers.

STUDY SUGGESTIONS

To understand the chapter you should know (1) the meaning and importance of key phrases and terms, (2) the contributions to California history of major personalities, and (3) the location and significance of geographic place names.

1. *Key terms and phrases*

argonauts
"around the Horn"
Battle of the Old Woman's
   Gun
Battle of San Pascual
Bear Flag Revolt
Boston ships
Cahuenga Capitulation
China trade
consul

the Donner party
forty-niners
mountain men
placer miners
pronunciomentos
sea otters
Sutter's Fort
Treaty of Guadalupe Hidalgo
Yankee whalers

2. *Major personalities*

John Bidwell
Kit Carson
Juan Flaco
John C. Frémont
Archibald H. Gillespie
William B. Ide

Commodore Thomas Ap
   Catesby Jones
General Stephen Kearny
Thomas O. Larkin
James Marshall
James Ohio Pattie

113

James K. Polk	Commodore Robert Stockton
John Slidell	Johann Sutter
Commodore John Sloat	General Mariano Vallejo
Jedediah Smith	

3. *Important geographic place names*

American River	Placerville
Cajon Pass	Sacramento River
Death Valley	San Fernando Valley
Donner Pass	San Gabriel River
Escondido	San Joaquin Valley
Isthmus of Panama	San Pedro
Kings River	Sonoma
Mazatlán	Strait of Magellan
the Mother Lode	Tehachapi Pass
New Helvetia	

FOR ADDITIONAL STUDY

John W. Caughey, *Gold Is the Cornerstone* (Berkeley, 1948).
Robert G. Cleland, *A History of California: The American Period* (New York, 1922).
——, *This Reckless Breed of Men* (New York, 1950).
Richard Henry Dana, *Two Years Before the Mast* (New York, 1840).
Bernard de Voto, *Across the Wide Missouri* (Cambridge, Mass., 1947).
——, *Year of Decision, 1846* (Boston, 1943).
John A. Hawgood, *America's Western Frontiers* (New York, 1967).
Oscar Lewis, *Sea Routes to the Gold Fields* (New York, 1949).
Ralph Moody, *The Old Trails West* (New York, 1963).
Allan Nevins, *Frémont, Pathmarker of the West* (New York, 1939).
Glenn W. Price, *The Origins of the War with Mexico* (Austin, 1967).
George R. Stewart, *Ordeal by Hunger: The Story of the Donner Party* (New York, 1960).
Irving Stone, *Immortal Wife* (New York, 1948).

•5•

STATEHOOD AND BEYOND

MILITARY GOVERNMENT

After the short-lived Bear Flag Republic ceased to exist, Commodore Stockton had on August 17, 1846, declared a state of martial law. During the Mexican War, therefore, California was treated as conquered territory, subject to military rule. Under international law such territory ordinarily retains its prior municipal institutions while the conqueror issues temporary laws and regulations. This was the case in California, where military rule and the civil administration of justice were combined to provide government for the province. The military commanders in California were cautious about handling civilian activities. Those sent to the region had been instructed to accommodate civilian desires, and they had all allowed a wide degree of local autonomy. Californians were living politically almost as much in a civilian environment as in a military one.

General Bennett Riley, California's last military governor, was a mature, amicable leader, who knew both how to obey orders and how to deal with an upset population. Although he originally had no intention of supporting local agitation for a civil government, he changed his mind after learning that Congress had once more adjourned without having provided for statehood. On June 3, 1849, Riley issued a proclamation that called for the selection of delegates to a general convention. Held at Monterey beginning on September 1, 1849, this gathering would form a state constitution and plan a territorial government.

North Beach, San Francisco, about 1860 (*H.G. Hills Collection, by courtesy of the Bancroft Library, University of California, Berkeley*)

THE CONSTITUTIONAL
CONVENTION OF 1849

The convention met on September 3, 1849, in Colton Hall, a newly constructed white building overlooking the town of Monterey and the Pacific Ocean. Forty-eight earnest delegates, the majority of American birth, were sworn in as members of the convention. The huge and angular Dr. Robert Semple of Sonoma, who had come to California as a covered-wagon pioneer, was elected president of the gathering. While none of the delegates were nationally known, they proved to be competent and devoted. The document they wrote was not the sudden creation of untutored gold hunters. It was the work of men with a purpose, men who had profited from their residence in California and who were interested in the future of the territory.

Nevertheless, the framing of this constitution was confronted with difficulties. Native Californians, earlier American settlers, and forty-niners reflected such different backgrounds that it seemed almost impossible to bring them to full agreement. They were unac-

116

Colton Hall, Monterey.
Scene of the 1849 Consti-
tutional Convention.
(From Dr. Gaines' collection)

General Bennett Riley, last
military governor of California.
(California State Library)

Robert Semple, Chairman of
the 1849 Constitutional
Convention.
(California State Library)

quainted with each other and without preconceived plans or policies.
The average age of the delegates was thirty-six; the oldest, José Antonio Carrillo, was fifty-three.

The native Californians numbered seven out of the forty-eight
delegates. Perhaps the most distinguished of these was General Vallejo. Although his personal fortunes suffered severely under American rule, with the loss of the practically unlimited lands on which he
had employed hundreds of Indian laborers, yet he wrote in his memoirs: "The inhabitants of California have no reason to complain of the
change of government, for if the rich have lost thousands of horses
and cattle, the poor have been bettered in condition."

Another foreign-born delegate was Johann Sutter, who by now
was regarded almost as an American. Clearly the most influential of
the American delegates was William M. Gwin, a professional politician of wide experience. He had openly come to California for political reasons and soon sought election to the United States Senate. His
knowledge of parliamentary procedure gave him a distinct advantage at the convention; his ability in debate, added to his powers of

118

leadership, marked him as the ablest politician of the group. Thomas O. Larkin, as the "first and last American consul to California," also lent his authority to the deliberations.

Debates of the Convention

Should the convention proceed at once to form a state constitution, or should it be content to establish a territorial government? This was a basic question. A few native Californians and conservative settlers from the South opposed state organization. By an overwhelming majority, however, the convention voted to proceed at once with forming a state constitution. This decision gave California the distinction of seeking admission into the Union without passing through the stage of being an organized American territory. Several existing state constitutions were on hand as resources, among them those of Iowa and New York, which were used extensively.

Next the Committee on the Constitution reported a Declaration of Rights, consisting of sixteen sections. After slight changes had been made, a delegate moved to insert an additional section: "Neither slavery nor involuntary servitude, unless for the punishment of crimes, shall ever be tolerated in this State." This vital proposal was, almost without debate, unanimously adopted. Because the miners did not want slaves working beside them, public sentiment was unquestionably in favor of a free state. The unanimous vote was rather surprising, however, because fifteen delegates had emigrated from southern slave states. California, entering the Union as the sixteenth free state, was to destroy forever the equilibrium between North and South. From the beginning California became a completely free state.

By far the most interesting debate of the convention concerned California's future boundary. This contest was sectional in character and slowed down the work of the convention. When California was ceded to the United States by Mexico, its vast territorial extent had not been strictly defined. The 42nd parallel of latitude, however, was generally conceded to form a definite boundary on the north, the Pacific Ocean on the west, and the treaty line between Upper and Lower California on the south. The point in dispute was the eastern border, which perhaps embraced the great desert east of the Sierra Nevada and even the basin inhabited by the Mormons. In the opinion of the Committee on the Boundary, Mexican California, estimated at nearly 450,000 square miles, was too vast for one state. It recommended as the eastern boundary the 116th parallel. This would have

119

placed the boundary at approximately the eastern border of today's state of Nevada. On this score disagreement was strong. Gwin took a leading part in favoring a large state. Semple argued that it was "not desirable that the State of California should extend her territory further east than the Sierra Nevada," a real natural boundary. A larger territory would prove administratively unwieldy. Moreover, the Mormons, who would certainly be affected if the boundary should be moved eastward, were not represented in the convention. Southerners also felt that Congress, already reflecting sectional discord, would never permit one state to settle by itself the question of slavery in so large a territory. The convention, therefore, agreed upon a relatively narrow state area, drawing its line of demarcation east of the Sierra crest, along the desert floor. It was hoped that this decision to restrict the size of California would make the new California constitution more acceptable to the United States Congress.

The desire to secure California's immediate admission into the Union prompted the delegates to bring their deliberations to an end.

Flood at Sacramento in January of 1850 (contemporary print).
(Courtesy of the Huntington Library)

The closing ceremonies of the constitutional convention took place on Saturday, October 13. As the delegates affixed their signatures to the constitution, a salute of thirty-one guns was fired at the Monterey presidio, just over the hill from Colton Hall, in honor of the thirty states then in the Union plus one for California, which was now ready for admission. After the cannonade ended, the crowd assembled outside Colton Hall cheered, and men tossed their hats in the air as California's newly adopted Great Seal was displayed for the first time.

This seal bears thirty-one stars, representing the states. Minerva, sprung from the brow of Jupiter, is the foreground figure, symbolic of California's admission to the Union without passing through territorial probation. A grizzly bear crouches at her feet; a miner, with rocker and bowl, illustrates "the golden wealth of the Sacramento"; and beyond the river, whose shipping typifies commercial greatness, rise the Sierra Nevada Mountains. At the top of the seal is the legend "EUREKA,"—the Greek word meaning "I have found it"—the state motto.

A NEW GOVERNMENT AND STATEHOOD

California's constitution of 1849 had illustrated once again the capacity of the American people for self-government under primitive con-

The Great Seal of the State of California

ditions. Despite numerous defects, it endured thirty years as the fundamental law of a growing state. Nevertheless, more was required to begin a new civilian government in California than the mere writing of a constitution. It had to be ratified before it could be put into effect. Copies of the constitution, printed in English and in Spanish, were quickly sent by messenger to virtually every town, camp, and ranch in California. On November 13, just a month after the close of the constitutional convention, it was ratified by an almost unanimous vote. Peter H. Burnett, a Democrat, was elected governor, and San Jose was selected as temporary capital. On December 20, the state government was actually established and Burnett was inaugurated. General Riley gracefully resigned his powers as governor. Whatever legal objections might be raised to putting a state government into operation before congressional approval of its status, Riley judged that these must yield to the "obvious necessities of the case." California was in almost every respect a state even though it had not yet been admitted to the Union.

Governor Burnett and the other new officials set to work carrying out the provisions of the constitution. The legislative body, consisting of a senate and an assembly, proceeded to convene in a lengthy session lasting until April 22, 1850. This first California legislature, as one of its earliest acts, named two senators to be sent to the federal Congress—Frémont and Gwin. In January 1850, the two men had set out for Washington, and in March they laid copies of the new state constitution before Congress. In long speeches before that body they requested the admission of California into the Union.

The issue was one that excited much interest in Congress. Southern senators and congressmen were considerably agitated at the prospect of the admission of a free state occupying so vast a portion of the recent Mexican cession. The balance of power between North and South seemed irretrievably slipping away.

After months of deadlock, Senator Henry Clay finally secured passage of his last great compromise. This series of bills, which is known as the Compromise of 1850, had parts to please both North and South. One of the provisions most welcomed in the North was the admission of California as a free state. On September 9, 1850, President Millard Fillmore affixed his signature to the admission bill; and California's senators and representatives, who had been standing by for months, immediately took their seats in Congress. News of California's admission reached San Francisco on October 18. For both that city and the state, this was a dramatic moment. All business was suspended, and the people poured into Portsmouth Square to

122

The state capitol building, Sacramento.
(Reprinted from California Real Estate Magazine. *Photograph by Albert Wray.)*

celebrate and to hear local orators boast of the fact that California was finally a full-fledged member of the Union. Admission Day has been a state holiday ever since.

Several cities desired to be selected as California's permanent state capital. The capital moved from San Jose to Vallejo and, in 1853, to Benicia. All were unsatisfactory. Sacramento made such a strong

123

bid for the capital that the legislature convened there in 1854. The city proved itself such a congenial and suitable place that it became firmly established as California's seat of government.

COMMERCIAL DEVELOPMENT

After the Gold Rush, California's commercial growth was irregular. One of the declining occupations, of course, was gold mining because the most precious deposits of ore were rather quickly exhausted. Some miners turned from gold to silver mining. A few entered the professions that depended for much of their activity at that time upon the mining industry—law, engineering, and banking. Former miners also settled down to running hardware stores, livery stables, and saloons. Greater numbers of people began to earn their living by retailing, wholesaling, warehousing, and processing goods. To the occupations represented by the rancher and miner were added such new trades as those of gunsmith, tanner, butcher, jeweler, cabinetmaker, and baker.

SAN FRANCISCO AFTER THE GOLD RUSH

San Francisco—historically and culturally—deserves to be called California's first city. After the Gold Rush the old Spanish hamlet grew out of its sand hills, its flapping canvas tents, lean-tos, and rickety frame shacks to become a city. In the twenty years between 1850 and 1870, San Francisco changed from a makeshift pueblo and trading post into a confident metropolis. A traveler who returned to a new gas-lit San Francisco after only a year's absence in the mines wrote:

> I really did not know where I was, did not recognize a single street, and was perfectly at a loss to think of such an entire change. Where I had left a crowded mass of low wooded huts and tents, I found a city in a great part built of brick, houses, pretty stores.

By the time the rancho days of the "splendid idle forties" were past, San Francisco's harbor had become a forest of masts. In 1851, a vistor counted 600 ships there. Sailors, traders, and miners had displaced rancheros in the city's life, and "flush times" had come to the village by the Golden Gate. Thousands of invading foreigners ushered out a sleepy Mexican past.

Although the citizens of San Francisco voted themselves a charter in 1850, few early residents expected to remain in the city permanently. Some American pioneers spoke of staying in California for only five years and, therefore, showed little interest in investing in such long-term projects as housing. Yet pressing civic problems demanded action. The fire hazard grew because of the large number of flimsy wooden structures that had been built. Housing became even more of a problem as the need for it increased drastically during the early fifties. In 1850, more than 36,000 immigrants, representing every race, creed, and culture, arrived in San Francisco by sea alone. Among them were spendthrifts, bankers, bandits, and gamblers. During the decade following the Gold Rush, a gambling spirit filled the city.

San Francisco actually consisted of several small settlements, which made the administration of law and order difficult. A sheltered little area called Happy Valley still contained about a thousand makeshift tents during the winter of 1850. Pleasant Valley opened onto an open beachfront from the middle of town. Sydney Town, around the base of Telegraph Hill to the north, became a hangout of ex-convicts from Australia. There were other outlying settlements—Little Chile, Spring Valley, and St. Ann Valley. All of these areas eventually merged into San Francisco

Six great fires swept over the city in a period of eighteen months. The first took place in December 1849, during which a million dollars' worth of canvas structures and the merchandise stored in them were consumed. A second great fire, even more disastrous, occurred in May 1850. After an interval of scarcely a month came a third fire. Following this, further erection of inflammable tents and cloth structures was prohibited. But lumber, so extensively used in local building, proved scarcely less combustible. Another serious fire occurred the following September. Most damaging of all was a disaster of May 4, 1851, which destroyed a large part of the town. San Francisco would eventually rebuild itself in brick and stone; until it did, the city was subjected seasonally to full-scale fires.

The growing metropolis also had its economic problems. After the Gold Rush, San Francisco prices, long subject to violent fluctuations, dropped sharply. Pickled beef and pork went from $60 to $10 per barrel; wheat flour decreased in price from $800 to $20 per barrel. Merchants could only guess what new changes to expect in supply and demand. The goal of most newcomers was to build themselves granite and marble mansions on the city's Nob Hill. Housing sites that had cost $15 before the rush reached $8,000 during its height, only to plummet below $100 later.

Among the more profitable enterprises of the time were the saloons and gambling establishments. There was often a stage and a piano in the back part of the saloons. Gambling also took place there, as well as in the bona-fide gambling houses. Some gambling parlors were elegantly decorated with plush furniture, chandeliers, and mirrors. The El Dorado, with its eight gaming tables, velvet upholstered chairs, and spacious bar, attracted perhaps the greatest crowds. In the plushier spots customers were expected to keep their derringers out of sight, unless attacked. A few of the wealthiest citizens of the town during this period got their start as professional faro dealers or card men.

Regardless of its unsteady economic and social conditions, San Francisco was concerned with culture from an early date. Education was one of its major interests. In September 1847, the first city public school committee met, and a school was opened in 1849. In 1851, the city added a superintendent of schools and a regular board of education. In addition, San Francisco became known for its outstanding museums and libraries. Later, this cultural development was supported by the mining fortunes of Nevada's Comstock Lode and by the riches of California's railroad kings.

Numerous books were written about San Francisco and California in this period. Characteristic of such early writing are travel accounts by pioneers who had originally come to California by sea. Among them, Richard Henry Dana's classic *Two Years Before the Mast* (1840) was one of the first books to introduce a pastoral California of the hide-and-tallow days to a wide reading public.

However, most of the early writing about California appeared in local journals. The most distinguished of such publications was the *Overland Monthly,* a little brown-covered magazine with a grizzly bear on its masthead, which began publication in July 1868. Bret Harte was its editor during the first few years. Harte had come to California in 1854 and had started out as a typesetter. His "The Outcasts of Poker Flat," published in the *Monthly* in 1869, strengthened the reputation created by his earlier stories and lead him to wider audiences. More than any other writer, Harte created a stereotype of the western miner as an unkempt, bearded, red-shirted rowdy.

MARK TWAIN

A then obscure writer, whose sketches reflected the best characteristics of western literature, became a literary immortal. This was Samuel Langhorne Clemens or Mark Twain. His descriptions of miners and mining camps in *Roughing It* are more realistic than Harte's, but

Twain's *Roughing It* is still considered primarily a humorous book. The story that made Twain famous almost overnight was "The Jumping Frog of Calaveras County." The national publicity he achieved as its author launched him on a great career.

Twain had made his mark in California and the West, and it had provided him with much material. His realistic and satirical examinations of society's shortcomings and hallowed beliefs were at the heart of his success. Out West, where conditions were crude, Twain was encouraged to write with directness and imagination; and his later work continued to show the humor and loose narrative style he had developed there.

THE VIGILANTES

California society remained in a turmoil after the Gold Rush. Discordant, brawling, and lawless elements had entered the new state, and they were bound to alter its future. "Respectable citizens" called for greater public morality; they were especially concerned with stamping out corruption in San Francisco. The failure of authorities to prosecute criminals often led to harsh punishment of such persons at the hands of private citizens who took the law into their own hands.

The need of the hour seemed to be for a strong organization to enforce the law. Rising to the occasion, the Committee of Vigilance of San Francisco organized itself in 1851 with about 200 members pledged "to watch, pursue, and bring to justice the outlaws infesting the city, through the regularly constituted courts, if possible, through more summary course, if necessary." The members determined that "no thief, burglar, incendiary, or assassin, shall escape punishment, either by the quibbles of the law, the insecurity of prisons, the carelessness or corruption of the police, or a laxity of those who pretend to administer justice." At the head of the committee was William T. Coleman.

Scarcely had the organization been formed when two sharp peals of the city's fire bell brought the members to its headquarters, the Fire Engine House. One John Jenkins had burglarized an office on Commercial Street, boldly carrying off its strongbox. Jenkins made the mistake of brazenly defying anyone to stop him. When several vigilantes sought to do so, he threw the strongbox into San Francisco Bay in an act of further contempt. When he was finally apprehended, the Committee of Vigilance showed little hesitation or mercy in dealing with him. They brought Jenkins to their head-

ECUTION OF JAMES P. CASEY AND CHARLES COR.
BY THE VIGILANCE COMMITTEE, OF SAN FRANCISCO.

Vigilante justice, 1856 (contemporary print).
(H. G. Hills Collection, courtesy of the Bancroft Library)

quarters, where the merchant Sam Brannan acted as his judge. Within a few hours, almost at the stroke of midnight, Jenkins was pronounced guilty. In the early morning hours the condemned man was taken to Portsmouth Square; a scaffold was hastily erected, a noose draped round his neck, and he was hanged. Although a coroner's jury charged Brannan and the other vigilantes with a hasty, indeed harsh, execution, San Francisco's "best citizens" approved the sentence heartily.

The record of sentences imposed by the first vigilance committee is as follows: hanged, four; whipped, one; deported, fourteen; ordered to leave the state, one; handed over to the "authorities," fifteen; discharged, forty-one. San Francisco's vigilante activities encouraged related movements in the interior and in the mining camps. Vigilance in a setting of rural isolation sometimes took even more vicious forms than it did in the cities. Whenever a mob got out of hand, foreigners were likely to bear the brunt of its fury. Immigrant miners, among them Chileans, Frenchmen, and Hawaiians, were frequently chased out of the better diggings.

After San Franciscans had dissolved their first vigilante brigades and the vision of the hangman's noose had faded from popular memory, criminal activity again increased. About a thousand unpunished homicides occurred in San Francisco from 1849 to 1856. On May 14, 1856, the murder of James King, editor of the *Daily Evening Bulletin,* by James Casey, a local politician, brought the city's corruption and lawlessness to a climax. Shortly thereafter, Casey was locked up in the city jail. Three days later, a crowd of several thousand vigilantes, enraged over this latest in a series of murders, seized Casey from the city jail and sentenced him to death. As King's solemn funeral cortege moved through the city streets, the vigilantes executed Casey.

Within two weeks almost 10,000 men had joined the vigilantes, with veterans of the 1851 group among the first to enroll. Each member, after taking a solemn oath, was known only by his assigned number. This San Francisco Vigilance Committe of 1856 again chose William T. Coleman as its head. The spirit of the 1856 committee was revealed by its constitution, which described the association as existing "for maintenance of peace and good order of society." A close examination of the record reveals that the distinction between vigilance and lynching was often lost sight of and that grave abuses were committed.

THE COMSTOCK LODE

Even in the 1870s, despite the great decline that followed the Gold Rush, California still surpassed other western states in mining activity. The story of the Comstock Lode belongs properly to the history of Nevada. Yet the financial dependence of that region upon San Francisco and the effects of this discovery in California were pronounced. Without California capital, the Comstock would never have been developed. Even the miners who worked the lode came from California. As early as 1853, various hard-rock prospectors had poked about the brush-strewn slopes of Mount Davidson, east of the Sierra. They had dug up a bluish-tinged ore which interfered with washing operations and which they cast aside as "that blasted blue stuff." In 1859, an assayer found that this "waste" was basically rich sulfide containing almost $4,800 per ton in silver as well as $1,600 per ton in gold. Almost overnight some 10,000 persons moved eastward on hastily constructed wagon roads that wound down the steep Nevada side of the Sierra. Until a railroad could be built, supplies had

129

to be hauled by mule and ox teams to Virginia City, Nevada, center of the boom.

By the 1860s, many companies floated mining stock on national security markets. William C. Ralston and his Bank of California invested heavily in the Comstock, transporting thousands of feet of heavy timber as well as machinery and other equipment over the Sierra—items essential in order to shore up deep tunnels that led to veins of silver fifty feet or more in width. The San Francisco financiers who made up "Ralston's Ring" turned the Comstock into a honeycomb of crisscrossing channels, tunnels, conduits, and shafts.

It took fourteen years to reach and to strip bare the richest ore pockets, known as the Big Bonanza. In 1873, the center of the lode was finally tapped and the silver boom approached its peak of production. That year future San Francisco mayor Adolph Sutro built an expensive new tunnel into the heart of the Comstock's ore bodies. This impressive engineering feat provided the hot sumps below the ground with ventilation, better access, and vital drainage facilities.

A national panic in 1873 resulted in slumps in both the production and the marketing of silver, signaling the beginning of trouble for investors in the lode. The failure of Ralston's Bank of California in 1875 set off a string of bankruptcies. For a time almost every bank in the state closed its doors. Serious unemployment added to the dark financial picture. Ralston was unable to save his own fortune. Distraught at the prospect of ruin, he met death either by suicide or by accident in the icy waters of San Francisco Bay. By 1880, the Comstock had permanently failed, but not before it had produced some of the most important personalities, incidents, and great personal fortunes of the West.

STAGECOACHES

California's economic development was closely related to the growth of transportation. The Far West's earliest mining rushes—that to the California gold areas after 1848 and that to the Comstock a few years later—greatly accelerated progress in transportation. During the 1850s, slow-moving mule and pack trains operated over regular routes in California.

Passengers on the early stagecoaches were warned that the trip might be a bone-jarring experience. The stage routes were often treacherous, crossing both arid wastes and rapid streams. Crude ferries over the latter only gradually gave way to permanent bridges. Few stages traveled at night for fear both of Indians and of dangerous

Going into the southern California mines by stagecoach, 1904. Diggings are in the canyon in the background. *(C. C. Pierce Collection, courtesy of the Huntington Library)*

potholes. Drivers were well paid for their arduous work. It was no easy job to drive the large teams of mixed mustangs, hitched to heavily loaded stages, along the rough and stony roads and over the steep grades of the Sierra. Drivers were expected to keep on schedule, and they had to know how to handle nervous teams of animals carefully. A good driver communicated with his mules or horses through movements of the reins. If he sometimes gave a dramatic crack of his whip as he got his wagon underway, it was more to impress spectators and passengers than the animals.

In 1851, there were few stage stations and only thirty-four post offices in all of California. So poor was delivery service that for six weeks during the harsh winter of 1852–1853 Los Angeles received no regular mail. The employment of dependable drivers and the establishment of new stage stations inevitably forced postal and parcel rates upward. In 1852, Wells, Fargo and Company, with its system of national connections, absorbed much local mail service, including the shipment of gold and other valuables. It established branches in the mining camps and towns of the new state. In a five-year period, Wells, Fargo transported $58,000,000 worth of gold into San Francisco alone. In time it also took on banking functions.

Nevertheless, local lines continued to provide the bulk of passenger service, as well as to transport a considerable proportion of the mail, both within California and overland from the Midwest. Congress voted through an overland mail bill in March 1857, requiring "the service to be performed with good four-horse coaches or spring wagons, suitable for the conveyance of passengers, as well as for the safety and security of the mails."

Hard-driving John Butterfield was the successful bidder for the franchise, and he started his cross-country stages moving toward California in September 1858. Butterfield demonstrated that, by using relays of horses, his coaches could cover the 2,800 miles between Tipton, Missouri, and San Francisco in twenty-four days, eighteen hours, and twenty-six minutes. The schedule called for an average speed of five miles an hour, day and night, with fresh horses waiting at ten-mile intervals. The passenger fare from Saint Louis to San Francisco was $200. Overland travelers, however, were a secondary cargo in comparison with the mails; they had the option of either preparing meals en route themselves or purchasing inferior, and usually cold, food at stations. Passengers received scant attention at the hands of busy station men and preoccupied drivers.

Ben Holladay, who had financial interests in stagecoach, steamboat, and, later, railroad transportation, purchased and united various stage lines. For a time Holladay boasted that he operated overland stages to California at a loss, in part because of the personal request of President Lincoln. In October 1866, Holladay's overland staging operations were sold to Wells, Fargo, which rapidly gained control of still other independent stage companies, including the old Butterfield Overland Mail Company interests. Had not sectional tension continued to keep the nation from settling upon a clear-cut railroad route, as recommended by various congressional surveys, overland staging probably would have disappeared before the Civil War. However, staging remained highly subsidized by the national government throughout that conflict.

The stagecoach route between Ventura and Santa Barbara hugged the surf.
(Title Insurance and Trust Company, Los Angeles)

OUTLAWS

Whether they worked for Ben Holladay or Wells, Fargo, western riders and drivers ran the risk of encountering road agents of all descriptions. Altogether, the Wells, Fargo stages were robbed 313 times. Outlaws, focusing particularly upon stage routes, would appear suddenly at a coach door, masked and armed, quickly relieve passengers of their valuables and the stage of its strong box, and then make off before the law arrived. Resistance meant instant shooting. The outlaws did not restrict their activities to robbing stages. They also preyed on lone horseback travelers or stole horses.

Chief among the California outlaws was Joaquin Murieta, whose name struck terror from one end of the state to the other. The Texas ranger Harry S. Love, an experienced manhunter hired by the state legislature to track him down, finally captured and killed a man supposed to be Murieta.

Fully as colorful as Murieta was Black Bart, a gentlemanly road agent who wore a long linen duster and a flour sack over his head. After nearly every robbery, he left behind a taunting verse signed Black Bart, the PO-8. To confuse his pursuers further, Bart's poetry was written in varying hands. One such poem was printed in a California mining paper:

> So here I've stood while wind and rain
> Have set the trees a-sobbin'
> And risked my life for that damned stage
> That wasn't worth the robbin'.

Black Bart, the PO-8

Bart inadvertently dropped a handkerchief at one robbery; its laundry mark led detectives to San Francisco, where they arrested a respected mining engineer who had been masquerading as Black Bart. He was sent to San Quentin Penitentiary for five years, served his sentence, and then disappeared forever.

SHIPS OF THE DESERT

A picturesque episode in the story of southwestern transportation began in 1855 with the authorization by Congress of a Camel Corps, as recommended by Secretary of War Jefferson Davis. He and other backers of this innovation believed that if camels could successfully be used in Africa and Asia, they might also flourish in the "Great American Desert." The projected "lightning dromedary express" made its first experimental trip westward to California from Arizona in only fifteen days, the camels swimming the Colorado River on their way. On January 8, 1858, the population of Los Angeles turned out to witness the appearance of the this first camel caravan.

Because the camel experiment gave promise of success, the army planned a regular caravan system, but this project proved short-lived. The "ships of the desert" developed sore legs and feet from the Arizona and Nevada trails, covered with cacti, prickly pear, and sagebrush. Exasperated mule drivers, furthermore, wanted nothing to do with the smelly "humpbacked brutes." In 1864, the last of the animals were sold at San Francisco. They were used thereafter for pleasure riding and in circuses. There is a story that other camels were turned loose in the desert, and that for years thereafter unbelieving travelers reported having seen their profiles in the distance.

THE PONY EXPRESS

Still another experiment in western transportation was to be tried out. This was the use of fast relays of horses to carry mail more efficiently between distant points than was possible by stage service. The Pony Express began to function on April 3, 1860, with the departure of a rider from Saint Joseph, Missouri, for California. The run of 1,966 miles was completed in nine days and twenty-three hours, or less than half the time required by the best stages; these usually took about twenty days to reach California from Saint Joseph. By means of this impressive record, national attention was attracted to the Pony Express.

The letters carried by the riders were written on the thinnest of paper; at first the rate of postage was $5 per half once, later reduced to $1.50 and finally to $1. The Pony Express, carrying its weekly mails without government subsidy, proved unprofitable despite its high postage rate. During its first eight months of service, Californians sent East only 172 letters, and less than a dozen were submitted to the company for westward transportation. Completion of a transcontinental telegraph line in 1861 ended the Pony Express. Though it had operated for only sixteen months, its demonstration of the practicality of a central route, which would serve as a forerunner of the Central Pacific Railroad, made the Pony Express nationally famous.

BANKING AND COMMERCIAL DEVELOPMENT

Related to the development of both mining and staging was banking. The earliest frontier bankers sometimes began as saloon keepers, as express and stage operators, or as businessmen with strong safes in the back of their stores. In that day of the double-eagle $20 gold piece and of two- and four-bit silver slugs, merchants charged as much as 5 percent interest a month for their banking service. As contrasted with modern banks, which lend out money to depositors and are consequently glad to have their accounts, these early banks considered keeping a miner's doeskin bag of nuggets or "poke" of dust quite a chore. A banking panic in 1855 ushered in a decade of depression, during which most Californians showed little faith in the stability of banks.

During the Civil War, the interruption of the flow of goods from the East encouraged the development of local industries and also converted California's major port of San Francisco into an export center, whose docks, warehouses, and piers were piled high with freight. Increasing numbers of ships passed through the Golden Gate carrying grain, flour, lumber, wool, mineral ores, and other products to world markets. More and more, these commodities were processed as well as produced in California. The period after the 1850s saw a great advance in California's commercial development as capital from the East was invested in California. The completion of a transcontinental railroad in 1869 also contributed to expansion by making vital raw materials more accessible and by further widening the export market. California was outgrowing the primitive economy of its frontier days. Diversified, reasonably self-sufficient, and endowed with remarkable natural resources, the state was on its way toward economic maturity.

THE AMERICANS CLAMOR FOR LAND

For the Spaniards, land always held a particular fascination and importance. Indeed, it was their very basis for measuring both wealth and status. By the time of the American conquest, there were over 800 Spanish and Mexican land grants in California.

Although the Treaty of Guadalupe Hidalgo, ending the Mexican War, had guaranteed resident Californians protection and security in the "free enjoyment of their liberty, property, and religion," increasing dissatisfaction over the large land grants was expressed by recent settlers. After 1850, old-time California residents, with many herds of cattle on their hands, faced increasing imports of stronger Texas longhorns. Many ranchers fell into debt, finding themselves caught in a fatal net of rising costs, falling income, and heightened competition. Unfortunately for them, more and more land-hungry American farmers were streaming into this cattle frontier. Almost all sought land.

Ranchos located near a creek or on lake frontage faced increasing problems. Overland cattle drovers stopped at such places to water their stock. American homesteaders who liked what they saw frequently became squatters, challenging the right of rancheros to hold their large land grants intact. Some incoming Americans justified seizures of land by pointing out that, unlike other areas of the United States, California had made available to the public almost no good free land. Still other American newcomers roamed about the country, living in their wagons and using up a free water supply and grazing areas; these nomads, too, often picked up unbranded calves and range animals.

The unsurveyed tracts were poorly defined, both as to origins and boundaries. Accurate surveys of grants generally did not exist, and most original boundary marks had disappeared or become unrecognizable. The original title to Rancho San José read: "A large oak was taken as a boundary, in which was placed the head of a beef and some of the limbs chopped." Sometimes an owner's cattle brand was burned into a tree. Such marks were quickly obliterated by nature and their existence was hard to prove. Further confusion arose because of numerous duplications and conflicts in the names and boundaries of grants. The Spanish and Mexican settlers, or *Californios,* had built few fences and had almost never quarreled over boundaries. There had been no reason for disputes over land, which had been plentiful and of slight value until the coming of Americans.

Viewed from the standpoint of the American pioneer, it was intolerable that "a few hundred despised Mexicans" should control vast tracts of the most fertile and desirable lands to the exclusion of American farmers. Yankees asked what right had the Vallejos, the Argüellos, or the Swiss Captain Sutter to regal estates?

Ultimately, the most important phase of the land question concerned how much land might be opened up within the state by the federal government—which parts of California would be declared public lands for sale? It took several decades to answer this question. The United States land survey of California was begun in 1851. Thereafter, large tracts of federal land became available, especially after the Homestead Act of 1862 was passed by Congress. California itself became a gigantic land dealer. The state was eventually granted 500,000 acres of land by the federal government for distribution. Many individual purchasers were attracted by the low prices of these federal lands, and some pressure was thereby taken off private landholdings that might otherwise have been subject to squatting.

SQUATTERS

Numerous American squatters settled around the bustling city of Sacramento. Nothing but force could dislodge the squatters, who seized vacant lots in the middle of the night, built weak "ribbon fences" around them, and erected flimsy shanties in the enclosures. Conflict was inevitable. On August 14, 1850, forty armed squatters attempted to regain possession of a lot which one of their party had recently occupied but from which he had been evicted. Sacramento's mayor ordered the squatters to give up their arms and to disperse. They refused to oblige, and in the riot that followed the mayor was wounded. Martial law was then declared, and an extraordinary police force of 500 men was summoned for duty. In the hectic days that followed, Sacramento Sheriff Joseph McKinney was shot and mortally wounded, and several squatters were killed. Not until two military companies arrived from San Francisco were the squatters removed and order restored. Squatting had also begun at an early date in and about San Francisco, and the practice was not discontinued until land titles were authoritatively settled by court decisions.

Sometimes squatting was done for speculative purposes. There were, in fact, "professional squatters," who hired themselves out to hold possession of coveted land. The usual equipment of such operators consisted of blankets to keep warm at night and firearms to fend off other poachers in the daytime. This system was especially common in mining regions. A prospector could not leave his claim untended for so much as a week and expect to find it unoccupied on his return—especially if he had not set up on his property a clear, written notice of ownership, with boundary stakes. Not all squatters were scoundrels. Many honestly believed that the grants on which they had settled were not actually the possession of others. Thus they took on in good faith the backbreaking job of land development.

THE LAND ACT OF 1851

A Federal Land Commission opened its hearings in San Francisco on January 2, 1852; it finally adjourned on March 3, 1856. During that four-year period, rancheros searched their homes for original grants from Mexican governors, ferreted maps out of the surveyor general's San Francisco archives, called upon friends and relatives to testify to their long possession of the land, and consulted lawyers—all to justify their titles. The burden of proof remained on the native Californians. They were at a disadvantage in other respects, too. None of the land commissioners either spoke or read the Spanish language. Claimants in southern California were handicapped by their distance from the place of sessions. Rancheros mortgaged their lands at high interest rates to pay legal fees, made trips to Washington, and waited hopefully for confirmation of their titles.

Attorneys demanded large fees for unraveling land-title problems, especially those involving vaguely defined, poorly surveyed, or overlapping boundaries; still other properties posed complex tax-delinquency problems. Supposedly "final" decisions of the Land Commission were repeatedly contested in both lower and upper courts. Numerous cases culminated in appeals to the United States

Supreme Court. Legal delays ran into many years. Confirmation of the patent to the Simi Rancho, as an extreme example, took twenty-four and a half years. From 1865 to 1880 alone, the owners of Rancho Palos Verdes underwent seventy-eight law suits, six partition suits, a dozen suits over the ejection of squatters, three condemnation proceedings, and other legal controversies outside the courts.

Litigation over pueblo land claims retarded the municipal settlement of both San Francisco and Los Angeles. The city of San Francisco answered several lengthy suits by claiming that, under Spanish legal tradition, it was, like every pueblo, entitled to four square leagues of land. At Los Angeles, the city fathers hopefully staked out claims to an area considerably larger than four square leagues, but these claims were whittled down. In 1866, President Andrew Johnson finally confirmed that city's titles to a tract of 17,000 acres.

Prominent politicians were on both sides of the squatter-versus-rancher issue. Among those who championed the rights of squatters were Governors J. Neely Johnson and John Bigler, as well as Senator William Gwin. Frémont lobbied for speedy confirmation of outstanding undecided land grants. His own large claim in the Mariposa region undoubtedly influenced his stand on the issue. Mariano Vallejo, who had been elected the Republican mayor of Sonoma, traveled to Washington to seek help in settling claims. He did get to visit with President Lincoln, but his land title disputes remained unresolved.

Though the *Californios* theoretically had recourse to the courts, the law was often interpreted by squatter judges and squatter juries and administered by squatter sheriffs. The formidable array of power on the side of the squatters at times led to "squatter compromises" by which squatters could buy land which they frequently already controlled with barbed wire and revolver.

A contemporary assessment of all this confusion over land in Henry George's *Progress and Poverty* (1871) stated:

> If the history of Mexican grants of California is ever written, it will be a history of greed, of perjury, of corruption, or spoilation, and high-handed robbery, for which it will be difficult to find a parallel....

The self-justification of the squatters does not alter the fact that they ruined legitimate landowners, enriched speculators, discouraged settlement, and retarded agricultural progress.

The 1860s were dismal years for California's ranchos and farms. In addition to a crop-destroying grasshopper invasion, came floods. Then, in the middle of the decade, there occurred a period of bone-

139

dry aridity. Falling farm prices after the Civil War and high property taxes reduced the fortunes of landowners, encouraging the concentration of vast holdings in the hands of lawyers and bankers. Both the *Californios* and the incoming Americans were hurt by the confusion over land ownership. The struggle over the old Spanish and Mexican land claims delayed the orderly growth of the state. Not until public confidence in land titles was restored did the normal development of California real estate become possible.

THE FOUNDING OF TOWNS

Often, as rancho holdings were broken up by controversies over legal titles, land fell into the hands of urban promoters and real estate speculators as communities sprang up on these sites which took the names of former ranchos. At first these "towns" were little more than country crossroads that later became farm supply centers.

Some town developers succeeded from the start. Among these was Phineas Banning, founder of Wilmington, a community located on an inlet of the sea south of the expanding pueblo of Los Angeles. Banning's Wilmington wharf and warehouses were built, in the period 1851–1858, on a harbor sheltered by a rock jetty. The harbor's channel was dug deep enough to float in barges and steam tugs carrying freight and passengers from ocean vessels anchored offshore.

Also in southern California, the city of Pasadena mushroomed out of Rancho San Pasqual, formerly the site of an Indian village located near the banks of the San Gabriel River. Manuel Garfias, who held the grant to the rancho by inheritance, faced grave economic problems. Repeated borrowing, at ruinous rates of interest, finally forced Garfias to sacrifice the rancho property. In 1859, he sold San Pasqual for $1,800. In 1875, the settlers chose the name Pasadena from the Chippewa Indian language, a name usually translated as "Crown of the Valley." In the early part of the twentieth century, this town, once dotted with clumps of oak and fields of poppies, was to transform itself into a winter playground of millionaires who would build mansions along its Orange Grove Avenue.

Various factors contributed to the rapid growth of towns like Pasadena: the low cost of land, the drastically increasing population pressures caused by the railroads, and the remarkable energy of town founders and developers in establishing irrigation and water facilities as well as local transportation. These speculators turned an arid countryside into prosperous cities. San Leandro, Pasadena, Wilmington,

140

Pasadena in 1876. *(Title Insurance and Trust Company, Los Angeles)*

and San Diego are examples of their pioneering enterprise and willingness to take risks.

THE GWIN-BRODERICK CONTROVERSY

California was one of the few states (Vermont, Kentucky, and Texas were others) that skipped the territorial stage of political organization. California's growth created an open field for ambitious eastern and southern politicians willing to migrate westward to fill a political vacuum. With President Zachary Taylor's election to the presidency in 1848, the Whig Party took over many eastern governmental positions, thereby releasing a flood of unemployed Democrats.

Among these were David Broderick of New York and William Gwin of Tennessee. In an atmosphere of relative political simplicity, these newcomers attained power partly because of the prevailing popular disinterest in state politics. In frontier areas the struggle for

141

Hotel del Coronado. This majestic hotel, built in 1887, is now a state historic landmark. Located in Coronado, the hotel is served by a yacht harbor in adjacent Glorietta Bay. One of the most beautiful bridges in the world connects Coronado with downtown San Diego. *(San Diego Convention and Visitors Bureau)*

existence did not leave the ordinary man much time for political activity or public service. Most settlers were absorbed in the processes of daily life, mending leaks in their cabin roofs, lining wells with bricks, and fencing property boundaries. Nor were old-time *Californios* inclined to make politics their profession; not many were trained in public oratory, so essential in those days to political victory.

Senator Gwin, as a southerner, made persistent efforts to promote sentiment in favor of slavery in the state legislature. The passage both of a fugitive slave act and of discriminatory laws against blacks seem strangely out of harmony with the antislavery record of California. Meanwhile, Broderick, one of the most remarkable personalities in the political annals of California, also a Democrat, vigorously opposed these pro-southern measures and stirred up statewide opposition to Gwin.

The intensity of the political rivalry between Gwin and Broderick has probably never been exceeded in California. It dominated

California politics during the 1850s, reaching its height after Broderick was elected senator in 1957. This bitter feud between the two California senators reflected the deep split in the Democratic Party on the national level. In 1859, Broderick was killed in a duel with Judge David S. Terry, a Gwin supporter. After the Terry–Broderick duel, Gwin, whose pro-southern views grew increasingly distasteful, became a political liability to the Democrats. In 1861, he was arrested as a disloyal person, and in the last years of the Civil War both Gwin and Terry went into exile in Mexico. The Democratic Party was temporarily wrecked both in the state and nation. The dispute had led to the downfall of both senators just as the national controversy over slavery had led to the Civil War.

CALIFORNIA BLACKS
BEFORE THE CIVIL WAR

Even before the Gold Rush, antislavery leaders frequently claimed that local conditions made slavery unlikely to succeed as a social system. Relatively few slaves had been brought into California from the South. There were, however, blacks in the original California pueblos and, later, a few black frontiersmen. Among the more prominent blacks in California were Jacob Dodson, a volunteer with Frémont on his 1842 expedition, James P. Beckwourth, and William A. Leidesdorff, vice consul to Mexico at Yerba Buena, who was of Danish-Negro parentage. In 1851, Biddy Mason, a young slave woman, crossed the desert on foot, driving a herd of sheep behind her master's wagon train. She later secured her freedom through the courts. Hard-working, frugal, and a shrewd investor, she amassed a fortune in real estate at Los Angeles.

Various blacks succeeded in striking it rich during the Gold Rush. In Brown's Valley, Fritz Vosburg, Abraham Holland, Gabriel Simms, and several other black miners operated the Sweet Vengeance mine most profitably. Others, among them Alvin Coffey, used gold mined in the Sierra to purchase freedom from their masters. While California's 1849 constitution excluded slavery, it did not spell out the rights of freed men. Not until after the Civil War did the federal courts fully guarantee those rights.

The census of 1850 lists some 1,000 black residents. By 1852, their number had grown to 2,200. Legally, none of these blacks were slaves. The terms of California's admission to the Union prohibited slavery, long before Lincoln, in 1863, issued his Emancipation Proc-

143

lamation. Yet California could not completely escape the side effects of slavery as a national institution. The California Fugitive Slave Act of 1851, passed at Gwin's behest, had provided that slaves brought in before the advent of statehood might be reclaimed and returned to slave states. This law was pronounced constitutional by the California Supreme Court. In numerous instances, however, slaves brought into California before its ban against slavery became effective were given their freedom by masters who wished to remain legally in the state.

The growth of California's black population is illustrated by the activities of Darius Stokes, a black pastor, who, by September, 1856, had founded fourteen "colored churches" in California. He claimed that the assessed valuation of property owned by the black population of San Francisco that year was $150,000 and that three-quarters of a million dollars had been sent back to the South by blacks to purchase freedom for members of their families. Stokes remarked that "men had paid as high as $2,000 each for their companions who were enslaved, to gain their freedom and bring them to this State." One had purchased eight of his own children and had paid $9,000 for them, having earned the money by washing clothes.

In 1855, the Convention of Colored Citizens of California met in San Francisco to formulate plans for improving the black's status. This organization was responsible for repeal of harsh and restrictive laws. A militant newspaper owned and edited by blacks, *The Elevator,* which was published under the motto, "Equality before the Law," became the voice of the Colored Convention's executive committee.

THE CIVIL WAR PERIOD

As disagreements between North and South grew, a decisive majority of Californians remained loyal to the Union. California was unable to free itself entirely from disloyal influences. Among the many southerners who were residents of California was General Albert Sidney Johnston, army commandant at the presidio of San Francisco. As open war threatened the United States, General Johnston voluntarily gave up his command to join the Confederate Army.

There was another attitude of opposition to the Union in addition to the southern one. Before President Lincoln's inauguration there was frequent talk of a Pacific Republic, under which California, instead of siding with either North or South, should found on the shores of the Pacific "a mighty republic, which may in the end prove

144

the greatest of all." The dream of a Pacific Republic finally died with a joint resolution of the legislature, adopted on May 17, 1861, which declared "that the people of California are devoted to the Constitution and Union now in the hour of trial and peril."

Though sympathy for the South was essentially an unpopular cause, disloyalty continued to appear in a variety of forms. Advocacy of secession also was heard in newspapers, in public speeches, and in sermons and prayers from the pulpit, as well as at private celebrations of Confederate victories and during arguments in barrooms. A few local papers heaped abuse upon Lincoln and his administration. But the citizens of California, having emphatically cast their vote for Lincoln in 1860, the next year chose the Republican Leland Stanford as their governor. Assuming office on January 10, 1862, Stanford was largely responsible for California's sustained loyalty during the Civil War.

During the war, to counteract secessionist sentiment by settlers from slaveholding states, the California legislature enacted numerous emergency measures. A new law made it a misdemeanor "to display rebel flags or devices." Illegal behavior also came to include "adherence to the enemy" either by "endorsing, defending, or cheering" the subversion or destruction of United States authority.

Meanwhile, Californians were being moved to new heights of sentiment for the Union caused by such orators as Thomas Starr King, a vigorous Unitarian preacher. Although King lived in California less than four years, this Bostonian was an extraordinary figure in the history of the state. After the outbreak of the Civil War, King became a major spokesman for the Union cause and contributed time and money to raise funds for the Sanitary Commission, forerunner of the Red Cross. His eloquence was so great that his supporters said of him: "King saved California for the Union."

Conscription was never enforced within the state. A total of about 15,000 men in California enlisted in the Union Army; many troops drilled at hometown armories and remained stationed where their military units were mustered into service. Although only a negligible military contribution toward the winning of the war can be claimed for California, her gold provided indispensable financial strength. California gold in considerable amounts flowed into the federal treasury, bolstering the nation's economy during the wartime period of unprecedented financial stress. The state also helped greatly to supply the Union armies with wool, wheat, and other materials.

145

The war helped California in other ways also. In particular, passage of the Pacific Railroad Bill of 1862 by Congress was made possible by the absence of those southern legislators who had blocked adoption of a northern railroad route. During 1863, work on the Central Pacific Railroad was begun at Sacramento. Lincoln's popularity remained so great in California that in 1864 he again received the state's votes for the presidency.

THE POSTWAR POLITICAL SCENE

Few California governors and senators achieved national stature in the period from the end of the Civil War to the turn of the century. One of the exceptions to this rule was former Governor Leland Stanford, who represented California in the United States Senate, serving there from 1885 until his death in 1893. Railroad builder, politician, and philanthropist, Stanford had risen from humble origins to create one of the largest fortunes, political and economic, in the West. A legislator of similar stature, repeatedly reelected to the Senate, was George Hearst, a multimillionaire mining engineer and father of the well-known publisher William Randolph Hearst.

In the years before the turn of the century, the Republicans were riding high; the Democrats captured the governorship and senatorial posts only occasionally. Both parties remained basically conservative, and voters seemed satisfied to follow national trends rather than to create significant local ones. Except for the anti-Chinese issue, most public concerns were those of the nation as a whole.

KEARNEY AND THE WORKINGMEN'S MOVEMENT

The origin of the Workingmen's Movement in California is best understood in the light of the severe economic depression which gripped the state at the time. Hordes of the unemployed were anxious to work for wages of $2 per day. Labor riots in large cities in the East also encouraged discord out West. Workingmen renewed demands for unionization and demonstrated vigorously for the eight-hour day as one means of sharing jobs more widely. By 1877, the general discontent had assumed a threatening aspect.

An unusually forceful labor leader arose in San Francisco to give direction to this dissatisfaction. Dennis Kearney, a native of Ireland, had arrived in California in 1868. A short, stout man with coarse

146

features and dark eyes, Kearney was a powerful speaker who possessed the ability to sway his hearers.

Unfortunately, Kearney injected the race issue into labor agitation. He kept repeating the popular slogan, "The Chinese Must Go!" As unemployment increased, Kearney charged that the Chinese were competing unfairly. The fact that 22,000 Chinese immigrants arrived in California's ports in 1876 added fuel to the flames Kearney had helped to light. San Francisco papers of the period, usually antilabor as well as anti-Chinese, were filled with reports of disturbances. In particular, the city's anti-Chinese labor riots of July 1877 posed an emergency which the police proved inadequate to meet. Kearney's men threatened to seize control of the state. Another Committee of Safety was formed by aroused citizens, under the presidency of William T. Coleman, "The Lion of the Vigilantes." Equipping itself with 6,000 hickory pick handles with which to quell rioting workers along the waterfront, Coleman's committee restored peace and order and stood by for further service.

Several months after these violent labor conflicts, Kearney founded the Workingmen's Party of California. Kearney's basic strategy was to accuse existing political groups of corruption and to demand more representation for labor's interests. He declared that every workingman should add a musket to his household effects, and predicted that within a year at least 21,000 laborers would be "well armed, well organized, and well able to demand and take what they will, despite the military, the police, and the 'safety committee.'"

Kearney delighted the workers with his strong language and threats of violence. In open-air meetings, held on a vacant lot in front of San Francisco's City Hall, Kearney pleaded for the support and cooperation of the laborers in the Workingmen's Movement. He proposed "to wrest the government from the hands of the rich and place it in those of the people" and "to rid the country of cheap Chinese labor." He hoped "to destroy land monopoly" and "to elect none but competent Workingmen and their friends to any office whatever." On one occasion the fiery Irishman suggested that "a little judicious hanging" would be the best course to pursue toward "robber-capitalists."

On January 21, 1878, the Workingmen's Party held its first state convention. The assembly made Kearney its chairman and adopted a platform stating that the government "has fallen into the hands of capitalists and their willing instruments." The party described Chinese labor as "a curse to our land, a menace to our liberties," and opposed the corruption of land monopolists, those "enemies of the

147

Workingmen." The Workingmen's Party soon became a powerful force in state politics. In 1878–1879 it elected various state supreme court judges, eleven state senators, and sixteen assemblymen.

Kearney's was the first organized attempt to rally the forces of labor in California. Many of the reform measures he advocated, progressive and advanced for their time, ultimately were adopted within the state. These included the now familiar eight-hour workday, a statewide public school system, reform of the banking system, and restrictions upon business profiteering and land monopoly. Kearney's Workingmen were more antimonopolistic than anticapitalistic. Yet they were considered radical and their leader dangerous. The Workingmen reached the peak of their political power at the time of the constitutional convention of 1879. Three years later the party had passed out of existence.

CALIFORNIA'S SECOND CONSTITUTIONAL CONVENTION

The constitution of 1849 had been formed to meet the needs of a frontier area anxious for admittance to the Union. Among its shortcomings, it lacked provisions for safeguarding public lands, for improving labor conditions, and for regulating the railroads and public utilities.

In September 1877, the electors that California normally sent to the national electoral college voted affirmatively on the question of holding a convention for the purpose of revising the constitution. The statewide election of delegates took place in June 1878. When the convention opened in September of that year, seventy-eight delegates registered as nonpartisans, fifty-one as representatives of the Workingmen's Party, eleven as Republicans, ten as Democrats, and two as independents. In general, the delegates spoke for three main groups. In descending order of influence, these were (1) businessmen and large landholders, represented at the convention by expert legal counsel and various incumbent state legislators; (2) farmers eager to reform existing railroad, water, and monopoly practices as well as what they felt to be unfair taxation; (3) city laborers, who owned even less property than heavily mortgaged farmers.

Taxation and the Railroad Issue

A topic of major importance at the convention was that of taxation. California's State Board of Equalization, which had actually been in

148

existence since 1870, was empowered to assess the value of *all* property taxable by the state government. Its duty would be "to equalize the valuation of taxable property in the several counties, and also to assess the franchise, roadway, road-bed, rails and rolling stock of all railroads operated in more than one county in the state."

This latter provision reflected the widespread discontent with the railroads. The railroads were held responsible for causing racial and labor difficulties by their importation of thousands of Chinese. The farmers at the convention were anxious to control the Southern Pacific. They charged that the railroad fraudulently influenced local elections, rigged high freight rates, and favored large shippers through the use of secret rebates. In particular, the Southern Pacific's quarrels with farmers who had settled on railroad lands blackened the reputation of the railroad. Railroad regulation at the convention, however, proved difficult to achieve. Although a state railroad commission was created, its powers were not extensive. The hardships that the farmers suffered on account of railroad abuses continued for many years after the constitutional convention.

Other Major Issues at the Convention

Popular dissatisfaction with the banks was demonstrated by the passage of a constitutional measure which provided that bank directors or trustees should be liable for moneys embezzled or misappropriated by bank officers. A prediction that bank owners and directors would leave the state because of this burdensome regulation proved false.

Anti-Chinese agitation was also a feature of the constitutional convention. The Workingmen delegates repeatedly urged the exclusion of Orientals from the nation. A number of anti-Chinese clauses were adopted almost unanimously as provisions of the new constitution.

Party lines disappeared when the convention considered educational matters. These were treated with dignity and foresight. A limitation against teaching any language but English was, after spirited discussion, stricken out of the proposed constitution. California's public school system was given what remains its basic shape, though it has, of course, been modified by numerous amendments from time to time. The University of California, already created by a legislative act of March 23, 1868, was accorded the higher legal status of a constitutional corporation.

Public Reception of the Constitution

The constitutional convention lasted over five months. The document it produced was ratified despite widespread opposition. California's present constitution consists of the document produced by the convention of 1879 plus more than 300 amendments. It is now seven times as long as the Constitution of the United States. In spite of the constitution's many technical defects, California has developed a workable and efficient governmental system.

STUDY SUGGESTIONS

To understand the chapter you should know (1) the meaning and importance of key phrases and terms, (2) the contributions to California history of major personalities, and (3) the location and significance of geographic place names.

1. *Key phrases and terms*

   Bank of California
   Californios
   Camel Corps
   Colton Hall
   Convention of Colored
     Citizens
   Committee of Vigilance of
     San Francisco
   Compromise of 1850 ·
   Comstock Lode
   The Elevator

   Great Seal
   Land Act of 1851
   Overland Monthly
   Pony Express
   Progress and Poverty
   Ralston's Ring
   Roughing It
   squatters
   Wells, Fargo and Company
   Workingmen's Party

2. *Major personalities*

   Black Bart
   David Broderick
   Peter H. Burnett
   Samuel Clemens
   William T. Coleman
   Ben Holladay
   William M. Gwin

   Bret Harte
   Dennis Kearney
   Joaquin Murieta
   General Bennett Riley
   Dr. Robert Semple
   Leland Stanford
   Adolph Sutro

3. *Important geographic place names*

   Great Basin
   Palos Verdes
   Pasadena

   Sacramento
   San Gabriel River
   Virginia City

150

FOR ADDITIONAL STUDY

Walter Van Tilburg Clark, *The Ox Bow Incident* (New York, 1942).

Robert G. Cleland, *Cattle on a Thousand Hills* (New York, 1951).

Samuel L. Clemens, *Roughing It* (Hartford, Conn., 1872).

Bernard De Voto, *Mark Twain's America* (Boston, 1932).

John F. Kennedy, *Profiles in Courage* (New York, 1961). See the Chapter on Daniel Webster and the Compromise of 1850.

Robert Kirsch and William S. Murphy (Eds.), *West of the West: Witnesses to the California Experience, 1542–1906* (New York, 1967).

Oscar Lewis, *The Silver Kings* (New York, 1947).

Ellis Lucia, *The Saga of Ben Holladay: Giant of the Old West* (New York, 1959).

George D. Lyman, *Ralston's Ring* (New York, 1937).

———, *The Saga of the Comstock* (New York, 1934).

Leonard Pitt, *The Decline of the Californios: A Social History of the Spanish-speaking Californians, 1846–1890* (Berkeley, 1970).

•6•

PERSISTENT
PROBLEMS
AND FEARS

For over a half century, California was beset by a variety of problems, some of them real, some exaggerated, and others imaginary. One of the most serious resulted from the long period of domination by the railroads over the state's politics and economics. Another was the persecution of the Chinese and, later, other Oriental minorities. No other state suffered from these problems in the same way. A discussion of their development shows how these unique factors have influenced the history of California.

THE OCTOPUS: THE RAILROAD ERA

Planning an Overland Railroad

The dream of a railroad across the North American continent had existed almost since the first railways were constructed in America, and during the 1840s, several men had devised various plans to connect the Middle West with the new American settlements along the Pacific Ocean.

The first transcontinental railroad was completed across Panama in 1855. The bulk of its traffic was either heading for or returning from California. Upon the arrival of passenger steamships on the Atlantic coast of Panama, trains were dispatched at almost any hour in order to meet connecting steamships on the opposite coast. Although the Panama link between Atlantic and Pacific served Californians moderately well, completion of a more direct transcontinental line in 1869 ended much of the need for this route to California and became largely responsible for the modern economic development of the state.

153

By 1850, the expense of getting to California by sea averaged $400, and the trip sometimes took 120 days or more. Overland stage service also remained expensive, slow, and uncomfortable. Advocates of a transcontinental railroad pointed out that such a trip might be made by rail for as little as $150 and in twenty days' time. This argument was made the basis of an appeal by Californians for congressional action. Obviously federal money was needed in large quantities to complete so vast a project. Objections were widely raised, particularly in those sections of the country that stood to benefit least from a connection between East and West. Others frankly doubted that a railroad could ever be constructed over the crest of either the Rockies or the Sierra.

Nevertheless, the idea of a Pacific railroad gained increasing acceptance in Washington. It became obvious that both for purposes of hauling mail, passengers, and freight more quickly, and for defense of the West Coast, a good rail route was seriously needed. There was generally no disagreement that such a route should cross the shortest possible distance because of the tremendous costs involved, but the question of the exact route westward was debated for years. Numerous routes were favored, the most heavily traveled trails tending to be considered most seriously for the ultimate choice.

Many questions arose to block passage of a railroad bill. Should construction and operation of the road be administered by the government outright? Or should the railroad be built and operated privately? How far would federal and state governments go toward financial encouragement and direct subsidies? What kind of land grants would prove most advisable?

As early as 1852, a route that swung generally southward through Texas, and then proceeded by way of the Gila Valley to Yuma, Arizona, and on to San Diego in California, was strongly advocated by southern interests. In 1853, the Gadsden Purchase acquired land from Mexico for this route.

The railroad cause, however, did not lack spokesmen to maintain public interest in the issue, and some of these were eloquent. The famed journalist Horace Greeley of the New York *Tribune*, who in 1859 made an overland trip to San Francisco, wielded an especially influential pen on behalf of a transcontinental railroad. In 1861, the outbreak of the Civil War pointed up decisively the necessity for the railroad and brought to an end all prospects of a southern route. Military and political considerations now became paramount. It was evident that the railroad was essential to bind the Pacific Coast safely to the Union.

Organization of the Central Pacific

On June 28, 1861, three California merchants founded the Central Pacific Railroad Company at Sacramento: Leland Stanford acted as president of the company, Collis P. Huntington as vice-president, and Mark Hopkins as treasurer. In a few years these three and Charles Crocker, who had joined them in the venture, came to be called the "Big Four." Originally, their enterprise relied less on their own efforts than on the almost single-handed determination of a young civil engineer, Theodore D. Judah. In 1855, at the age of twenty-eight, Judah had laid out the rails of the Sacramento Valley Railroad to serve the mining regions along the slopes of the Sierra Nevada. By the late fifties, Judah was advancing some bold engineering concepts, which he felt would make possible the construction of a railroad over the Sierra. For such efforts he was ridiculed in both Washington and California and was often called Crazy Judah. By personal lobbying in Washington, he was finally able to bring effective pressure to bear on individual congressmen for passage of a railroad bill. Also, it was actually Judah who had interested Stanford, Huntington, Hopkins, and Crocker in the railroad project.

Leland Stanford, Sr., railroad tycoon, politician, and philanthropist, about 1875.
(*The Bancroft Library*)

Congress, on July 1, 1862, passed the Pacific Railroad Act. In addition to the 400-foot right of way, a generous government land subsidy was given the railroad builders. Numerous sections of this terrain stretched off in checkerboard fashion on either side of the track almost as far as the eye could see. In all, the railroad builders were entitled to 1,280,000 acres of public land for every 100 miles of track they laid plus some $3 million in credit for each of the two railroad construction companies. Both the Central Pacific and Union Pacific railroad companies were to construct at least twenty-five miles of road a year, and the thirty-year government bonds (at 6 percent interest) authorized for the railroad could not be redeemed for cash until at least forty miles of road had been constructed. Although the transcontinental railroad would be built by these two separate corporations, Congress stipulated that the entire road should be operated "as one connected, continuous line." Actually this was to be done only theoretically. The Central Pacific and Union Pacific companies remained separate entities. Both companies were empowered to and did issue the contracts for construction of their section of the transcontinental railroad. On the western end of the line the Central Pacific remained supreme.

Judah and his partners had also convinced Congress to grant them, in the bill, a federal loan subsidy of $16,000 per mile for track laid across level land, $32,000 a mile in the foothills, and $48,000 per mile across mountain areas. Judah's partners devised a plan to collect, for part of the construction, twice the subsidy to which they were entitled. Their strategy was simply to prove to Congress that the foothills of the Sierra Nevada began further west than was the case. This reasoning, duly written into the bill, in effect "moved" the mountains to within only ten miles of Sacramento—near the center of the great Central Valley of California!

In a few years all except Judah were multimillionaires. Judah reputedly was en route to seek eastern capital with which to buy out his greedy partners when he was stricken with a fatal attack of yellow fever, which he had contracted in Panama on a previous trip to the East Coast.

The provisions of the Pacific Railroad Act of 1862, generous as they were, were increased in 1864. In that year the Central Pacific officers, together with the backers of the Union Pacific, achieved passage of an amendatory act which doubled the land grants and increased financial inducements. The fact that the enormous obstacles to construction of the railroad could be overcome only by vast sums of money, the pressure created by the war, and the inexperience of Congress in dealing with such a gigantic project—all help explain why the legislation of that era was so loosely written. It was wholly natural, in an age of untrammeled business expansion, that construction of the first transcontinental railroad should have been left to private initiative.

Construction of the Railroad

Actual building operations were begun by the Central Pacific in 1863, a year and a half before the first track laying by the Union Pacific Company. Building eastward from Sacramento, the Central Pacific had to ship its machinery and supplies from the East around Cape Horn or via Panama at great expense. Union Pacific crews, on the other hand, moving west from Omaha, were able to transport heavy supplies over the track they had already laid. The Sierra Nevada presented an even more formidable obstacle to the engineers of the Central Pacific than the Rocky Mountains were to offer to those of the Union Pacific. The California mountains, however, did supply timber for ties, trestles, and the long stretches of snow sheds required in midwinter—a resource at first lacking to the Union Pacific as it worked its way across the relatively treeless Great Plains.

In order to cut a roadway through the rock walls of the Sierra, Central Pacific construction crews used picks, shovels, black blasting powder, mortar, axes, ladders, wheelbarrows, and dumpcarts, in addition to thousands of laborers. For a labor force, the Central Pacific relied chiefly on 15,000 Chinese, whom Crocker had imported for this purpose. Crews of these expendable "Celestials," a name taken from the Celestial Empire of China, tied by ropes around their middles, chipped at the sides of Sierra cliffs 7,000 feet high for wages of less than $2 per day. After they had chiseled out a crude footing along the steep canyon walls, other Chinese would make use of this toehold in blasting out a roadway for the track. Despite irksome delays, due largely to financial difficulties, the Central Pacific crossed the Sierra Nevada summit in December 1867, at an elevation of 7,047 feet; and from there the work of the crews was speeded by the less rugged terrain and the previously completed section of the road. They soon crossed the state line and began construction in Nevada.

The Union Pacific relied mainly on Irish immigrants for its construction crews. There was a lively sense of rivalry between the two companies, and it became especially intense when Crocker announced a schedule of a mile of track for every working day. His Chinese—known as Crocker's Pets—responded wholeheartedly to

157

Chinese construction workers on the Central Pacific Railroad at "Cape Horn,"
a strategic point in the crossing of the Sierra Crest (contemporary print).
(Courtesy of the Huntington Library)

every new demand made upon them. By June 1868, they had
reached Reno, but it was not until early in 1869 that the most fever-
ish construction occurred. On one day the Union Pacific's Irishmen
laid six miles of track; Crocker's Chinese countered with seven miles
and ultimately set a record with ten miles and fifty-six feet of track
laid in just under twelve hours. That day Crocker reputedly won a
bet of $10,000 because of their labor.

The government subsidy was, of course, based upon mileage of
track laid, and each railroad was on that account alone eager to cover
as much ground as possible. As the distance between the rival construction crews lessened, their competition became even more keen.
For a time grading crews worked within a few hundred yards of each
other along parallel lines, since they could not agree as to where the
tracks should join. Early in May 1869, government railroad commissioners ruled that the two lines should meet at a little summit in
northern Utah Territory called Promontory Point, 56 miles west of
Ogden, 1,086 miles from Omaha, and 689 miles from Sacramento.

There the gap was closed, finally fulfilling the edict of Congress that "the rails shall meet and connect, and form one continuous line."

The Golden Spike

It remained only to drive the last spike. On May 10, 1869, on desolate Promontory Point, the formal ceremony was performed, uniting Atlantic and Pacific with bands of steel. Two bonnet-stacked, wood-burning locomotives faced each other on the new tracks, one headed east, the other west. California's polished laurel tie was put in place and her spike of gold produced. President Stanford of the Central Pacific and Vice-President Thomas C. Durant of the Union Pacific proceeded to drive this last spike while the locomotive whistles screamed. Each blow of the silver sledge was announced via telegraphic connection to eastern cities, where the event was celebrated by the ringing of bells. Stanford was the only member of the Big Four to put in an appearance at the ceremony.

It was a memorable day for California, as for the nation as a whole. San Francisco celebrated for three days. The telegraph announced: "The last rail is laid! The last spike is driven! The Pacific Railroad is completed!" At Sacramento, the bells and whistles of thirty locomotives joined in a chorus with the bells of the city's churches and fire houses.

Now it took only seven days to travel the 3,167 miles, over numerous separate railroad lines, from Sacramento to New York. Successful completion of the largest engineering job yet undertaken in North America was a decisive event in California history. In 1869, exactly 100 years after the settlement of the Pacific province by the Portolá-Serra expedition of 1769, California's frontier isolation had finally come to a close.

The Southern Pacific

After the Big Four completed the transcontinental line, they began to develop railroad mileage within California. They enriched themselves by transferring control of the Central Pacific to a holding company called the Southern Pacific. Under this name they bought up local lines and constructed many new ones, thereby consolidating all of their enterprises and eventually creating a railroad system covering hundreds of miles from San Francisco and Los Angeles to terminuses as far away as New Orleans, Louisiana, and Portland, Oregon.

Wedding of the rails, Promontory Point, Utah, May 10, 1869.
(Union Pacific Railroad)

The early railroad had needed and received government subsidies in the form of money and land. As the railroad grew in power, it began to take over politics and government in the state. In 1880, at Mussel Slough, near the town of Hanford in Kings County, a bitter dispute between farmers and the railroad even resulted in the loss of several lives. Some settlers, after improving plots of land, found that the original price they had agreed upon had been raised. They refused to pay, and the Southern Pacific tried to evict them. A bloody battle was fought between the two groups, in which seven persons were shot to death and an eighth wounded. A number of settlers were then tried because they had resisted the law, and were convicted and sent to prison for protecting what they believed to be their property.

The railroad's land-management policies, as dramatized by this incident, and its further struggles with farmers, caused tension against it to mount steadily in California. However, full regulation would have to await the reforms of the Progressive Movement just prior to World War I.

The Boom of the Eighties

The boom in California's urban growth toward the end of the nineteenth century was closely connected with the railroads. The new flood of population descended upon the state from 1870 to 1890, seeking to substitute harsh winters with sunshine. Whether they settled down as town dwellers or farmers, the new residents became their own best customers and created a boom that fed on itself.

The movement of population reached its peak in 1887, the year that the Atchison, Topeka, and Santa Fe Railroad first arrived at Los Angeles. This event touched off a bitter rate war with the Southern Pacific. At the height of the rivalry, passenger fares from the middle West to southern California dropped from $125 to as little as $1. More than 200,000 persons came to California in 1887 by railroad. Dozens of towns sprang up immediately in Los Angeles County, and colleges, banks and other institutions were also founded. Within less than two years, 100 communities had been born inside the borders of the county. Though lacking in coal and metals, and isolated on the far side of North America without a fully developed harbor, Los Angeles had embarked on a period of fantastic growth—the result of skillful realty advertising and the lure of climate as well as of the railroad competition.

The Decline of the Big Four

Ultimately the power of the railroads was resented by the farmers, the politicians, and the general public. The antirailroad feeling was encouraged in many ways. David D. Colton had been a close associate of Huntington, Stanford, and Crocker during the period after 1874 when they were lobbying for government aid for the building of Southern Pacific lines from Yuma, Arizona, into New Mexico. After Colton died suddenly in 1878, his widow was dissatisfied with the

161

Street scene in downtown Los Angeles, 1889. *(C. C. Pierce Collection, courtesy of the Huntington Library)*

financial settlement she received from the Big Four. Mrs. Colton publicly released several hundred of the personal and business letters Huntington had written to her husband. The letters, which provided an inside view of Huntington's selfish use of power to influence legislation, supported the popular beliefs concerning the railroad machine. In 1887, when Huntington was called to appear before the United States Railway Commission, he even admitted that he would have considered it perfectly proper to pay the salaries, fees, and expenses of the entire Arizona territorial legislature in order to get legislation passed. He apologized neither for his methods nor for his objectives. As Huntington put it: "I've been in business fifty years, and practiced the usual methods known among business men to accomplish certain objects. . . . My record as a business man is pretty well known among business men and there is nothing in it I am ashamed of." Although the Big Four had voted themselves huge dividends, they had made no attempt during the period of their greatest prosperity to pay off their government loans. Huntington used every means at his command to prevent such measures. Within a few years he was left alone to carry on both this fight and others against the building of rival transcontinental systems; Hopkins died in 1878, Crocker in 1888, and Stanford in 1893.

Each of the four men had amassed a fortune in excess of $50 million. They had built huge homes on Nob Hill. Gilt-edged Victo-

Corner of Colorado and Fair Oaks in Pasadena as it looked in the 1800s.
(Title Insurance and Trust Company, Los Angeles)

163

rian residences like that of Charles Crocker, with its ornate carvings, rococo bell towers, and intricate verandas, overlooked spacious lawns. Popular legend has it that in the vicinity of the Hopkins' mansion there were so many brass fences that one man was kept busy just polishing them. However, not all of their money was selfishly spent; in 1890, Stanford founded Stanford University as a memorial to his son.

Toward the end of the century, a financial writer estimated Huntington's fortune to be $70 million. He owned enough railroad trackage to connect the North and the South poles, and he literally could travel from Newport News, Virginia, to San Francisco without ever riding on anyone else's rails. He also owned sawmills, steamship lines, and coal mines. During the 1880s and 1890s, Huntington continued, nevertheless, to maintain that the railroad had performed primarily a public service. He restated his conviction that no impropriety had occurred in his lobbying and that he had operated entirely within the business ethics allowable in an age later labeled as one dominated by "Robber Barons."

The national press, however, charged that Huntington wanted what amounted to cancellation of the railroad's debts to the government. And the San Francisco *Examiner,* under young William Randolph Hearst, published frequent articles criticizing Huntington and the Central Pacific. These articles were accompanied by cartoons that showed Huntington leading the governor of California around on a leash.

Another public controversy in the last days of Huntington's career was the Los Angeles free-harbor fight. That city was clearly on its way toward becoming the largest in California. Only one deficiency threatened to halt this expansion—lack of a suitable harbor. Federal funds were sought to build the expensive facilities necessary for a modern harbor. Two sites, San Pedro and Santa Monica, were available. Huntington favored construction of a deep harbor at Santa Monica, principally because the Southern Pacific controlled all the railroad approaches to that location. An aroused Los Angeles citizenry organized a Free Harbor League whose object was to secure the appropriation for San Pedro. The term "free harbor" sprang from the feeling that the new port should not be dominated by the railroad. The Terminal Railroad, a minor competitor of the powerful Southern Pacific, had access to San Pedro, a fact that gave Los Angeles at least some assurance that access to its future harbor would not be the exclusive province of the Huntington monopoly. The Free Harbor Leaguers with the aid of the Los Angeles *Times* and the city's

San Francisco mansions built on Nob Hill by the railroad tycoons, Mark Hopkins (left) and Leland Stanford (right). *(H. G. Hills Collection, courtesy of the Bancroft Library)*

Chamber of Commerce battled to prevent Huntington from achieving his goal of having the federal funds allocated to Santa Monica. The free-harbor fight ended with San Pedro being designated as the site of Los Angeles' port.

In 1900, the tough and flinty Collis P. Huntington reached the end of his life. Shortly after his death, his nephew, Henry, sold the control of the Southern Pacific to E. H. Harriman. Only when the magnificent Henry E. Huntington Library and Art Gallery was founded in San Marino, after the turn of the century, did the Huntington name begin to increase in stature.

One should not, however, conclude that the power of the railroad was significantly weakened by the death of the last of the Big Four. When the Harriman interests took over the Southern Pacific at the opening of the century, the railroad machine was, if anything, politically stronger than at any time in the past. Yet, the new tide of reform was rising ever higher in California and nationally, gaining particular impetus from reform-minded President Theodore Roosevelt.

Railroading, A Changing Industry

The dominant position held by railroads at the turn of the century has since been confronted with serious challenges. First, the completion of the Panama Canal in 1914 increased competition on coast-to-coast routes. Then, the ever increasing use of the private automobile and the development of improved highways led to a reduction in rail commuter service and the substitution of trucks and buses for short hauls. The huge transportation demands and fuel shortages of World War II temporarily reversed the pattern, and railroading reached all-time highs in both passenger miles and freight tonnage. Highway building and private auto ownership regained momentum after the war, but it was the tremendous increase in air travel that made the operation of trains like the *Golden State Limited, California Zephyr,* and *City of San Francisco* unprofitable.

Union Station in Los Angeles, the last of the great train stations in America; it was built in 1939 on a site made available by the demolition of Los Angeles' Old Chinatown. *(Santa Fe Railway)*

166

The *Super Chief.* *(Santa Fe Railway)*

It is not surprising that the railroads were happy to transfer their passenger service to AMTRAK in 1971. Unlike many of the eastern counterparts, however, California's railroads have maintained good profit records on their freight operations. Such innovations as containerized cargoes and piggy-back freight have helped them keep pace with rapidly changing transportation technology. Commuter rail service has all but disappeared except in the San Francisco region where the futuristic Bay Area Rapid Transit (BART) system provides an alternative to the private automobile. Los Angeles voters have three times rejected bond issues that would have provided a comparable system for their smog-choked basin.

ORIENTAL MINORITIES

Many immigrant strains have contributed to the development of California. As we have seen, the railroad to the East was built largely with Chinese labor. California's growth was furthered, too, by the efforts of Japanese farmers in the Central Valley, of Italian and French wine growers in the north, and of Swiss and German dairymen along the Coast Range. The presence of these immigrants made

California relatively receptive, especially in comparison with other western states, to foreign ideas, food, styles of clothing, and patterns of life. Yet it is true that California's history includes episodes of suspicion, harshness, and violence toward foreigners and minority groups. During the nineteenth century, Orientals faced an especially tough battle for acceptance. Their mistreatment is perhaps best summed up in the phrase, "He doesn't have a Chinaman's chance."

Early Chinese Immigration

In 1844, Caleb Cushing, minister plenipotentiary from the United States, went to China to negotiate for the opening of Chinese ports to American trade. Partly as a result of a treaty of trade and friendship which Cushing signed with China, contact between California and the Orient began to increase. In 1847, the first small band of Chinese immigrants found their way into the state. Orientals showed themselves to be particularly adaptable and faithful workers and were, at first, treated with consideration. In the mines, on railroads and ranches, in laundries and hotel kitchens, in cigar factories, and in private homes, they seemed to have a passion for work and, furthermore, were content with meager wages.

The first serious dissatisfaction with the Chinese appeared in the mines where, in spite of their small daily earnings, the Chinese through hard work and frugality sometimes accumulated more gold than did extravagant whites. Although they were usually patient, peace loving, and hard working, when the Chinese got in the way of aggressive whites, they often became the victims of sharp accusations and violence. Some diggings were frankly closed to them and other foreigners.

"California for the Americans!" was a cry increasingly heard in the cities as well as in the mining camps. When the financial panic of 1854 brought prices down with a crash, ruining business houses and causing grave unrest, feeling against the Chinese reached new heights. Miners by the thousands drifted back to San Francisco, only to find that they could not get jobs. The presence in that city of large numbers of Chinese was held chiefly responsible for white unemployment. White workers complained bitterly that the Orientals, by undercutting wages, deprived them of work. Prejudice among whites extended even to little children, who were encouraged by some of their elders to practice public disrespect and insult against the Chinese. By the late 1850s, mistreatment of them was of daily occurrence. San Francisco's notorious 1855 Pigtail Ordinance re-

168

quired Chinese men convicted of breaking the law to have their pigtails cut off one inch from the head. In 1871, nearly a score of Chinese were massacred in a Los Angeles race riot. This episode, one of the bloodiest in the history of the state, was ignored by the law.

Meanwhile, in spite of prejudice and persecution, "Little China" was steadily growing in San Francisco. The mysteries of Chinatown

Chinese grocery store in San Francisco, about 1890. (*Wyland Stanley Collection, courtesy of the Bancroft Library. Photograph by I. W. Taber.*)

held a great attraction for the curious—especially tourists. Smoke-filled gambling dens flourished, and backroom saloons, secret passages, deep basements, and hidden recesses teemed with activity, day and night.

The mass of the Chinese who continued to come to California did so under conditions only slightly better than slavery. When the Central Pacific Railroad was being built, Mark Hopkins supervised the founding of the "Six Companies" to recruit, transport, and utilize Chinese labor on a large scale. This enterprise was responsible for much of the immigration in the early 1860s—about 9,000 Chinese in all. In contrast to the Chinese who had come earlier as miners, the new arrivals had among them many undesirables who were impoverished, undernourished, and frequently sickly.

The newspapers charged the Chinese with unfair competition especially in mining, construction work, cigar making, and the lesser trades. Critics also accused the Orientals unjustly of draining the countryside of substantial sums of money, supposedly sent to China. The Chinese were regarded as the "Yellow Peril," a threat to "Christian values and Republican government." In 1871, Governor Newton Booth was elected to office on an anti-Chinese platform. Laboring groups kept up the anti-immigrant pressure, and in June 1882, the Democratic state convention passed a resolution against further Oriental immigration. Both major parties were, in fact, anti-Chinese—on a national as well as state level. In 1882, President Chester Arthur signed a bipartisan exclusion bill which temporarily stopped Chinese immigration.

Japanese Immigration

Many Japanese began to enter California in the late nineteenth century. Like the Chinese, they experienced reasonable treatment at first. Not until 1891 did the Japanese immigration into the United States for a single year exceed 1,000. Acquisition of Hawaii in 1898 was followed by a heavy two-year influx of both Japanese and Chinese from these islands, and public opinion was, therefore, aroused anew against all Orientals. Soon strong opposition to the Japanese was being voiced in California.

The first specifically anti-Japanese exclusion meeting was held in 1905 at San Francisco, resulting in the organization of an Asiatic Exclusion League. The San Francisco Board of Education recommended the establishment of separate schools for Chinese and Japanese. When a "separate school order" was issued, requiring the transfer of a majority of San Francisco's 93 Japanese pupils to a separate school, great indignation was aroused in Japan, and diplomatic protests were promptly lodged with the American government. The Japanese objected as much to the inclusion of their children in a school with the Chinese as to any other discrimination. President Theodore Roosevelt insisted that the national government was a party to the controversy, stating: "As soon as legislative or any other action by any state affects a foreign nation, then the affair becomes one for the Nation, and the state should deal with the foreign power purely through the Nation." The mayor of San Francisco and members of the school board journeyed to Washington to confer with President Roosevelt who persuaded them to give up their segregated school policy.

In contrast to the Chinese, who as a rule seemed placidly uninterested in material success, the Japanese were often ambitious and enterprising. Japanese farmers, for example, worked impressively long hours, expecting the same of all the members of their families. Because of their enterprise, the Japanese were depicted by the unfriendly press as efficient, shrewd, and conniving.

In order to avert an international crisis with Japan, Roosevelt called for further negotiations, which resulted in the well-known "Gentlemen's Agreement." Under this agreement, which became effective in 1908, Japanese immigration was severely curtailed in exchange for the promise of better treatment for Japanese-Americans.

The institution of Japanese "picture-bride" marriages offended exclusionists. A Japanese laborer in America, unable to go home to be married, often made the acquaintance of his future wife through a go-between who arranged an exchange of photographs. After the couple agreed to become man and wife, the wedding ceremony was largely a matter of legal documents.

The California Alien Land Act, which became effective in 1913, provided that "aliens not eligible for citizenship may inherit or devise real estate only as prescribed by treaty," that real property acquired by such aliens would eventually be returned to the state, and that agricultural lands could not be leased to such aliens for periods to exceed three years. There were, however, ways in which the Japanese could avoid these provisions. One of these was to gain control of land by registering it in the name of another landowner who was a citizen. By the leasing and subleasing of land, the Japanese came to control increasingly large truck-farm acreages of crops such as lettuce, celery, tomatoes, beans, and strawberries. And the more

171

land the Japanese acquired, the more they were feared as an economic threat.

Laws were passed against Orientals in Oregon, Idaho, and other western states, but California's legislation was the harshest. The Anti-Alien Initiative Measure of 1920 prohibited the owning of land by native-born Japanese or the leasing of farm land to them. Under its terms, the Japanese born in their native homeland were forbidden even to hold an interest in any company owning real property. Finally, the U.S. Immigration Act of 1924 put an end to the Gentlemen's Agreement. Oriental immigration became virtually impossible. Certainly the later deterioration of relations between Japan and the United States was in part caused by attitudes related to such immigration difficulties.

Japanese Relocation During World War II

Just before World War II, as the United States and Japan were becoming increasingly antagonistic, feeling against the Japanese had been mounting. The Japanese immigrants' position became economically stronger over the years. As fishermen, cannery workers, gardeners and farmers, they still awakened the hostility of Caucasian competitors.

Immediately after the Pearl Harbor attack on December 7, 1941, the rule of the Hawaiian Islands was turned over to the commanding general of the United States Army in the Pacific and remained in his hands until 1944. Fear naturally spread to the mainland, especially during 1942 after a lone Japanese submarine surfaced at Goleta, near Santa Barbara, and fired a shell which splintered the end of a wooden jetty. Frightened residents put their houses up for sale and made plans to flee. On February 25, 1942, the California press erroneously reported that Japanese planes had bombed Los Angeles and its environs the night before, heavily damaging defense installations. Antiaircraft fire had indeed been shot into the sky against imaginary aircraft, and the jittery, ill-informed populace was ready for the worst.

At this point racial attitudes were mixed with the argument of the military authorities that the California Japanese were too close to the airfields, army installations, and navy bases in the state. The fact that there was no evidence whatsoever that any of the Japanese were disloyal did not influence the military's considerations, and the military prevailed. This was disastrous for the Japanese. A policy of

172

internment at specified locations in the state and elsewhere away from the Pacific Coast was instituted. Many had to sell their homes, businesses, and land at a fraction of their value. The Japanese-Americans suffered a property loss estimated at $365 million. Radios, arms, and other suspicious-looking personal effects were confiscated from them. German and Italian aliens were also interned, but in most cases quickly released.

A total of 112,000 West Coast Japanese, two-thirds of whom were American citizens, were subject to relocation. Thousands were actually taken from their homes and businesses and herded into the interior. Some Japanese were given the choice of "relocation" along the eastern seaboard. Others were sent to Tule Lake, Manzanar, and similar internment centers were the evacuees lived behind barbed wire under military guard. They were charged with no crime, but were merely considered potential enemies by the Department of the Army, and no defender, in the government or outside it, arose to invoke the protection of the Constitution on their behalf.

Large numbers of Japanese-Americans enlisted for military duty. As the 442nd Regimental Combat Team, they fought heroically in Italy and France, thereby attesting to the loyalty of the Japanese-Americans. Only about 65,000 of the Japanese who had been forced to leave the West Coast ever returned. Some settled in the Middle West and in the East. Historians who have studied this forced evacuation in the calmer atmosphere of the postwar years have generally concluded that it was a grievous violation of the constitutional rights of these individuals. The United States Supreme Court has, however, refused to pay claims made by the many Japanese who have appealed to the Court.

Recent Oriental Immigration

When the 1965 Immigration Act removed the exclusionary national origin quotas in effect since 1924, a large increase in immigration from the Far East occurred. At first most of the new immigrants were Chinese and Korean. More recently a large number of displaced Vietnamese have made their home in California. Most of the newly arriving Chinese joined existing Chinese communities. Meanwhile, identifiable Korean and Vietnamese neighborhoods were established.

Changes in Social and Political Status

In 1970, Japanese Americans constituted approximately 1 percent of California's population. Their academic and professional achievements as well as their adaptation to the general "middle-class" culture has earned them the reputation as America's most successful ethnic minority.

In 1970, the Chinese population of California was also just under 1 percent, much of it concentrated in San Francisco's Chinatown. Heavily influenced by their ethnic heritage, the Chinese community was seriously challenged by the increasing flow of recent, often less tradition-bound, newcomers from Hong Kong and Taiwan. The San Francisco Chinese were also upset by a court-ordered busing plan which took their children away from neighborhood schools. Overall, the Chinese Americans are considered hard-working, family-centered, and law-abiding citizens.

Although prejudice against Orientals was not totally overcome, the old hostilities gradually weakened. This was demonstrated by the 1974 election of March Fong Eu, a Chinese-American, to the statewide office of secretary of state and by the 1976 election of Samuel I. Hayakawa, a Japanese-American professor, as United States Senator.

174

CRITICS AND REFORMERS

The many problems confronting California's citizens at the turn of the century were the subject of numerous books and newspaper stories. A leader in this effort was the already mentioned Henry George, who had held a half-dozen jobs along the San Francisco waterfront before he turned to the career of economic analysis that made him world famous. He had been a seaman and a printer, and he even tried to support himself by prospecting for gold. George once reminisced: "I was, in fact, what would now be called a tramp. I had a little money, but I slept in barns to save it and had a rough time generally." George became a newspaper reporter and editor with an intense ambition to voice the complaints of the working people.

In his *Progress and Poverty* (1880), he protested against the presence of poverty and wealth side by side in so rich a land. In California idle land was everywhere before his eyes, and he may well have exaggerated the importance of the issue. His book sold 3 million copies. It made George a champion of the landless "laboring masses" and won him the respect even of persons who opposed his socialistic ideas.

March Fong Eu

175

S. I. Hayakawa

Thorstein Veblen, the economist who originated an influential "theory of the leisure class," taught at Stanford University. After a period of residence in the East, he returned to California in 1926 and lived there until his death in 1929.

An original California thinker was Josiah Royce. Born in 1855, at Grass Valley, Royce had little in his pioneer background to suggest that he would one day sail out of San Francisco to teach philosophy at Harvard. Like Henry George, he conceived and published his initial writing in California. He, too, was incensed, perhaps a bit more objectively, at the abuses of the land monopolists and of the railroad. In 1875, Royce sent his first essay to the *Overland Monthly*. By 1882, he was on the Harvard faculty. Royce became, along with William James, one of the most influential American philosophers, basing his theories on the principle of individuality and human will rather than upon the role of intellect. An idealist and nonconformist, Royce rejected the notion of any monopoly in state or national politics; he expressed his distaste for railroad domination with particular effectiveness in a novel entitled *The Feud of Oakfield Creek* (1887) and reviewed the early history of his native state in the book *California, From the Conquest in 1846 to the Second Vigilance Committee* (1886).

Another native son, the novelist Frank Norris, was a bitter critic of monopolies in general and the railroads in particular. Shortly before his death at the age of thirty-two, Norris wrote about his work: "I never truckled. I never took off the hat to fashion and held it out for pennies. I told them the truth. They liked it or they didn't like it." Norris' most famous work was *The Octopus* (1901), which portrayed the clash between the railroads and the farmers, describing the rails as steel tentacles. Norris was an important figure in the history of American social protest.

The writing of Frank Norris exerted a deep influence upon a better known writer, Jack London. In such works as *The Call of the Wild* (1903) and *The Sea Wolf* (1904), London displayed both skill as a storyteller and his deep feelings for his fellow men. Although for a time an active Socialist, London eventually became discouraged with the cause.

A writer of a different sort, the brilliant, acid-tongued, and vindictive Ambrose Bierce had the distinction of dominating the California literary world for several decades with his witty and opinionated diatribes. His journalistic targets were many, from disreputable politicians to untalented young authors. He also launched some devastating articles aimed at the Southern Pacific railway interests. His *The Devil's Dictionary* (1911) was a series of ironic definitions. Bierce's career ended at the pinnacle of his success. His disappearance in 1913, when he was seventy, is as mysterious as his most controversial writings. It is assumed that, disillusioned and tired, he went to revolution-torn Mexico and that he died there. He was never again heard from.

Bierce's publisher was William Randolph Hearst, who in 1887 received the San Francisco *Examiner* as a gift from his father, Senator George Hearst. Through his personal genius, unlimited energy, and willingness to invest vast amounts of his father's money, Hearst made the *Examiner* the most powerful paper on the West Coast. His reputation as a young and energetic publisher was first made by his attacks on the Southern Pacific in California. In many other respects, the young Hearst appeared in the role of a reformist crusader, but by the 1930s he was to bear little resemblance to the liberal of earlier decades. Hearst came to believe that reform had gone quite far enough and that the forces of conservatism must rally to reverse the abusive power of labor unions, of state and national government, and, in particular, of dangerous New Dealers.

Throughout most of the eighty-eight years of his life, Hearst made his power felt even at the international level through his chain of some thirty newspapers, thirteen magazines, and many radio stations. He came to be associated with a remarkable number of issues and events. Prominent among these were the Spanish-American

San Simeon, William Randolph Hearst's estate on a hilltop overlooking the Pacific, is now owned by the State of California and is open to the public.
(Union Pacific Railroad)

The Japanese Tea Garden, an attractive feature of Golden Gate Park since 1894.
(San Francisco Visitors Bureau)

War (which he almost surely helped cause); hatred of the two Roosevelts; opposition to United States entry into both World Wars; suppression of radicals and Oriental minorities; and distrust of the League of Nations as well as of most other forms of internationalism. In promoting his various prejudices, Hearst achieved mixed results. Thoughtful people were often offended by his convictions and repelled by his taste.

Orson Welles' 1940 film entitled *Citizen Kane* drew a skillful picture of the egotisms and personal imperialism of the aging genius. Hearst, who even dreamed of the Presidency, was always dramatic and usually controversial. His biography seems as unreal as the lurid articles that filled his Sunday supplement, "The American Weekly."

At Los Angeles, General Harrison Gray Otis acquired the *Times* in 1881. This paper, whose ownership passed into the hands of Harry Chandler and his descendants, played a vital role in the growth of Los Angeles; it became embroiled in a number of important civic issues, among them what came to be known as the Free Harbor struggle, the Owens River water controversy, and union difficulties. By the 1970s, the *Times* was one of the most successful newspapers

179

in the United States. It was Los Angeles' only morning daily and led the nation in lines of advertising.

STUDY SUGGESTIONS

To understand the chapter you should know (1) the meaning and importance of key phrases and terms, (2) the contributions to California history of major personalities, and (3) the location and significance of geographic place names.

1. Key phrases and terms

AMTRAK
Atchison, Topeka, and
 Santa Fe Railroad
BART
the "Big Four"
California Alien Land Act
Celestials
Central Pacific Railroad
Citizen Kane
the Colton letters
Crocker's Pets
The Devil's Dictionary
Gadsden Purchase
"Gentlemen's Agreement"
golden spike
Huntington Library

Immigration Act of 1965
Japanese relocation
Los Angeles *Times*
Manazanar
The Octopus
Pacific Railroad Act of 1862
picture brides
Pigtail Ordinance
San Francisco *Examiner*
San Simeon
Six Companies
Southern Pacific Railroad
Super Chief
Union Pacific Railroad
Yellow Peril

2. Major personalities

Ambrose Bierce
Harry Chandler
David D. Colton
Charles Crocker
Caleb Cushing
Henry George
S. I. Hayakawa
William Randolph Hearst
Mark Hopkins
Collis P. Huntington

Henry E. Huntington
Theodore D. Judah
Jack London
March Fong Eu
Frank Norris
Harrison Gray Otis
Theodore Roosevelt
Josiah Royce
Thorstein Veblen

180

3. *Important geographic place names*

Goleta	Santa Barbara
Hanford	Santa Monica
Promontory Point	Tule Lake
San Marino	

FOR ADDITIONAL STUDY

Dee Brown, *Hear that Lonesome Whistle Blow* (New York, 1977).

Glenn S. Dumke, *The Boom of the 'Eighties in Southern California* (San Marino, 1944).

Henry George, *Progress and Poverty* (New York, 1880).

Daisuke Kitagawa, *Issei and Nisei: The Internment Years* (New York, 1967).

George Kraus, *High Road to Promontory* (Palo Alto, 1969).

Oscar Lewis, *The Big Four* (New York, 1938).

Stanford M. Lyman, *The Asian in the West* (Reno, 1970).

Frank Norris, *The Octopus* (New York, 1901).

W. A. Swanberg, *Citizen Hearst* (New York, 1961).

Jeanne Wakasuki, *Farewell to Manzanar* (Houston, 1973).

Staten W. Webster, *Ethnic Minority Groups* (Scranton, Penn., 1972).

Michi Weglyn, *Years of Infamy* (New York, 1976).

•7•

"THE DESERT SHALL REJOICE"

The economy of many agricultural states depends heavily on some single crop, such as corn, cotton, dairy products, or beef. California, however, as the nation's leader in agricultural output, produces more than 200 farm products. By the mid-nineteenth century, California's agricultural pattern had become genuinely diversified, due partly to a varied climate, but also to the European methods of artificial irrigation introduced centuries before by the Spanish padres. The consumption within the state of its beef, wheat, and citrus production steadily increased. California's needs were not confined to food alone, however. A demand for lumber led to the development of a lumber industry. California's forest reserves, thus, constituted another of its natural assets.

CATTLE AND SHEEP RANCHING

Ranching had long been a major California enterprise. By the early 1860s, more than 3 million cattle roamed the hills and the valleys of California. The influx of population accelerated the growth of sheep herding, which profited from the demands for wool and meat.

When sheepmen erected sheds and fences and their lambs overcropped the ranges, trouble flared up between them and the cattlemen. Fences impounded roaming cattle in search of free grass. With their ranges overstocked, cattlemen were in no mood to see the easy movement of their animals checked by barbed wire. In this conflict, which occasionally reached the stage of violence, the sheepmen seldom emerged victorious. The cattlemen were more powerful and better organized. A few dry summers and a few severe winters drove small ranchers out, leaving behind the large cattle outfits. Sheepmen often fell into the category of small operators, and as such suffered especially from the control of water by the large cattle ranches.

Complicating the plight of cattle owners during the sixties was a further factor that had been traditionally friendly to them—the weather. A devastating drought in 1863—1864 kept the California skies cloudless for months on end. The bleached skeletons of thousands of animals dotted the valleys and hillsides. Many hundreds of thousands of cattle, starved for green grass and water, perished. The price of land slumped, and southern California range lands sold for as little as ten cents per acre by the late 1860s. The lure of cheap lands, however, brought new settlers, and by the mid-seventies population pressure drove the price of land upward again.

Over the years, California's cattle herds, roaming the ranges without supervision, had deteriorated. They had become scrawny, mangy, and bony, and their numbers had been drastically reduced by the drought. Heavier, meatier strains were imported, and fenced-in ranges became increasingly common.

DAIRYING, HOG RAISING, AND CEREAL PRODUCTION

Relatively little use had been made of either butter or milk during the Mexican period of California's history, the chief value of cattle being in hides and tallow. In a new era there gradually developed a considerable production of dairy products in response to the demands of the growing population. Dairies close to large centers of population, using labor-saving devices and modern methods, helped make Los Angeles County first in the nation in dairy production.

After the Civil War, the cultivation of crops for both human and animal consumption gradually superseded cattle ranching in value of operations. Among the most important of such crops were various kinds of grain, which often could be grown successfully without expensive irrigation. In addition, wheat and corn were in demand on international markets and therefore had the advantage of being only partially dependent on local economic changes. California's climate and soil were splendidly suited to growing these grains. Whereas the state had imported most of its grain during the Gold Rush, within a few years vast new ranches in its Central Valley made California more than self-sufficient as a producer of oats, barley, corn, and other cereals.

By the 1870s, California wheat in particular had become an important export crop. The state produced an unusually hard, dry, white grain, especially popular with British millers. By 1890, during

184

a period of extensive national expansion of wheat acreage, California ranked second among all the states in wheat production.

THE CITRUS INDUSTRY

California's citrus fruits, one of the state's most important crops, include lemons, tangerines, and grapefruit. But the real symbol and overwhelming source of strength of the citrus industry is the orange. In the mission period, orange groves were relatively small and un-

White faced cattle grazing under live oaks near Pacheco Pass in the Coast Range. *(Reprinted from California Real Estate Magazine. Photograph by Albert Wrey.)*

The grain harvest in San Fernando Valley, about 1900.
(C. C. Pierce Collection, courtesy of the Huntington Library)

developed, producing pithy, thick-skinned, and often sour fruit. One of the earliest orange groves in California was planted at San Gabriel Mission in 1804.

The first trainload of oranges was sent eastward to Saint Louis in 1877, soon after the Southern Pacific Railroad made its services available to Los Angeles. Eventually, orange growing spread widely throughout Los Angeles, Riverside, Orange, San Bernardino, San Diego, Ventura, and Santa Barbara counties. Trees were also planted in the Imperial, Coachella, and Sacramento valleys as far north as Oroville and Chico.

Frost was a hazard to the orange industry. In the winter months, temperatures sometimes fall below freezing in California's orange groves. To protect against frost oil heaters, called "smudge pots," that burned cheap crude oil were used. Nearby city dwellers, whose house furnishings, draperies, and rugs were sometimes covered with soot from the oil burners, complained bitterly. Eventually, the orchards were protected against cold damage by wind machines, which keep air currents in motion to prevent frost.

As the orange industry grew, new markets had to be found to absorb increased production, and a more efficient means of servicing these markets needed to be devised. Accordingly, the California Fruit Growers Exchange, a cooperative marketing organization, was incorporated in 1905. Its trade name, Sunkist, was used in a vigorous advertising campaign which set out to add the orange to the American breakfast diet. California's Chamber of Commerce, the Los Angeles All-Year Club, and dozens of other booster organizations soon joined in the campaign begun by the citrus industry.

Orange groves, palm trees and the snowcapped San Bernadino Mountains, in the 1920s. *(From Dr. Rolle's collection)*

THE WINE INDUSTRY

An important part of the agricultural history of California has been the development of its wine industry. A combination of the proper climate and soil, particularly in northern California, gave wine making a propitious start. And Europeans skilled in the care of vines arrived early in the region. Today, more than 90 percent of the United States grape crop and most of the wine production comes from California.

In 1770, the year after the first Franciscans arrived in California, the missionaries set out a small patch of grape cuttings at San Diego. Vines were also planted at Missions San Gabriel, Santa Barbara, and San Luis Obispo, where they bore grapes for over 100 years. The first vineyard planted at San Gabriel contained 3,000 such vines. In 1857, a group of Germans formed the Los Angeles Vineyard Society on lands which they had bought about thirty miles southeast of Los Angeles, not far from the ocean. They gave their tract the name Anaheim from its location in the Santa Ana Valley and the German word for home, *heim.* Around their property the Germans built a fence five and a half miles long, consisting of 40,000 willow poles, each eight feet long, of which six feet projected above the ground. They defended their fence by a ditch four feet deep, six feet wide at the top, sloping downward to a breadth of one foot at its bottom. The willow poles took root to form a living wall around the colony. Such "fortifications" were constructed mainly to keep out roving herds of cattle. With water from the Santa Ana River, the Germans irrigated their vineyards. Among these settlers only one man originally understood the art of wine making, but all went about the new work with patient industry.

In the mid-1880s, wine growing became fashionable, especially among the rich. One of the largest vineyards in the state belonged to Senator Leland Stanford, who owned 3,060,000 vines near Mission San José. Senator James Graham Fair, a forty-niner and Comstock millionaire, built a winery near Petaluma. Senator George Hearst owned a vineyard in Sonoma County, and E. J. "Lucky" Baldwin grew grapes at Santa Anita in sandy and hot southern California.

By the 1880s, no organization planted quite so many grapes as did the Italian-Swiss Agricultural Colony at Asti. Its 1897 vintage was so large that there were insufficient barrels in all California to hold the wine. A reservoir had to be chiseled out of solid rock, which became the largest wine tank in the world; when empty, this huge vat could accommodate a dance floor for 200 persons.

E. J. "Lucky" Baldwin, who became enormously wealthy as a speculator in the Comstock Lode and led in the development of the San Gabriel Valley. *(Title Insurance and Trust Company Los Angeles)*

As California wines began to win national and foreign prizes for their excellence, many new wineries appeared, not only in the Sonoma Valley, but also at Napa and in the San Joaquin–Sacramento Valley. At Cucamonga, in southern California, the Guasti family owned the largest vineyard in the world. Much of California's grape crop is dried for raisins, which amount to 75 percent of United States production.

RECLAMATION AND IRRIGATION

In recent years, a large part of California's agricultural production has consisted of vegetables. Extensive reclamation of swampy land and irrigation of dry terrain has opened up vast new areas for farming operations. All sorts of crops, from artichokes to watermelons, can now be grown in almost every one of California's fifty-eight counties.

One of the first regions to undergo reclamation was the large triangle of land lying within the fork formed by the Sacramento and San Joaquin rivers. This area of over 500,000 acres, once consisting of a group of islands and swampy plains, began to be transformed by the end of the nineteenth century along with other low-lying delta land.

The large-scale irrigation of California land began in 1887 with the passage of the Wright Act by the state legislature. The act, which

189

This plank road that crossed the sand dunes between the
Colorado River and Imperial Valley was used between 1914 and 1926.
(Title Insurance and Trust Company, Los Angeles)

provided for the organization of irrigation districts by farmers without allotting funds for their assistance, was an agricultural milestone. The Imperial Valley is a notable example of an early irrigation project. Sometimes called the American Nile area, this valley is located in the dry and hot southeastern part of the state. Through irrigation, it has been transformed from a waterless, sandy basin into a garden of abundance.

George Chaffey, a Canadian, planned this irrigation project for the Imperial Valley. By diverting the waters of the Colorado River, Chaffey made it possible for the Imperial Land Company to sell the land in the valley and bring in a large number of settlers by 1900. However, the opening of the area nearly proved catastrophic. In 1905, a serious flood began that lasted almost two years, created the Salton Sea, and threatened to drown the whole valley. This torrent

The Salton Sea. *(Title Insurance and Trust Company, Los Angeles)*

was caused when almost the entire river turned into the canal channel and flowed by gravity into the valley which was below sea level. In Febuary 1907, with the help of the Southern Pacific Railroad, the rampaging flood was stopped, and the river was diverted back into its old bed. Once the flood damage was repaired, the Imperial region grew into a rich agricultural community. The Salton Sea has now become an important water sports center.

Farther northward, east of Palm Springs, the Coachella Valley proved to be another marvel of productivity with the assistance of irrigation. Crops in this valley have the particular advantage of an early harvest, providing fresh fruit "out of season" to the lucrative eastern market.

WATER PROJECTS

Development of California's water resources, long of great importance to agricultural growth as well as to industry, became an increasingly crucial issue in the twentieth century. The vast immigration into the state that accompanied the advent of the automobile could not possibly have been supported without an adequate water supply. Large cities and small farming communities alike were obliged to find new sources of water when local wells and streams began to fail them. From 1900, hundreds of millions of dollars were spent on dams, wells, canals, reservoirs, catchment basins, and aqueducts. Especially in semiarid southern California, irrigated agriculture—once ridiculed by farmers—became widespread. At the same time, the new communities of the state's southland were wisely building upon the water conservation experiments of Chaffey, who had led the way toward replenishing the dwindling water supplies of older communities.

Los Angeles and the Owens Valley Project

Los Angeles displayed particular interest in Chaffey's techniques, which included the diversion of streams, the creation of lakes, and the storage of subsurface water. Los Angeles faced a genuine water crisis when it became apparent that the city's reservoirs were barely able to take in enough water to equal their outflow. The city *had* to find new sources of water. Its solution to the dilemma was to tap the Owens River in the far-off southern Sierra—a scheme that became one of the most controversial projects in the history of the state. In 1904, chief city engineer William Mulholland recommended that a bond issue be put on the ballot to provide funds for construction of an aqueduct that would traverse the 238 miles from the Owens Valley to Los Angeles. Mulholland argued that building such an aqueduct was the only way to relieve the shortages created by continued heavy reliance upon the Los Angeles River.

The bond issue was passed, and the project got under way. Using an army of several thousand workers, Mulholland completed his complex network of tunnels and trenches in less than five years. In November 1913, to celebrate a feat that was then considered second only to the building of the Panama Canal, a two-day celebration was held at the San Fernando Valley spillway where the new concrete aqueduct terminated.

In spite of the enthusiastic celebration and the newspaper accounts that generally described the construction feat in glowing terms, a bitter controversy developed over the project. Violent criticism of Mulholland and the City of Los Angeles came from the ranchers and farmers who had been forced to evacuate their Owens

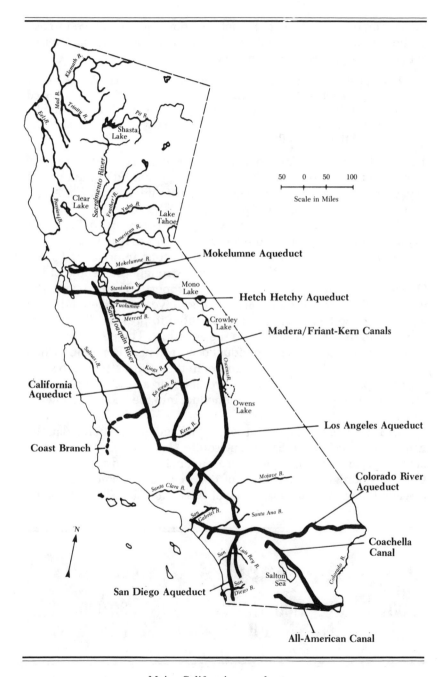

Major California aqueducts

Valley homes under threat of eviction. Sportsmen who loved to fish in the remote valley, as well as other outdoorsmen and naturalists, joined in the protest. They charged:

> Los Angeles gets its water by one of the costliest, crookedest, most unscrupulous deals ever perpetrated. . . . The City of the Angels moved through this valley like a devastating plague. It was ruthless, stupid, cruel, and crooked. It deliberately ruined the Owens Valley. It stole the waters of the Owens River.

The reputation of Los Angeles as a looter of water resources properly belonging to a pastoral paradise has, in fact, persisted to the present day, with many critics convinced that private interests in Los Angeles benefited most from the Owens Valley Project.

The citizens of Owens Valley appealed in vain to President Theodore Roosevelt, but Roosevelt sided with Los Angeles. The valley residents continued to regard the project as an organized swindle. Three demonstrations illustrate how strongly the people of the Owens Valley felt about the loss of their property. The first occurred when ranchers near Big Pine armed themselves with rifles and stood guard over the headgate to Big Pine Ditch to prevent diversion of water from the Owens River into the aqueduct. The next attempt to impede the progress of the aqueduct occurred near Lone Pine when a spillway was dislodged by dynamite. In their third attempt to sabotage the project, the ranchers were able for a short time to turn practically the entire flow of the aqueduct into the bed of the Owens River.

In 1928, renewed criticism of Mulholland arose when a dam he had constructed in the San Francisquito Canyon near the town of Saugus, as part of the Owens River Aqueduct, buckled and collapsed. Close to midnight on March 12 of that year, an avalanche of water cascaded down the narrow valley of the Santa Clara River to Santa

'All the News All the Time   Los Angeles Times   In Three Parts — 44 Pages

Vol. XLVII.   WEDNESDAY MORNING, MARCH 14, 1928. C   DAILY, FIVE CENTS   SUNDAY, TEN CENTS

200 DEAD, 300 MISSING, $7,000,000 LOSS IN ST. FRANCIS DAM DISASTER

Paula, fifty miles away, and on to the sea. Houses, trees, telephone poles, fences, bridges, and railroad tracks were swept away and 385 people were killed. Courageously, Mulholland accepted the blame for having built the dam in a poor location and thus ended his career of public service on an unhappy note. He is, however, generally remembered as the father of large-scale water development in California.

A second major disaster was narrowly averted in 1971 when engineers drained the Van Norman Reservoir after it had been severely weakened by the San Fernando earthquake. Located above the heavily populated northwest portion of the valley, this huge reservoir is an important link in the Owens Valley Project.

San Francisco's Aqueduct

Like Los Angeles, San Francisco also had to cope with a growing water shortage in the early years of the twentieth century. Although located in an area of heavier rainfall, the city's demands for water would soon exceed the supply. Civic leaders had long been eyeing the scenic Hetch Hetchy Valley of the Tuolumne River near Yosemite National Park as a future source of water. Conservationists, however, objected strongly to the San Francisco plan, which would permanently flood the rugged valley. Their protests to the United States Department of the Interior helped to retard construction of the proposed dam for years. Federal authorization, however, came in 1913 when Franklin K. Lane, former city and county attorney of San Francisco, became federal secretary of the interior. San Francisco finally completed its 186-mile-long Hetch Hetchy aqueduct and power network in 1931.

John Muir (1838–1914) was one of the leading opponents of the Hetch Hetchy Dam. Muir's strong feeling for the majesty of the Sierra peaks and for the natural treasures of the great valley of the Yosemite attracted many readers. He spent much of his life out of doors, tramping all over the California back country. As an influential defender of the forest, mountains, and wildlife against human encroachment, he encouraged President Theodore Roosevelt to set up the National Park System. The Sierra Club, which he founded, continues to champion the causes which Muir so eloquently advocated. One of its recent victories was in stopping the development of the Mineral King wilderness into a gigantic resort by the Disney Corporation.

195

The Boulder Canyon Project

By 1923, even while controversy over the Owens Valley Project was still a public issue, Los Angeles faced the same situation that had led it to embark on that water-development measure almost twenty years before. In 1922, representatives of Colorado, Wyoming, Utah, New Mexico, Arizona, Nevada, and California met in Santa Fe, New Mexico, to sign an agreement on the use of the waters of the Colorado River. This agreement provided for development of the basin of that river for the common use of the participating states. The project was to be undertaken jointly by the federal government, the states, and local municipalities. The aims of the measure were to protect the Imperial Valley against flooding, to provide water supplies for several states, and to generate hydroelectric power.

Most of the major cities of Los Angeles County formed a Metropolitan Water District to coordinate the transportation and distribution of water and power to southern California. Hoover Dam, the project's dominant structure, was built in Nevada near Las Vegas. It was one of the largest construction jobs in the world. The dam, 1,282

John Muir, famous naturalist, and founder of the Sierra Club wrote about the natural wonders of California, such as Yosemite and the redwoods. *(Photograph by Bradley and Rulofson, San Francisco (no date). Courtesy of the Bancroft Library)*

feet high, required the combined efforts of six large construction companies employing 10,000 workers. An artificial lake 242 miles long, Lake Mead, was created by the dam. Despite opposition from private utility companies, from army engineers, and from the state of Arizona, Hoover Dam was completed on March 1, 1936. Soon its generators pumped electrical energy into homes, farms, and industrial plants throughout the Southwest. With its power-generating capacity, and its unequaled water resources, the Boulder Canyon project proved to be of special significance to Los Angeles and southern California. Downstream, along the California–Arizona border, a huge reservoir lake named Lake Havasu was impounded behind Parker Dam. The Metropolitan Water District built this costly diversion dam to deflect water westward through an aqueduct 242 miles long to Los Angeles. Piercing through six mountain ranges, the aqueduct provided water to the district, which supplies water to most southern California cities.

Water for the Central Valley

Farther north, particularly in the interior of the state, the 1930s saw California's farmers becoming increasingly concerned over the water supplies needed for agricultural growth. The solution seemed to lie in channeling wasted flood waters to the dry and dusty farms located far from the rivers. One of the most obvious sources of water was the Sacramento River. This river had been so silted up by mining operations that navigation was difficult and floods were frequent. Millions of dollars of damage occurred every time the rivers of the central valley went on the rampage. The other great river of the Central Valley was the long, twisting San Joaquin, which joins with the Sacramento from the south and empties into San Francisco Bay. To conserve and to redistribute the flow of both rivers, a plan for harnessing their water resources passed the state legislature in 1933. This scheme, the Central Valley Project, also proposed to generate large quantities of electric power by impounding part of the waters of the Sacramento, San Joaquin, and various lesser streams. Opposition to the measure came from private utility companies, particularly the Pacific Gas and Electric Company, which looked upon the Central Valley Project as unfair government intervention. They sponsored a public referendum in 1933, to rescind the legislation; however, the voters upheld the project.

With this issue settled, there still remained the problem of raising money to build the costly system. When a state bond issue could

This giant pipe brings Colorado River water from Parker Dam to Los Angeles.
(Title Insurance and Trust Company, Los Angeles)

not be sold because of the Great Depression, the state appealed to the federal government for assistance. As a result, California's water program in the Central Valley was declared a national reclamation project. Congress authorized the construction of Shasta Dam as the first step. The project not only saves water for the summer dry season, but also, through a system of canals, takes water from the north to the dry southern areas of the Central Valley.

AGRICULTURE BETWEEN THE TWO WORLD WARS

California's agricultural development benefited from new water and power supplies and from land-conservation measures. As in other farm areas of the country, agricultural yield in California spiraled upward while the acreage of the average farm decreased and the value of farm land boomed.

The major problem of the interwar years was not agricultural production but, rather, finding the means to increase sales and consumption of the greatly expanded variety of products which California grew. As elsewhere in the country, crops were plowed under during the depression of the 1930s, at the very time when needy refugees from the Dust Bowl regions of the Middle West were going hungry. To sustain a profitable price level, vineyardists, orange-grove owners, and ranchers redoubled their search for new markets to absorb the greater yields that resulted from better knowledge about spraying, fertilizing, and irrigating crops. Prohibition worked a devastating hardship upon grape growers and wineries, which tried to market their products in nonalcoholic forms such as "wine bricks" and grape bars.

The fruit and vegetable farms of the Central Valley came to resemble big-business operations in their impersonality and in their greater efficiency. A cheap migrant labor market, widespread unemployment, increasing mechanization, and specialized production combined to boost output still further. Agricultural centers were influenced by industrialization. Fresno, in the San Joaquin Valley, a city served by two railroads and various truck lines, reflected the new pattern of growth. An important transportation center, Fresno gradually became a clearing center for the distribution of fresh fruits and vegetables, cotton, livestock, wine, dairy products, and such dried fruits as raisins, apricots, and prunes. In addition, it became a supply center for nearby mountain recreation sites and tourist traffic and a local headquarters for petroleum, hardware, grocery, and appliance

199

firms. Other valley towns—Stockton, Visalia, Madera, Merced, Modesto, and Bakersfield—grew into similarly important market centers.

Whether the times were good, as from 1923 to 1929, or bad, as from 1930 to 1937, California's agricultural establishment was geared to deliver an uninterrupted flow of farm products. As world and national economic conditions improved after the depression, consumption of these products began to rise sharply once more.

THE CALIFORNIA WATER PROJECT

By the late forties, it became evident that even Hoover Dam and the Boulder Canyon Project could not permanently provide water for a growing southern California. Overuse of wells in coastal locations often causes the intrusion of seawater into freshwater wells. In the Los Angeles basin of southern California, and to the north in Suisun Bay and along the Sacramento–San Joaquin Delta, such intrusions have caused serious pollution of existing supplies.

In 1955, construction of the federally financed Trinity River Project, a new unit of the Central Valley Project, was begun. Portions of the San Joaquin Valley Project were expanded, and in particular the Kings River was harnessed. But none of these developments provided a solution to the water needs of urban centers outside the San Joaquin Valley. Along California's northwest coast—where 41 percent of the state's water resources originated—the rivers continued to empty most of their water into the ocean.

Feather River Project

A new approach to the conservation of California's wasted water resources had to be found. As early as 1948, advocates of a huge new plan began to speak up in the state legislature. This was the Feather River Project. The Feather is the most important tributary of the Sacramento River. To achieve the purpose of the Feather River Project—to harness the energy and to conserve and distribute the waters of the Feather—a series of costly dams and 638 miles of canals, tunnels, and siphons had to be constructed. The main portion of this system, which runs along the west side of the Central Valley, is known as the California Aqueduct. The cost of creating this capacity was originally estimated to be in excess of $1.75 million. But this project was only part of an $11 billion statewide master plan, which would be under construction over a period of sixty years until the year 2020. During 1957, work began on "the world's largest earth-fill dam," the 770-foot-high Oroville Dam, located on the Feather River above Sacramento. When completed in 1968, it was the first step in a great downhill "natural stairway" of untapped hydroelectric power and water. Work on other parts of the project was held up because of sectional disputes and funding.

In the 1950s, a time-consuming debate over whether state or federal funds should be used—added to quarrels between northern and southern California—hampered further development of the Feather River Project. Even after construction had begun on the Oroville Dam, California's legislature continued to argue many points. Southern legislators were against appropriating money for water which could be recaptured by northern "counties of origin." The wetter north required flood control as urgently as the south needed water.

A persistent objection to the Feather River Project was the prospect of "unjust enrichment" of large landowners. Many argued for a 160-acre limitation on the use of cheap water provided by the

Lake Oroville. *(State of California, Department of Water Resources)*

201

general taxpayer. Such a provision already applied to federally funded projects. The sponsors of the limitation feared the further increase of "corporation farmers," whose thousands of productive acres would be nourished by water paid for by others. It was also pointed out that cheap subsidized water development in the San Joaquin Valley would produce more agricultural surpluses, already stockpiled with tax dollars by the federal government. A leading stumbling block to adoption of the Feather River Project was its great cost. For a time the water problem threatened to dominate and disrupt state politics.

Not until after the election of Governor Edmund G. "Pat" Brown in 1958 was the legislative deadlock on the statewide master plan broken. In a comprehensive water message to the legislature, Brown expressed regret that in a state so magnificently endowed by nature,

> it has become the fashion in recent years to dwell on our water problems as being awesome and impossibly complicated. . . . The result has been delay and frustration. This stalemate must come to an end. If we take courage and put our fears behind us, we can replace narrow sectional differences with confident, pioneering leadership.

The California Aqueduct

In 1960, Governor Brown's water program was placed before the voters. With its passage, work began on the long-delayed Feather River Project, which with a number of additional elements came to be known as the California Water Project. Key elements in this system are the Delta Project, the San Luis Dam, the Castaic Reservoir, Lake Silverwood, Lake Perris, and the 444-mile California Aqueduct, which connects them. The Delta Project consists of a network of canals and pumping stations in the low-lying portions of the Sacramento and San Joaquin valleys. Located in Merced County, the 310-foot-high San Luis Dam provides a reservoir for water which is used to irrigate the dry western and southern portions of the San Joaquin Valley. The Castaic complex connects the California Aqueduct with the older Owens River Project on the south side of the Tehachapi Mountains. Because of its twin lakes, its electric generating capacity can be used to supplement existing sources at peak load and the same system can pump the water back into the upper level when demand is low. Lake Silverwood in San Bernardino County and Lake Perris in Riverside County provide supplementary water to these regions, the latter also ties in with the Colorado River Aqueduct.

By 1990, the yield of the entire facility will be 4.5 million acre-feet, of which nearly one-half has been allotted to the Metropolitan Water District, which is paying nearly 70 percent of the project's costs.

Because of its north-to-south flow, the California Aqueduct provided no relief from the serious northern California drought of 1975

California Aqueduct, Stanislaus County.
(State of California, Department of Water Resources)

to 1977. Southern California had to conserve in its water usage because of the cutback in the flow, but Marin County and other northern areas were hit hardest by the dry cycle.

Observers have repeatedly pointed to another possible way of solving the water problem—large-scale desalination of sea water by mechanical means. However, such a process would be tremendously costly. The popular conception of the economic feasibility of converting ocean water into fresh water has little foundation in fact. However, during the early sixties, the state explored desalination. A desalination laboratory erected at Point Loma near San Diego with federal funds has begun active experimentation. California cannot afford to ignore any possible means of developing its total water resources.

California suffered an apparent setback in the 1960s when the United States Supreme Court, after many years of disputes on allocation of Colorado River water, decided in favor of Arizona. In 1964, Secretary of the Interior Stewart Udall, a former Arizona congressman, announced further curtailment of California's use of the river's water. In 1977, the 160-acre limitation issue reached the Supreme Court again. This time the question was whether the Coachella–Imperial Valley System should continue to be exempted from this provision.

CONTINUED AGRICULTURAL PRODUCTIVITY

California has become an industrial state without ceasing to be an agricultural one. Aided by irrigation projects, a vigorous farm lobby, and government agricultural agencies, farm acreage continues to expand though the actual number of farms decreases annually. Farmers and their dependents represent only 10 percent of the state's population. California's cash farm income is the highest for any state in the Union. In 1960, Fresno County headed the nation's 3,134 counties in agricultural production for the twelfth year. Tulare County was in second place, while Kern County was third.

The chief reason that California has remained the leading agricultural state in the nation is that it continues to produce over 200 different crops. The state is first nationally in the production of dozens of crops, ranging from almonds and artichokes to tomatoes and walnuts. It supplies more than one-fourth of the fruit and vegetables commercially grown in the United States. Though faced with heavy competition from Florida, California still contributes much of the nation's citrus production to domestic markets.

The small family-run farm has shown itself incapable of competing successfully; consequently it is tending to be replaced by large mechanized "agri-businesses" such as Kern County Land Company and the Irvine Ranch Company. By adopting the techniques of industry, these large corporations increased the size of the average farm and took advantage of technology and corporate managerial skills. Large growers extended their operations into shipping, processing, and marketing, sometimes controlling agriculture from planting through sale of the final product. Today's California cattlemen sometimes breed, feed, finish, ship, and sell their own livestock; a few even grow their own feeds. Some large rancher-farmers rely upon two-way radios to keep contact with employees; they buy costly harvesters, tractors, and automatic potato pickers. This mechanization is a far cry from the nineteenth century's horse-drawn plows, haystacks, and milk wagons. Large capital investments are necessary to carry on the new agriculture.

Agriculture has, of course, yielded large areas of farm land to real estate subdivisions, industrial plants, and highways. Real estate promoters today even "process the desert" to prepare new housing tracts. The decline of Los Angeles from its position as the first agricultural county in the nation has been caused by its shift toward industrialization. The annexation of the agricultural San Fernando Valley in 1915 brought 170 square miles of farm land into the Los Angeles city limits. Now the fields and orchards have given way to people, with over 1 million people living in San Fernando Valley. Yet Los Angeles today still ranks among the nation's most productive agricultural counties. Its 520 dairies with 112,000 milk cows are housed virtually on the doorsteps of urban consumers.

Heavy migration into Los Angeles and Orange counties has made the sight of orange orchards (once a symbol of southern California) a memory of the past. As late as 1930, orange growing was clearly the first agricultural crop in the state with dairies second and livestock third. But orange groves occupy too much land. As ten newcomers step across the state line in search of sunshine and a better life, California loses an average of one more acre of farm land. Yet, California remains the nation's first farm state. True, crops have changed. The state's first agricultural activity today is the raising of livestock; dairying is the second largest; cotton has become the third largest crop; and grapes, the fourth. Orange growing has tumbled to sixth place.

An exception to the haphazard pattern of development of land formerly devoted to agriculture has been accomplished by the Irvine Ranch Company in Orange County. The 88,000 acre parcel of land held by the company represented the bulk of three Spanish ranchos which had been owned by several generations of the Irvine family. In 1960, 10,000 acres were set aside for an entirely new city to be centered around a proposed branch of the University of California. Architect William L. Pereira's master plan projected a thriving community of 50,000 which focused on the new campus.

One should not lose sight of California's food-processing industry. Aside from widespread fruit and vegetable canning operations, the state remains a significant center of commercial poultry raising, dairying, and fish canning. Over 80 percent of the wine consumed nationally comes from California wineries. Fish and shellfish landed at California ports annually exceed a billion pounds, the largest catch of any state in the Union. Fish canneries are located at San Francisco, Monterey, San Pedro, and San Diego, and the number of persons engaged in commercial fishing is more than 10,000. These canneries have to meet stiff foreign competition.

University of California, Irvine. *(Stu Shaffer)*

MIGRATORY FARM WORKERS

Although increasingly mechanized, modern agriculture still requires large numbers of hand laborers to hoe and thin sugar beets, cut spinach, feed livestock, and prune grape vineyards. During both winter and summer, fruit, vegetable, and cotton pickers range throughout the state looking for work. Uncertain market conditions and the maladjustment between labor demands and the supply of workers keep wages depressed. Migrant laborers, traditionally nonunionized, are also dependent upon the harvest itself. A bad freeze or drought period drastically reduces their income. They live in substandard housing, are rarely fed adequately, and their children seldom complete even a grade-school education.

Migrants, foreign and domestic, wander from farm to farm, following the harvests as birds follow the sun. Until recently, their wages were low and their working conditions poor. Even worse were the hovels in which they lived. Whole shipments of them, including women and children, slept in abandoned barns, adobe huts, empty corrals, on straw in warehouses—any place where rent was not demanded. Many of the structures in which they lived had dirt floors or tin roofs with no ceilings. Cheese cloth or flour sacks were hung over the window openings to keep insects out, but flies, attracted by primitive toilet facilities, found their way into sleeping areas. Poorer "houses" were patched together from scraps of lumber, flattened oil cans, old signboards, or tar paper. They had no indoor water pipes or cooking facilities. Migrants often cooked outside over open fires in warm weather and inside out of wash tubs when it rained. These laborers were the modern equivalent of the poorest nineteenth-century squatter—wretchedly clad, housed, and fed and unwanted.

Braceros and Illegals

In California the migrants include large numbers of Chicano (Mexican-American) farm workers. The low wages Mexicans received north of the border seemed good by Mexican standards. Between 1942 and 1964, as many as 750,000 of these workers entered the United States legally as supplementary farm laborers, or *braceros.* "Illegals," or "wetbacks" (as they were sometimes called), slipped across the border, defying efforts of the Border Patrol to prevent their entry. Man-snatching *coyotes,* or middlemen, made a business of hiding laborers and even stealing and marketing whole labor crews to employers. The Mexican government protested the illegal

207

profiteering that resulted from the exploitation of Mexican labor in California and elsewhere.

The combined effect of the drastic curtailment of the *bracero* program in 1964 and the first time ever imposition of a legal limit on Western Hemisphere immigration imposed by the 1965 Immigration Act, compounded by high inflation and high unemployment in Mexico created great pressure for illegal immigration. By 1977, when an estimated 50,000 persons crossed the border each month, there may have been as many as 8 to 10 million illegals in the southwestern states. When President Carter suggested a plan for increased border security coupled with a blanket amnesty for earlier "illegals," the pressure on the border increased markedly. While the overwhelming majority of these border-crossers quietly blended into the existing Chicano communities in East Los Angeles and other urban areas where they had no great difficulty obtaining low-paying jobs, the farm workers could not be so easily absorbed, and they became the most visible Mexican work force.

UNIONIZING FARM LABOR

The IWW (Industrial Workers of the World) tried unsuccessfully to unionize the Central Valley before World War I, and later, in the 1930s, the AFL and CIO also failed. It was not until the 1960s that unions were finally able to represent the farm workers with some success. During 1960, the Agricultural Workers Organizing Committee obtained wage increases of 12 to 17 cents for each box of peaches picked and from 15 to 17 cents per box for tomatoes. In 1961 the Teamster's Union signed a union-shop contract at Salinas with various large ranches. But these were sporadic gains, without general significance. California's army of migrants found the growers' resistance virtually impregnable. The Council of California Growers insisted that their unstable and unpredictable "industry" did not lend itself to traditional unionization. They claimed that once a crop was ready to harvest, strikes were an impossibility, as they could not shut down picking operations to negotiate.

The disorganization which had long plagued seasonal farm laborers seemed to end in 1965, when a massive strike of grape harvesters took place in Delano. The strikers, many of whom were Chicanos, wanted union recognition, better housing and working conditions, unemployment insurance, and the right to bargain collectively. Farm owners often refused to discuss these demands, and some even dusted the strikers with insecticides. Nonunion laborers imported by the growers met aggressive picket lines shouting *"Viva la Huelga!"* Then labor organizers imposed a statewide sympathetic boycott upon Delano grapes and beverages, and a few chain stores agreed not to stock these items. Leaflets explaining the boycott flooded into stores which had not agreed to ban such merchandise. The strike was backed by the Congress of Racial Equality (CORE) and various student groups, with support from local clergymen.

Cesar Chavez and the United Farm Workers

Personally leading the farm workers was Cesar Chavez, a magnetic idealist who had spent his youth in the labor camps of Imperial Valley. Chavez and his grape strikers marched 300 miles to Sacramento to protest working conditions. In August 1966, Chavez began to reap the fruits of his organizing efforts, when grape pickers employed by the powerful DiGiorgio Fruit Corporation voted in favor of his union against the Teamsters, who had tried to organize them. By the fall of 1967, Chavez had also struck against the Giumarra Vineyards—the largest table grape growers in the world.

Shy and sad in appearance, Chavez became the new, charismatic, mobilizer of a once despised heritage. His checkered shirt and blue jeans characterized a wish to remain close to his people. Chavez, who came from their ranks, knew what it was to do "stoop work," picking grapes or harvesting lettuce all day long. He made up for lack of a formal education by extensive reading, particularly the autobiography of India's Mahatma Gandhi, which had a profound effect upon him. Like Gandhi, he refused to allow violence to enter into his fight for Chicanos and other farm workers.

In 1968, Chavez completed a twenty-five-day hunger fast. Senator Robert Kennedy joined him at the close of the fast, expressing sympathy (after the senator's assassination Ethel Kennedy, his widow, continued the family's support for Chavez). The year 1968 saw nine smaller strikes among California's farm workers and intensification of the boycott against the purchasing of grapes.

In 1970, when the big grape strike was approaching its fifth year and many believed that the growers would never give in, Chavez intensified picketing and invited student groups as well as militant Chicano organizations to help the farm labor cause. At last, a group of Central Valley grape growers agreed to sign contracts. They were soon followed by a majority of the Coachella growers.

Chavez's persistence produced a minimum wage for his pickers of $1.70 per hour, heretofore an unheard of rate of pay. Further-

209

Cesar Chavez. *(United Farm Workers of America. Photograph by Cathy Murphy.)*

more as crates containing union grapes displaying the United Farm Workers Union (UFWU) label were stocked in the nation's stores, sales of union grapes jumped. Both stores and growers wanted what they once had labeled the "Trotsky eagle." The walls of resistance erected by the grape growers came tumbling down as the majority of growers signed labor contracts. In 1978, the boycott of nonunion grapes was officially ended.

By late 1970, the UFWU was admitted into the AFL-CIO. There was no turning back from the war against mechanized agriculture. "Brown Power," as Mexican-American efforts were called by many, had never before attained similar results. Chavez, now speaking out against depersonalized agribusiness, labor contractors, and "body merchants," sought to enhance the dignity of his union's members. He turned to challenging the lettuce-growing industry, moving the battle from the San Joaquin and Coachella valleys to its main site, the Salinas Valley. There he faced the same management attempts to break a strike that he had encountered with the grape growers. On December 4, 1970, he was jailed without bail for refusing to obey an injunction. This court action drew further national attention to his lettuce boycott, and he was released. But trouble in the fields was not over.

Throughout most of the seventies Chavez and his union engaged in bitter organizational disputes with the Teamsters Union. Finally, in 1977, with indirect assistance from Governor Jerry Brown's support for unionization of farm laborers, Chavez and the Teamsters agreed to divide the turf. Field work would be reserved for UFWU and the Teamsters would concentrate on processing plants.

STUDY SUGGESTIONS

To understand the chapter you should know (1) the meaning and importance of key phrases and terms, (2) the contributions to California history of major personalities, and (3) the location and significance of geographic place names.

1. Key phrases and terms

aqueduct	Metropolitan Water District
bracero	160-acre limitation
California Aqueduct	Owens Valley Project
Castaic Reservoir	reclamation
corporation farmers	Shasta Dam
desalination	Sierra Club
Feather River Project	smudge pots
Hetch Hetchy Valley	Sunkist
Hoover Dam	UFWU
illegals	Van Norman Reservoir
Irvine Ranch Company	*Viva la Huelga!*
Mexican-American	Wright Act of 1887

2. Major personalities

George Chaffey	William Mulholland
Cesar Chavez	William Pereira
Robert F. Kennedy	Stewart Udall
John Muir	

3. Important geographic place names

Anaheim	Cucamonga
Asti	Fresno
Bakersfield	Imperial Valley
Coachella Valley	Kings River

Owens Valley
Palm Springs
Salton Sea
Santa Ana River
Santa Anita

Santa Paula
Sonoma Valley
Stockton
Yosemite

FOR ADDITIONAL STUDY

Robert G. Cleland, *California in Our Time* (New York, 1947).
———, *The Irvine Ranch* (San Marino, 1966).
Sheridan Downey, *They Would Rule the Valley* (San Francisco, 1947).
Carey McWilliams, *Factories in the Fields* (Boston, 1939).
Peter Matthiessen, *Sal Si Puedes: Cesar Chavez and the New American Revolution* (New York, 1973).
Remi Nadeau, *The Water Seekers* (New York, 1950).
Vincent Ostrom, *Water and Politics* (Los Angeles, 1953).
Harold Bell Wright, *The Winning of Barbara Worth* (New York, 1911).

·8·

CALIFORNIA AS SYMBOL AND MYTH

Several generations of Americans viewed California as the land of golden opportunity, the "Last Frontier." That this utopia failed to materialize for all made it seem like a dream; that it succeeded for so many is what kept the vision alive. Some came for sunshine; some came for money; some sought a fresh start. They came by the tens of thousands. Neither they, nor California, would ever be quite the same again.

REFORM IN SAN FRANCISCO

At the turn of the century Californians seemed ready to clean up politics in all levels of government. San Francisco was particularly ripe for reform. In 1902, a labor-backed political machine, the Union Labor Party, captured the city administration and installed a theater musician, Eugene E. Schmitz, as mayor, with Abraham Ruef, an extremely clever attorney, as the power and brains behind the throne. Ruef collected bribes, blackmailed legitimate businesses, and extorted graft through a variety of protection rackets.

In 1905, the San Francisco *Bulletin* began publishing a series of articles by Fremont Older, its reformist editor, exposing the city regime. But just as a full-scale campaign to overthrow Ruef and Schmitz began, a disaster struck San Francisco. This catastrophe was to throw new light on the city's administration.

213

Earthquake and Fire

At 5:16 A.M. on April 18, 1906, a loud rumbling noise awakened thousands at San Francisco. Then came a creaking and grinding sound as flimsy buildings were suddenly twisted off their foundations. More substantial brick structures fell into the streets. Yawning fissures opened up in the earth. Electric wires, which fell into the city's streets, set off fires that swept through block after block of apartments and residences. When volunteer firemen attached their hoses to hydrants, no water came out of the mains. Not only were pipes broken, but in some instances, it was discovered, the city's fire hydrants had never even been hooked up to its water system. Firemen fought, even without water, to stamp out the advancing flames. But the fire moved relentlessly on. Panic-stricken property owners stood on the roofs of their buildings with strips of carpet, beating out the flames.

As the fire spread, General Frederick Funston, commandant of the Presidio of San Francisco, charged into the city and proceeded to dynamite more than a quarter mile of wooden and stone mansions along Van Ness, one of its most beautiful streets. Explosion and burning took an awesome toll in the fire, which raged for three days and two nights before it burned itself out. Over 500 city blocks had been destroyed and along with them most of the city's business houses, banks, churches, and newspaper offices. The quake and fire caused a total property loss in San Francisco of $200 million and 452 people had lost their lives. At nearby Palo Alto, Stanford University's newly constructed buildings were largely demolished by the quake.

For weeks 300,000 homeless people were forced to live in army tents pitched on vacant lots, along the streets, and in Golden Gate Park. Campers, some clad in their best Sunday clothes, munched on rations of shredded-wheat biscuits and drank beef tea. Hundreds of tins of corned beef were also distributed by the Red Cross. By standing in lines several blocks long, children could get free oranges and milk.

Reform

Even as the work of rebuilding the devastated city began, definite plans for the destruction of the brazen Ruef–Schmitz machine were being formed. After months of detective work, the great "San Francisco graft prosecution" began, in November 1906, with the indictments of Ruef and Schmitz for extortion. Whereas the bribe takers,

Results of the San Francisco earthquake, April 23, 1906. *(H. G. Hills Collection, courtesy of the Bancroft Library. Photographed by T. E. Hecht.)*

Ruef and Schmitz, were condemned for their crookedness, the bribe givers, it was argued, had been blackjacked into making deals with the thieving politicians who ran the city.

The San Francisco graft trials lasted more than two years. Of all the defendants, only Abe Ruef finally went to the penitentiary. He was sentenced to fourteen years for bribery, but after four years and seven months at San Quentin, he was freed. As for Ruef's political associate, Mayor Schmitz, the California Supreme Court reversed his conviction.

The spirit of municipal reform, meanwhile, had resulted in emergency action elsewhere, particularly at Los Angeles. In that city, a "good-government" movement took shape under Dr. John R. Haynes, a wealthy physician and an especially severe critic of the influence of the Southern Pacific. Through the influence of Dr. Haynes and his civic-minded fellow citizens, Los Angeles became one of the first cities in the nation to adopt the measures of initiative, referendum, and recall as part of its charter. During 1907, the electorate recalled Mayor Arthur C. Harper in what was the first use of the recall technique in the United States.

HIRAM JOHNSON AND THE LINCOLN-ROOSEVELT LEAGUE

In 1907, the Lincoln-Roosevelt League was founded by liberal Republicans. Their aim was to free the Republican Party in California from domination by corrupt interests. President Theodore Roosevelt himself gave his blessing to the group, which was made up generally of well-educated, independent-minded business and professional men. The platform of the league pledged to free the state from domination by the Southern Pacific.

In 1910, it ran Hiram W. Johnson as its candidate for governor. Johnson had already achieved fame as a prosecutor in the San Francisco graft prosecutions. Now forty-four, a stubborn and steel-nerved politician, Johnson knew how to put the diffuse talents of his supporters to best use. He won the governorship against four other candidates.

Seemingly overnight, the league succeeded in an objective that neither the Republicans nor the Democrats had been able to accomplish in a generation—the overthrow of one of the nation's most entrenched political systems. The legislature of 1911 enacted fundamental reform measures, racking up a record that was the envy of progressives in every state of the Union and receiving praise from

216

President Roosevelt. Measures providing for statewide initiative, referendum, and recall were among the first to be adopted. Then came laws designed to cut down the powers of political machines and bosses by requiring local offices to be elected on a nonpartisan basis. Cross-filing was also instituted; this device, which was repealed in 1959, allowed a candidate to run in the primary elections of more than one party.

The state legislature of 1911 also added a total of twenty-three amendments to the state constitution, all of which were subsequently adopted by the voters. These amendments concerned such issues as control of public utilities, workmen's compensation, conservation of natural resources, income tax provisions, and women's suffrage. Other progressive measures included a comprehensive civil service law and the establishment of a legal minimum wage for women and minor children. These reforms seem routine enough today, but in their time the measures enacted by the California progressives were

Hiram Johnson (Republican), Governor, 1910–1917; United States Senator, 1917–1945. *(California State Library)*

major innovations. The major achievement of the progressive victory in California was the removal of the Southern Pacific from state and local politics. As governor from 1911 to 1917, Johnson and his progressive state legislature helped make sure that the railroads would be the servants, not the masters, of the people.

THE PROGRESSIVE PARTY AND ITS DECLINE

When Theodore Roosevelt failed in his attempt to obtain a third-term nomination in 1912, his progressive followers bolted the Republican Party and formed the Progressive Party. Roosevelt was nominated for the presidency with California's Governor Johnson as his running mate. The pair carried California by a narrow margin, but their major objective was lost because many Republicans remained loyal to Taft. The election put Woodrow Wilson in the White House with only 40 percent of the popular vote. The split in Republican ranks gave 435 electroral votes to Wilson, only 88 to Roosevelt, and 8 to Taft. In 1914, Johnson was returned to the governorship under the Progressive banner.

The confusion caused by the national election of 1912 was felt again in the presidential campaign of 1916 when Republican Charles Evans Hughes ran against President Woodrow Wilson. In theory the Republican Party was reunited. When Hughes visited California, he kept in poor contact with Governor Johnson. Both men were momentarily in the same hotel in Long Beach without meeting. Justly or not, Johnson felt snubbed by Hughes.

Johnson did not campaign vigorously for Hughes. Had he done so any more than half-heartedly, he could, some believed, have swung the state for Hughes. The voting was so close that Hughes retired on election eve in the belief that he had been elected. The next morning he learned that California's vote was still in the balance. Two days later, California's thirteen electoral votes finally went to Wilson, leaving Hughes twelve votes short of the presidency. Meanwhile, Johnson won a seat in the senate for himself.

In the crucial postwar election year of 1920, Johnson hopefully believed that he might capture the Republican presidential nomination. Like Theodore Roosevelt, who had died in 1919, Johnson vigorously opposed United States entry into the League of Nations. Johnson won the state presidential primary, however, only to see his hopes dashed in the Republican National Convention by the nomination of Ohio Senator Warren G. Harding.

218

Despite their decline in the period after World War I, the Progressives had not only cleaned up state and local government but also improved its efficiency. Without seeking to destroy the capitalistic economic structure, they had called attention to its weaknesses. Their chief California goal, "to kick the Southern Pacific out of state politics forever," was attained.

THE CITIES FLOURISH

The San Francisco earthquake and fire stimulated the growth of neighboring communities. In San Francisco itself the heavy damage gave years of booming employment to the building trades. Civic leaders insisted on rebuilding the city on a more magnificent and more enduring scale.

Farther south, the same spirit of improvement and expansion was exhibited. Once the bitter struggle over the location of Los Angeles' new harbor had ended with the selection of San Pedro in preference to Santa Monica, Angelenos went on to develop a great port. In 1909, the consolidation of San Pedro and Wilmington with Los Angeles was accomplished by connecting them with a "shoe-string" of land 500 feet wide and 15 miles long.

The new port facilities, whose construction was followed by formal opening of the Panama Canal in 1914, made Los Angeles one of the world's most important harbor cities. By 1924, Los Angeles had surpassed San Francisco in total annual tonnage. Meanwhile, the city itself was expanding rapidly as a population shift occurred from northern California southward. Los Angeles first reached and then surrounded Beverly Hills. Next it pushed its boundaries over the Hollywood Hills toward San Fernando. The city eventually included more than 450 square miles of land. Though it became one of the largest cities in the world in area, it seemed to lack a central section such as most cities have, and thus "LA" has been referred to as "a group of suburbs in search of a city."

Transportation was a vital factor in the growth of both San Francisco and Los Angeles during this period. San Francisco's Key Route Electric Railway and Henry Huntington's Pacific Electric in Los Angeles were unifying forces for both cities. However, in Los Angeles, transportation continued to be more of a problem than in the metropolitan area of San Francisco. By the mid-1920s, Los Angeles County contained more than forty incorporated cities within its limits, and its transport facilities were already strained.

219

CALIFORNIA AND WORLD WAR I

The prosperity of California was stimulated by World War I. Though the state was remote from the zones of combat, it quickly became involved in the national war effort. Manufacturing and the food-processing industries, including meat packing and fruit and fish canning, as well as lumber, mineral, and oil production now flourished with renewed vigor. In agriculture the war spurred the production of certain crops in particular. Cotton, for example, grew in demand because of its use in the millions of new uniforms that had to be supplied to soldiers. Taking up the slogan, "Food Will Win the War!" the state sent huge quantities of grains, fruits, meats, and vegetables into Allied storehouses. In manpower, California contributed more than 150,000 soldiers to the Allied forces.

The 1920s brought a housing boom that produced a number of new towns. Realtors developed large tracts of former countryside. The suburbs became dotted with small frame bungalows, which retired Iowa farmers, for example, might buy for as little as $1,000, as well as larger and more expensive homes for those who preferred white "Spanish-style" stucco with palm trees in their yards.

California's mining industry also benefited from World War I. With the demands for gold, silver, salt, soda, potash, cement, and

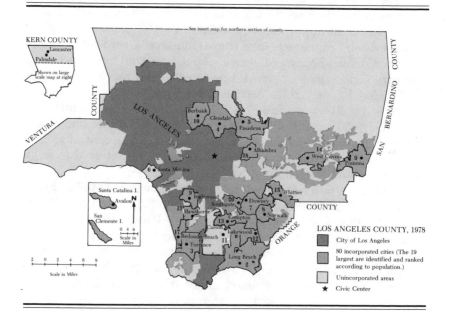

various clays greater than ever, miners developed new methods of extraction that increased production. Farmers and fishermen disliked the increasingly destructive methods of the mining industry. Hydraulic and dredger mining ruined hundreds of square miles of rich agricultural lands. Millions of tons of earth were washed into the rivers, filling their beds with boulders and yellow mud and making navigation difficult. When winter rains fell upon rivers filled with mining debris, the result was often torrential floods, which deposited sand and clay over wide areas and caused serious erosion.

THE RISE OF THE OIL INDUSTRY

California's black gold has played an important part in the history of the state. From the time of the Franciscan padres, petroleum was known to exist in the subsoil. Roaming cattle would sometimes fall into the tar and pitch sumps of southern California, as the animals of prehistoric times had done. Asphalt from the natural brea beds at Los

Edward L. Doheny (wearing straw hat in center of picture) at ceremonies noting the discovery of oil in Los Angeles in 1892 (photograph taken in 1938). *(Title Insurance and Trust Company, Los Angeles)*

Angeles was used for roofing from the Mexican period onward. Natural seepages of surface oil and tar also existed in other areas.

The first oil production west of Pennsylvania occurred in California's Ventura County without the drilling of wells at all. This operation began in 1859, when George S. Gilbert, a whale-oil merchant, erected a small pot still with which he was producing kerosene for lighting and lubricating oil. His still burned down, however, and he became a merchant at Ventura.

The Philadelphia & California Petroleum Company drilled the first oil well in southern California in 1865. In the mid-1870s, the California Star Oil Company began drilling in southern California's Newhall Basin. Despite the production of kerosene for illumination, tar for roofing, and oil for lubrication, the petroleum industry in those years before the invention of the internal combustion engine suffered from a limited market and poor refining methods.

Edward L. Doheny

The career of Edward L. Doheny is one of the most venturesome in the history of American capitalism. When Doheny came to Los Angeles in 1892, he noticed on the streets of the city the presence of brea, or tarry pitch, which clung to the wheels of passing carriages and carts, and he traced this substance to a center of oil seepage downtown near Westlake Park. Doheny and a partner leased a city lot and began to dig. When they had, with pick and shovel, reached a depth of 50 feet, the pair struck a gas pocket that almost asphyxiated them. They then employed a driller, who, at 600 feet, brought in a well with a capacity of forty-five barrels per day. This started a frantic oil boom that caused 2,300 wells to be dug in Los Angeles within the next five years.

A strange, new skyline sprang up in the area of the old pueblo, still no more than a formless, sprawling community of muddy and crooked streets. Greasy little refineries—most of them shantylike structures—were noisily hammered together. Black derricks were erected in both the front and the back yards of numerous residents. Some of these Angelenos became wealthy, but many others got nothing for their trouble except expensive drilling bills, uprooted gardens, and clouds of dry dust which coated their houses. A particularly rich oil field was discovered in the area of the Rancho La Brea Pits, from which local amateur scientists had been unearthing the bones of prehistoric animals since asphalt diggers, working in tar seeps, had found part of a saber-tooth cat.

222

In 1977, the array of animal bones found in the famous La Brea Tar Pits of Hancock Park were put on display in a museum which is located at the site of the discoveries. The exhibits include extinct species of lions, ground sloths, camels, mammoths and mastodons. A single human skeleton was also found, that of a woman who lived approximately 9,000 years ago.

Oil Field in the Central Valley. *(Standard Oil Company of California)*

In 1894, the Union Oil Company succeeded in converting a railroad locomotive to burn oil instead of coal. This attempt to create a market for fuel oil was a success, and the Santa Fe and the Southern Pacific railroads switched from costly imported coal to the less expensive locally produced fuel oil. Encouraged by this new market, the oil industry embarked upon expanded operations. Doheny branched out beyond California to Peru and Mexico, where he not only drilled for oil, but also developed the techniques of paving roads with asphalt.

The Oil Boom of the Twenties

California's greatest oil discoveries were made in 1920 at Huntington Beach near Los Angeles, and in 1921 at Santa Fe Springs and Signal Hill. These three fields contained such vast pools of oil that their discovery upset national prices. Standard Oil Company of California proceeded to develop the Huntington Beach area. Meanwhile, Union Oil concentrated on Santa Fe Springs, while the third major field, Signal Hill, was the site of increasing activity on the part of the Shell Oil Company. Throughout the twenties, California led in the field of western oil production.

Doheny attracted national notoriety through his eagerness to obtain the Elk Hills reserves in Kern County. It was revealed that he had secretly sent a satchel with $100,000 in it to Secretary of the Interior Albert B. Fall, "an old prospector friend," who held control of the Elk Hills reserves and of others at Teapot Dome, Wyoming. Secretary Fall claimed that the money was only a loan, but a tremendous scandal followed the revelation that he planned to lease these oil reserves to Doheny. Both Fall and Doheny were indicted for bribery and conspiracy. Fall was convicted and sentenced to prison although Doheny, surprisingly, escaped punishment; in effect, he was acquitted of giving the bribe that Fall was convicted of accepting.

THE COMING OF THE AUTOMOBILE

The oil industry depended for much of its market on the demands of the new automobile age. In the 1920s, the auto underwent a transformation from a sputtering plaything of the rich, which frightened ladies and horses, to a vital necessity of the working classes of the United States. From the beginning, the automobile was more popular and necessary in California than any other state in the

An early beach scene in southern California.
(Title Insurance and Trust Company, Los Angeles)

Union. The manufacturers of automobiles themselves, however, remained centered for the most part in the large cities of the East and Midwest. Service stations sprang up everywhere, providing—in addition to gasoline and minor adjustments—free air, road maps, and restrooms for the convenience of dusty motorists.

Perhaps nowhere did the automobile change the mode of life more than in the rural West. Along with the phonograph, the radio, and the movies, the auto broke down the isolation of those who lived on farms and ranches. Gradually, too, automobiles stimulated the decentralization of cities by making it possible for people to live at some distance from their work. In the years 1910–1930, California began to pull itself out of the mud, as the state's rutted country lanes were converted into two-laned ribbons of concrete. These, in turn, gave way after the 1930s to four-lane macadamized highways, which remained in use until the advent of still larger freeways in the 1940s. The increasingly urgent need for roads imposed an unending financial strain upon the state.

Railroad towns were displaced by crossroads with garages, filling stations, hot-dog stands, giant oranges, and wooden tourist bungalows. Good weather, low gasoline prices, and thousands of miles of paved highways, plus ready access to desert, beach, and mountain, helped make Californians more and more automobile- and vacation-minded. In addition, thousands of tourists were brought to the state each year by persistent advertising, which especially emphasized California's constancy of sunshine. The most popular resorts were the beaches from Santa Barbara to San Diego, Lake Tahoe, Sequoia and Yosemite Valley in the High Sierra, and Palm Springs in the desert. Even Death Valley became a winter tourist attraction. Winter sports in the highest mountains, especially skiing, grew as popular as hunting, fishing, boating, and swimming in the spring and summer.

The Automobile Age had many side effects. The control of traffic became a matter of great importance and complexity. Public transportation declined. Slick used-car dealers like Honest John and Mad Man Muntz sold cars formerly owned and cared for by those proverbial "little old ladies from Pasadena." California was truly on wheels.

THE LABOR MOVEMENT

During the years after the turn of the century, tensions between laborers and employers grew. As they had earlier in the Workingmen's Movement, San Francisco workers resorted to political activity again in 1901 through formation of the Union Labor Party. San Francisco became one of the most effectively organized labor strongholds in the country, a center from which labor agitators operated vigorously in the interior and in the many coastal valleys of the state.

The Wobblies

In 1905 the Industrial Workers of the World (IWW), a socialist-oriented group of unionists, turned its attention to the Far West. In particular, the IWW was developing plans to organize California's many seasonal and part-time workers into "One Big Union." Among these migratory laborers were field hands, lumberjacks, and cannery workers. As already noted in Chapter 7, the hours of labor on most farms and ranches were very long and pay was extremely low. Furthermore, increased use of farm machinery annually lessened the need for such workers' services.

These conditions drew the attention of the IWW. Agitators set to work throughout the state, with their greatest activity occurring in the years 1908–1912. By 1910, they had recruited about 1,000 migratory farm laborers as members. Those who became members of the IWW were referred to as Wobblies, belonging to an "I Won't

226

Work" movement, while local police officials regarded the organization as an outlaw labor group. Soapbox orators were arrested at
meetings and rallies sponsored by the IWW, fire hoses were turned
on its members, and field workers were warned not to join the IWW.
Municipal officials took no action when organization headquarters in
various cities were mysteriously burned.

In spite of such treatment, the IWW, held mass meetings at
which orators charged that employment agencies had demanded
high fees from workers for jobs that were nonexistent. Because of the
continued IWW agitation, most California towns came to set aside
certain areas where public speaking was forbidden. After further
incidents with local police, the most serious of which took place at
Fresno and San Diego, various cities adopted strict laws aimed
against the IWW. Leaders of the organization often violated such
ordinances, sometimes because of ignorance of the law. In other
cases, however, they did so in defiance, deliberately conducting demonstrations and defying restrictive laws.

Subscribing as it did to the Marxian concept of class struggle and
to anarchist ideas, the organization threatened the position, property, and security of all but the poorest, most oppressed workers.
Other workers distrusted the Wobblies because of their attempts to
obtain equal rights for Chinese and Mexican workers. Employers
naturally hated their techniques. Though their leaders were jailed,
clubbed, driven out of their headquarters, and even killed, the Wobblies still continued their activities.

The IWW campaign to organize migratory workers reached a
peak of violence in 1913 on a large farm in the Sacramento Valley.
At stake were the conditions under which laborers—men, women,
and children—were forced to live and work on the farm, known as
the Durst Ranch. Virtually no provision had been made to house the
workers decently or to provide basic sanitation for them. Eight toilets
existed for the use of 2,800 persons. The owners of the ranch had
advertised for many more workers than they could actually use and
then paid the ones they hired wages as low as 75 cents per day. A
ranch-owned store, furthermore, held back 10 percent of these meager wages, forcing field hands to purchase food and supplies at high
prices. The workers, under the leadership of the IWW, called a strike.
When a sheriff's posse sought to arrest the leaders of the strike, a
pistol was fired, and a full-scale riot followed. The sheriff and the local
district attorney, as well as several workers, were killed. Governor
Hiram Johnson called out the National Guard and brought in detectives to investigate. As a result of the incident, the IWW organization

was ruined in the Sacramento Valley. Two of its leaders were convicted of murder and sentenced to life imprisonment.

The riot, nevertheless, led to attempts on the part of the state to improve the welfare of migratory workers. The California legislature, with its attention drawn to the problem of seasonal labor, passed several bills toward this end though such measures were not very effective. Late in 1913, a disgruntled agitator who called himself "General" Kelley marched an "army" of several thousand unemployed farm workers to Sacramento to demand relief, but Kelley's men were driven off by armed guards after attempting to camp on the capitol grounds.

Bombing of the Los Angeles Times

The bombing of the Los Angeles *Times* set back the labor movement in California. The blast occurred at 1:07 A.M. on October 1, 1910, just as the morning edition went to press. In the explosion, heard for more than ten miles, twenty persons were killed and many more injured, while the *Times* building was reduced to a pile of rubble. Tension between the paper and labor oganizers, which had existed before the bombing, increased even more. The owner of the *Times*, General Harrison Gray Otis, blamed irresponsible labor leaders for the bombing. The labor leaders denied that a bomb had caused the blast and accused the *Times* of operating a faulty plant, which union spokesmen called a gas-leaking firetrap. It was only after a lengthy and dramatic trial that the incident was established as an act of union violence.

In 1911, three labor agitators—Ortie McManigal and James B. and John J. McNamara—were brought to trial, accused of organizing the bombing. Labor retained the nationally famous defense lawyer Clarence Darrow, who was known for his opposition to both violence and capital punishment. The testimony against the McNamara brothers was too incriminating for Darrow to win their acquittal. Acting on his advice, they changed their pleas from not guilty to guilty, and, after a mysterious compromise with both prosecution and judge, they were sent to the state penitentiary. James drew a sentence of life imprisonment and John one of fifteen years. McManigal was freed because he had "turned state's evidence."

Mooney and Billings

In the midst of the boom brought on by World War I, strikes were considered unpatriotic by many. President Wilson had proclaimed

Destruction by fire of the Los Angeles *Times* Building, 1910.
(C. C. Pierce Collection, courtesy of the Huntington Library.
Photographed by C. C. Tarter.)

July 22, 1916, Preparedness Day when the nation was to demonstrate
its unity and fitness for service in case war were ever declared. At San
Francisco, militant advocates of the open shop helped organize a
patriotic parade as a Preparedness Day demonstration. Meanwhile,
a serious longshoremen's strike was under way. The combination was
enough to make employers and union organizers especially edgy
about their differences. In the midst of this uneasy situation, a suit-
case containing a bomb, left by someone on a city sidewalk on Market
Street, exploded, killing nine persons and injuring forty others.

Two radical union leaders, Thomas J. Mooney and Warren K.
Billings, were arrested and accused of the crime. Newspapers joined
in the strong public reaction to the Preparedness Day incident and
the Mooney–Billings trial. The press printed a story on the day the

trial began that Mooney and Billings had been part of a conspiracy to assassinate Governor Hiram Johnson. There was also talk connecting the two men with the "Reds." Both Billings and Mooney presented alibis designed to clear themselves of the bombing, but they were found guilty. Mooney was sentenced to be hanged, and Billings received a life term in the state penitentiary.

A rally in Petrograd, Russia, helped focus international attention on the case. The White House was deluged by protests from labor leaders. Under these circumstances, President Wilson appointed an investigative committee, whose overall conclusion was that there was insufficent evidence to find anyone guilty. As a result of Wilson's intervention in the interest of wartime unity, Mooney's punishment was commuted to life imprisonment. Nevertheless, the public remembered that, during the trial, the prosecution had proved Mooney's association with the McNamara brothers—convicted earlier of planning the explosion of the Los Angeles *Times*—and antilabor sentiment continued to run high.

The issue of Mooney's and Billings' guilt remained a burning one. Numerous Californians felt that Mooney and Billings were dangerous men: "They may not be guilty of the bomb explosion, but they belong where they are." From the moment Mooney and Billings went behind the bars of San Quentin Penitentiary, however, labor embarked upon a twenty-year campaign to free the two men, calling them martyrs. Their case continued to attract attention all over the world. After innumerable petitions and appeals, at last, in 1939, Governor Culbert L. Olson pardoned both men as the first act of his administration.

Continued Labor Strife

In the later New Deal years, the organized labor movement in California showed new force. As more industries moved to the West Coast, the growth in the number of workers offered new opportunities for labor leaders. In the 1930s, the CIO attracted a large following among previously unorganized laborers, who were encouraged by the industry-wide bargaining techniques of John L. Lewis, the vigorous and effective CIO president. Lewis personally turned his attention to those unskilled laborers in California's fields and factories who had once been the target of IWW organizers. For a time it appeared that Lewis might actually be able to unionize even farm workers.

Waterfront workers at San Francisco were unhappy with their Longshoremen's Association, considering it a company union through which shippers controlled hiring and most other labor conditions. Their discontent paved the way for the entrance of radicalism into the maritime labor movement, which now acquired new leaders. Among these, Harry Bridges, a spellbinding Australian-born longshoreman, began to attract much attention in the early 1930s by complaining that a speed-up of waterfront operations caused many accidents among the longshoremen. To combat the shippers, Bridges reorganized the International Longshoremen's Association (ILA).

Although his enemies called Bridges a dangerous alien radical, if not a Communist, thousands of longshoremen up and down the Pacific Coast stood behind his authoritarian but effective ILA leadership. By 1934, his power was such that he staged a strike which affected shipping from San Diego to Seattle.

The center of the great maritime strike of 1934 was San Francisco. The ILA tied up the port for ninety days. In sympathy with the longshoremen, sailors marched off their ships, warehousemen quit their jobs, teamsters abandoned their trucks and lift-vans. Hundreds of vessels lay idle in San Francisco Bay, while cargoes rotted and rusted on piers and in warehouses.

Bitterness on both sides of this massive labor dispute made arbitration difficult. President Roosevelt tried in vain to achieve a settlement. The attempt by employers to use strikebreakers only aggravated matters. On July 5, "Bloody Thursday," violence erupted when the San Francisco police moved against picket lines with tear gas. Before it was over, two union pickets had been shot to death, and over a hundred men, including police, had been wounded. On July 14, ILA leaders appealed to all unions not already involved in the sympathy strikes to join in protesting the action of the police. The entire San Francisco area was paralyzed in the most severe disturbance the city had undergone since the earthquake and fire of 1906.

Disputes among union leaders themselves finally helped end the strike. The more conservative ones felt that this outbreak, especially the general strike, damaged the long-term interests of unionism; this was too high a price to pay for short-term victory against management. As allied union members returned to work in the late summer of 1934, only the longshoremen remained out on strike. Finally, the longshoremen won certain concessions from management, including higher wages. Though the strike had resulted in what seemed to be a victory for labor, the public was not to forget that the price had been violence.

Bridges remained a controversial character, and demands were made for his deportation. A congressional committee on un-American activities charged that the new International Longshoremen and Warehousemen's Union, which he now headed, was under Communist leadership and control. Antiunion newspapers joined in denouncing Bridges, but they found it difficult to prove the charges of Communism against him. Bridges retained his power along the Pacific Coast and eventually expanded it to Hawaii.

THE GREAT DEPRESSION

After the collapse of the stock market in October 1929, the nation's economic situation grew worse. President Herbert Hoover's administration seemed powerless to stop the downward trend. Unemployment spread throughout the West, and at the same time the strength of California unionism declined. In the fields its farm labor remained nonunion and in the cities unemployed workers found themselves in intense competition for jobs. The bargaining power of union leaders was weakened; labor spokesmen were in no position to demand the closed shop or to insist upon better working conditions of any sort.

In the presidential elections of 1932, the Democratic candidate was Franklin Delano Roosevelt, governor of New York. Roosevelt's campaign took him to the major cities of the Far West, and many thousands of Californians reponded to his magnetic personal appeal. Roosevelt offered hope to the downhearted and discouraged. When election day came, California voted overwhelmingly for Roosevelt.

While Roosevelt campaigned, however, the economic situation grew worse. Overproduction caused unemployment to spread still further. Once prosperous industries, farms, and real estate developments were going bankrupt. Within a few months, many banks were threatened with collapse. California Governor James Rolph, Jr., ordered a bank holiday on March 2, 1933. By March 4, the day of President Roosevelt's inauguration, almost every state governor had declared a bank holiday or had imposed severe restrictions on withdrawals. The country faced economic paralysis with the scarcity of money in some cases reducing business to a barter system. Roosevelt's New Deal was built around the "Three Rs": relief, recovery, and reform. Initially the most important of these, for California and for every other state, was relief.

The Okies and Arkies

Thousands of new migrant farm workers descended upon the state in the depression years and thus added their needs to those of other citizens. The state published a warning to migrants not to come to California to seek jobs. However, rumors of high wages and comfortable conditions out West caused many to make a trip that they were later to regret.

The newcomers who were from the parched Dust Bowl areas of the Middle West were generally known as Okies or Arkies from their origins in Oklahoma and Arkansas. Their trek overland in rickety flivvers and jalopies, with brooms and pails tied onto running boards and the tops of the vehicles heaped with mattresses, children, and blankets, has been well described in John Steinbeck's famous novel *The Grapes of Wrath*. Because the labor situation was already depressed, a state law was passed to close the border to people without money or jobs. Later, in 1941, the United States Supreme Court declared such laws unconstitutional.

The migrant workers who came to California in the 1930s settled mostly in the farming regions of the Central Valley area. There, job conditions remained more depressing than elsewhere in the state. These immigrants resembled the homesteading pioneers of the nineteenth century, except that they had no homesteads. Housed often in rude tar-paper shacks, many of them were in need of direct relief. Farm owners became accustomed to paying the starvation wages which the newcomers were forced to accept. Themselves faced with bankruptcy, the owners could not spend money they did not have to improve working conditions.

Folksinger Woody Guthrie mirrored the confusion and public intolerance over what to do about the Okies and Arkies. This prejudice was born of a combination of insecurity, embarrassment, and shame concerning one's fellow Americans, caught in a tragic social and economic web. Guthrie, like Steinbeck, embodied the depression years. Born in an Oklahoma oil boom town, he went on the road at age thirteen. During his move across the land, he spent several years at Los Angeles, where he sang for thirty minutes a day on a local radio station. Guthrie preached optimism, spoke for "the little man" and "the drifting families," and voiced both strength and bitterness in his "talking blues."

Guthrie, who composed over a thousand songs, is perhaps best remembered for his "folk national anthem" entitled "This Land Is Your Land."

233

This land is your land and this land is my land,
   From California to the New York Island,
   From the redwood forest to the Gulf Stream waters,
   This land was made for you and me.
As I went a walking that ribbon of highway
   I saw above me that endless skyway,
   I saw before me that golden valley,
   This land was made for you and me.
I roamed and rambled, and I followed my footsteps
   To the sparkling sands of her diamond deserts,
   All around me, a voice was sounding,
   This land was made for you and me.
When the sun come shining and I was strolling,
   The wheat fields waving, the dust clouds rolling,
   A voice was chanting and the fog was lifting,
   This land was made for you and me.*

Federal Relief and Work Programs

Throughout the nation, the pattern of depression relief that was to become best known was that administered by the federal government. Dozens of new federal agencies, known by the alphabetic abbreviations of their titles, were established to perform a number of functions designed to bring back prosperity. Often these organizations worked in partnership with state agencies, so that relief and employment were administered with a particular view to local needs.

Mention has been made of the use of federal funds to construct Hoover Dam and of the national government's participation in the Central Valley Project. Other federally financed power, reclamation, flood control, and navigation projects were also to affect the future of California. Poor people depended upon receiving weekly government checks to sustain them until they could get jobs. In addition to this direct relief, agencies of the federal government provided a variety of employment opportunities. Unemployed young men, were given jobs in the Civilian Conservation Corps (CCC). This project pushed through construction of mountain trails and firebreaks on federal forest lands and the state parks. Others worked on Works Progress Administration (WPA) or Public Works Administration (PWA) construction projects.

Though criticized as extravagant and bitterly resisted by conservatives, these activities improved conditions of economic hardship.

*"This Land Is Your Land," words and music by Woody Guthrie. TRO copyright © 1956 and 1958 Ludlow Music, Inc., New York, N.Y. Used by permission.

Certainly no state benefited more from the federal relief program than California, where hundreds of new schools, parks, roads, and beach facilities were built during the depression.

FADDISTS AND UTOPIAN SCHEMES

Southern California had long been deluged with large numbers of migrants armed with solutions to most of mankind's age-old problems from economics to health. One of the first of these was Helena Modjeska, a Polish actress who established a utopian community at Anaheim in 1876. Spiritualism also flourished in California. A few diet faddists went so far as to preach that they could conquer illness by mixing "spiritual power" with such foods as "mushroomburgers" and date milk shakes. In addition, there were Yogi mystics, Swami palm readers, rain makers, Hindu Fakirs, and other occultists of every description. Earnest devotees—including sentimental elderly persons and aging former movie stars—invested time, money, and effort in these strange goings on.

California's mild climate created problems, because it attracted thousands of older people. Even during the depression, the oldsters seemed to believe that sunny California would, in one way or another, support them. Dependent on a modest investment income, seriously reduced due to the nation's economic difficulties, they suffered acutely from the collapse of banks and building and loan associations. These elderly people tended to be attracted by a variety of schemes that promised to solve their problems by redistributing the wealth.

Among such plans was the movement known as technocracy. Technocracy's chief advocate was Howard Scott, an engineer who wanted to create a utopian society in the 1930s by eliminating poverty. With great enthusiasm, he urged the harnessing of society's "energy" for the benefit of mankind. To achieve the best use of both human and natural resources, Scott proposed to place technical experts in control of industry and government. A corps of technocracy spokesmen, equipped with blueprints, explained Scott's proposed engineering civilization in almost every California community.

Like technocracy, the other utopian social plans that the depression years seemed to encourage were almost always identified with some one personality. One of these was the controversial Upton Sinclair, who had been, since the Progressive era, a well-known crusading author and journalist. A familiar figure in liberal causes, he was also a founder of the American Civil Liberties Union in California. While Sinclair continued his writing career, he repeatedly ran for office on the Socialist ticket. In 1920, he unsuccessfully sought a congressional seat for the first time. Two years later, he ran for the senate and, in 1926 and 1930, became the Socialist candidate for governor.

Sinclair's last attempt at public office was in 1934, when he won the Democratic nomination for governor. Sinclair's program attracted many of California's older people as well as its poor and unemployed. His EPIC ("End Poverty in California") Plan was, in fact, tailor-made for the discontented and downhearted, of which California had more than its share. One of the measures Sinclair advocated was a monthly pension of $50 for widows, the aged, and the physically handicapped. In addition, he argued for inheritance and income taxes, a tax on idle land, and a program to stimulate employment and business. Sinclair believed that small homeowners should be exempt from taxation and that state ownership and operation of farms and factories would cure unemployment.

Although Sinclair's program held much the same appeal for the masses of unemployed as did President Roosevelt's New Deal, Sinclair did not gain Roosevelt's endorsement. The President considered Sinclair's program radical and impractical. Other New Dealers regarded Sinclair as an extremist—a visionary whose socialistic notions were unworkable and even dangerous. During one of the most bitterly contested of California's gubernatorial elections, the conservative press, radio, and movie industry united in a campaign against Sinclair. Sinclair's opponent was Republican Frank F. Merriam, who, as lieutenant governor, had in 1934 succeeded to the governorship upon the death of Governor Rolph. In November, Merriam received 1,138,620 votes as against Sinclair's 879,537. Sinclair was to remain remarkably active as a novelist, but his office-seeking days were over.

Cure-all promoters appeared with other economic schemes. Among these popular leaders was Dr. Francis E. Townsend, a retired physician who sold real estate at Long Beach. With the slogan "Youth for work and age for leisure," he proposed, in 1934, his Townsend Old-Age Pension Plan, a supposedly foolproof scheme that would provide a monthly pension of $200 for every person over the age of sixty—provided the entire payment was spent within three months.

Dr. Townsend led a national "crusade" via the 5,000 clubs organized in his name. The plan aroused wide opposition among those who considered it unsound. Faithful subscribers to Townsend's newspaper continued to read it long after his plan had any chance of adoption. Remnants of the Townsend movement exist even today.

In 1938, yet another visionary plan came to the fore—the "Thirty Dollars Every Thursday" or "Ham and Eggs" proposal. Its sponsors, who suggested giving a pension to every unemployed person in the state over the age of fifty, were in some ways even more radical than Townsend. Pushed by professional politicians in the state elections of 1938, the measure came close to adoption, despite the fact that well-informed critics labeled it the height of economic irresponsibility. This movement, as well as the EPIC Plan and Dr. Townsend's pension scheme, can perhaps best be understood in terms of the despair and confused thinking of the depression years.

THE OLSON ADMINISTRATION

Despite the popularity of the New Deal—which helped Franklin Roosevelt to sweep the state in four successive national elections—there was only one Democratic state administration in California during the first half of the twentieth century. Until Governor Culbert L. Olson came to power in 1938, Californians had not seated a Democratic chief executive since Governor James H. Budd, who left office in 1899. Only a few Democrats had been elected to the legislature.

The Olson regime in California was expected to inaugurate a "New Deal in miniature." Olson was a frank advocate of FDR's ideas and was a former backer of Sinclair's EPIC Plan. Although Olson tried to solve such problems as California's migrant-labor situation, an economy-minded Republican legislature refused to support his reform program. Not only was Olson unable to secure passage through the legislature of his principal social measures, but his administration was also hurt by poor appointments. However, his first official act—the freeing of Tom Mooney in 1939—remained his most dramatic one. Olson also achieved moderate reform of the California prison system and of its mental-hygiene and youth-correction programs. He was defeated for reelection by Earl Warren in 1942.

AN AGE OF PROSPERITY

In the twenties and thirties, despite the serious national depression, California's business increased. To finance California's massive construction needs, the banking industry continued to develop. This was a period in which existing banks were consolidated into large-scale institutions capable of loaning millions of dollars annually. The largest of all, eventually, was the Bank of Italy, later the Bank of America. Founded in 1904 at San Francisco by Amadeo Pietro Giannini, son of an Italian immigrant, it developed a system of branch banking that came to dwarf the activities of other California banks. Geared to the needs of the small depositor, Giannini's system soon spread beyond the boundaries of the state, and even of the nation. Ultimately, the Bank of America became the largest bank in the world, thereby helping to gain a new financial status for California, and especially for San Francisco, where the institution's headquarters remained.

By 1925, Los Angeles ranked first economically among California cities. By 1930, 2.3 million people lived within a thirty-mile radius of the city (though the population of Los Angeles proper was much less). Only in the early thirties did LA develop a genuine civic center with its new Spanish-style Union passenger railroad terminal and nearby complex of municipal government buildings. Between 1930

The Golden Gate Bridge. *(Union Pacific Railroad)*

and 1940, the city also celebrated its 150th anniversary, was host to the 1932 Olympics in a new coliseum, saw the arrival of the first streamlined transcontinental trains, built an observatory at Griffith Park, constructed a metropolitan water system, and laid the groundwork for what was to become an important wartime aircraft industry.

San Francisco's growth, though less spectacular, also remained impressive. The city by the bay strengthened its opera, symphony orchestra, and museums; improved Golden Gate Park; and built remarkable bridges to supplant colorful ferry boats. On May 27, 1939, the day the Golden Gate Bridge opened, 200,000 people walked across the span. That same year San Francisco held the Golden Gate International Exposition, the World's Fair of the West. San Francisco had always been a tourist mecca with its exotic Chinatown, distinctive cable cars, fine restaurants, and the famous Golden Gate through which ships stream in constant procession.

WARTIME CHANGES

During the years preceding United States entrance into World War II, Californians became disturbed over the threat posed by the European dictators and the Japanese military clique. The unexpected attack upon Pearl Harbor in Hawaii by carrier-launched Japanese dive bombers on December 7, 1941, created a new economic and social climate in California. Not only did thousands of defense workers pour into the state, but also soldiers, sailors, and airmen came by the hundreds of thousands for training or to be shipped oversea. Military posts became virtual cities, with their own supply, transportation, and postal facilities. A big army depot was Fort Ord, located between Monterey and Salinas. Camp Pendleton, near Oceanside, became a massive West Coast base for the marines. San Diego, Long Beach, and Mare Island, already major naval bases, increased their facilities, and there were expanded air training centers at March Field, the El Toro Marine Air Depot, and the Alameda Naval Air Station.

Industrial Expansion and Housing Shortages

Even before the attack on Pearl Harbor, California's shipyards hammered out ships for the Allied powers. An industrial revival took place in the San Francisco Bay area. The shipyards of the Henry J. Kaiser enterprises began to build cruisers, destroyers, and other vessels. The labor force at Kaiser's Richmond Yard alone came to num-

ber more than 100,000. Kaiser also constructed the largest steel mill
in the West in a vineyard at Fontana.

Firms that produced steel, chemicals, textiles, and machine tools
had been on a wartime footing before 1941. Others converted, after
Pearl Harbor, to the production of tanks, jeeps, and munitions. As
civilian workers swarmed into the state, its towns expanded overnight. Typical was Vallejo, which jumped from a population of 20,-
000 in 1941 to 100,000 in 1943. Thousands of workers lived in trailer
parks and commuted to work, traveling as much as three or four
hours per day.

The Aircraft Industry

No segment of the California economy grew more rapidly than the
aircraft industry. Airplanes had been produced in the state since the
years before World War I. Thus, when World War II came, an aircraft
industry already existed.

In 1910, the first public aviation meet in America was held near
Los Angeles. This event drew almost 200,000 spectators, who saw
Glen Curtis make the first successful West Coast flight, a thrilling
spectacle that lasted for two whole minutes. Southern California's
aircraft designers broke into the national news in 1927. That
year Charles A. Lindbergh, "The Lone Eagle," commissioned San
Diego's Ryan Aeronautical Corporation to build his "Spirit of Saint
Louis," in which "Lindy" flew the Atlantic. In 1932, Robert
Gross headed a group that bought Lockheed Aircraft Company.
Lindbergh, Wiley Post, and Amelia Earhart began to set flying
records in the company's planes, which earned an international
reputation.

By 1941, placement of orders for war planes by foreign governments and by our own government had made California's aircraft
companies vital to the rearmament program of the free nations of the
world. Douglas, which built the Flying Fortress (B-17), and Lockheed, which produced the P-38 fighter, were the cornerstones of
American air power. Other plants, notably Consolidated Vultee,
North American, Northrop, and the Hughes aircraft companies, expanded spectacularly. The millions of dollars in government funds
that poured into California's new steel mills, shipyards, and aircraft
factories brought about a massive growth of the state's economy
and population. After the war the aircraft companies diversified
their activities and produced radar equipment, missiles, and jet
aircraft.

FOUNDING THE UNITED NATIONS

In April 1945, as the war in Europe was drawing to a close, representatives of forty-six nations met at San Francisco to transform a wartime alliance against the Axis powers into a permanent structure for world peace. Despite almost constant disagreement between American and Russian delegates, the United Nations Charter was signed at San Francisco on June 26 by the delegates of all nations participating. Thus, San Francisco is forever associated with the UN Charter, whose purpose, as stated in its opening words, is "to save succeeding generations from the scourge of war." Covering the Charter Conference as a reporter for the Hearst papers, was a young man recently released from active duty with the United States Navy. His name was John F. Kennedy.

POSTWAR ADJUSTMENTS

California faced many problems at the end of the war. Only a few war contracts for production of aircraft and ships were extended beyond September 2, 1945, the date of Japan's surrender. California began the process of reconversion from a war-stimulated economy to a peacetime one. It was feared that the wartime labor force would leave California. In actuality, however, a startlingly high number of veterans returned to California, which they had first visited while on military duty. The United States Veterans Administration estimated that more than half of California's resident World War II veterans came from other states. Most of the GI's who poured back into California found satisfactory work. The migration into the state generated new employment to take the place of discontinued war industry.

The war not only stimulated existing industries, but also helped develop many new ones. This adjustment was long overdue in California, where the economy was dependent upon too few major industries, among them orange growing, the movies, and oil. The war, furthermore, made the state prominent in the economy of the nation. It allowed California a larger share of the nation's wealth and population. California in the postwar years grew faster than almost any other part of the nation.

ANOTHER BOOM

In the postwar years, California's new residents sought better houses and more clothing, food, and services. Wartime facilities had often

241

been flimsy and temporary. Great quantities of apartment houses, homes, schools, and facilities of all sorts had to be built. Business construction boomed.

There seemed to be no end to the migration into the state as the once tranquil paradise became crowded with people and automobiles. Despite the smog, which made city throats rasp and eyes smart, its growth continued. The state's highways became so jammed that California recorded the highest accident rate in the nation. Its schoolrooms grew so crowded that schools were forced to offer classes in several shifts.

The shortage of postwar housing was severe, and the Korean War (1950–1953) aggravated conditions further. Public housing projects, however, were often resisted by community groups. In small towns and big cities alike, acres of raw, green lumber framework and innumerable stacks of bricks and sacks of cement went into thousands of new dwellings. Large-scale tract development occurred at the new postwar cities of Westchester, Lakewood, and West Covina in southern California and at Burlinghame and Lafayette in the north.

Massive freeway expansion, closely tied to the building boom, occurred throughout the state. By the 1950s, the state was spending more than $1 million per working day on new freeways and highways designed to relieve traffic congestion. This sum was bound to increase. The federal government also contributed heavily to highway projects. By 1960, total auto registration was close to 8 million as two- and three-car families became commonplace. California's highway engineers planned a 12,500-mile statewide freeway system, to be built during the 1960s and 1970s. This system would link all cities in the state with a population of 5,000 or more and would further serve to tie these cities into the federal highway program.

Los Angeles and San Francisco both undertook reconstruction of their civic centers after 1950. At Los Angeles new buildings, twenty to forty stories high, were constructed to house federal, state, county, and city government offices. This became the largest group of government buildings outside the national capital. Another Los Angeles project featured redevelopment, with federal aid, of a rundown area, Bunker Hill, into a residential and commercial site. This work followed years of controversy between the city fathers and residents ousted by the project, mostly elderly and dependent on a small income.

Los Angeles grew more rapidly than any part of California after the war. It was the only major city in the nation that had not lost

242

The Los Angeles Bonaventure
Hotel, in downtown Los
Angeles *(Paul C. Lasley)*

residents to its suburbs in the decade preceding. Los Angeles County
with a population count of 6,038,771 persons was, in 1960, the most
populous county in the United States. (It continued this ranking in
the 1970 census too. For a population breakdown of the county in
1970, see the Appendix.)

As the shift from single-family homes to apartments continued,
the city skyline changed markedly. Construction became vertical
rather than horizontal. Rising land costs made it uneconomical to
build single-family dwellings in many areas. In the 1950s, a new style
of architecture bagan to convert downtown Los Angeles and its
nearby Wilshire district into an area of multistoried apartments and
office buildings, built of "high-rise" lightweight metal and much window glass. Construction of the first modern skyscrapers followed the
1956 repeal of an earthquake-conscious height limit.

At San Franscisco, planners suggested constructing tunnels under San Francisco Bay to handle the increasing flow of traffic in and
out of the traffic-clogged city. San Francisco's population remained
almost constant since the war, but its many suburbs grew spectacularly. Unlike Los Angeles, which could spread out in all directions for
many miles, San Francisco is hemmed in by water on three sides. In

243

San Francisco skyline viewed from Treasure Island. *(San Francisco Visitors Bureau. Photograph by George Knight.)*

addition to this, once the city and county of San Francisco were combined, there was no place to expand the territory of the city except by filling in the bay.

TWO ASIAN WARS

Defense activities curtailed or cancelled after World War II were renewed as a result of the Korean War. A new round of government orders opened up branch plants of the major aircraft companies that had been closed since World War II. A large group of aircraft, missile component, and instrument workers came to rely upon government contracts for their jobs. Although this meant great unemployment whenever defense expenditures were cut, the continuing "cold war" with the Soviet Union and the "hot war" in Vietnam (1955–1975) kept the contracts coming at a rapid though uneven pace.

SPACE AGE DEVELOPMENTS

California remains a center of military activity, much of which has implications for its future, notably man's conquest of outer space. Since 1954, California has been engaged in missile, rocket, and outer-space research and technology. And in the late fifties, the Pacific

Missile Range, extending several hundred miles along the California coast and far into the Pacific Ocean, became the scene of mounting military activity. A major launching site was located at the Vandenberg Air Force Base, just north of Lompoc.

As a major center of science and technology, the position of southern California became the largest complex of military production in the entire nation. The Los Angeles region is as well known for its missiles as for its movies. The former aircraft industry has become, in large measure, a missiles industry.

In the early 1960s North American's El Segundo plant developed the prototypes of the B-70 bomber, the most powerful yet designed. This same company produced the X-15 supersonic rocket plane as well as the guidance and control systems of the Boeing Company's Minuteman missile. North American's Rocketdyne Division powered thirty-six out of forty of the first American space probes. Rocketdyne also developed the H-1 Saturn engine and designed weather satellites. North American became the prime contractor of the Apollo moonship.

The Lockheed Corporation of Burbank and Sunnyvale, like North American, remained active both in missile and aircraft production. Its F-104 Starfighters were used throughout the world. Lockheed, in addition to producing the Polaris submarine missile for the United States Navy, was the prime contractor for the Midas system of detecting ICBM (intercontinental ballistic missile) firings. Lockheed played a part as well in the development of the Agena and Polaris missiles and in the Samos "spy-in-the-sky" satellite. By the 1970s Lockheed's L-1011 (Tristar) wide-bodied jet transport became a major air carrier.

Competing with that airplane is the McDonnell-Douglas wide-bodied DC-10. That firm has also manufactured the Thor-Able booster rocket, with the aid of the Aerojet General Corporation of Azusa and North American's Rocketdyne Division. Douglas also worked on the Nike-Zeus and Skybolt ballistic missiles.

At San Diego, Convair (later General Dynamics), builder of the F-106 Delta Dart and the 880 jet airliner, also grew into a missile-designing organization. Its prize product was the Atlas ICBM, a missile with a range of almost ten thousand miles.

STUDY SUGGESTIONS

To understand this chapter you should know (1) the meaning and importance of key phrases and terms, (2) the contributions to Califor-

nia history of major personalities, and (3) the location and significance
of geographic place names.

1. *Key phrases and terms*

aircraft
Bank of America
Camp Pendleton
Civilian Conservation
   Corps
cross-filing
Durst Ranch
Elk Hills reserves
EPIC
Fort Ord
The Grapes of Wrath
initiative, referendum,
   and recall
International Long-
   shoremen's Association
Korean War

La Brea Pits
Lincoln–Roosevelt League
Lockheed Corporation
Mare Island
missiles
Okies
Pacific Electric
Progressive Party of 1912
Ruef–Schmitz machine
Space program
technocracy
"Three Rs" of the New Deal
Times bombing
Union Labor Party
Vandenberg Air Force Base
Wobblies

2. *Major personalities*

Warren K. Billings
Harry Bridges
Glen Curtis
Edward L. Doheny
Amelia Earhart
Albert B. Fall
General Funston
Amadeo P. Giannini
Woody Guthrie
Dr. John R. Haynes
Hiram W. Johnson

Henry J. Kaiser
the McNamara brothers
Helena Modjeska
Thomas J. Mooney
Fremont Older
Abraham Ruef
Howard Scott
Upton Sinclair
Dr. Francis E. Townsend

3. *Important geographic place names*

Beverly Hills
Fontana
Golden Gate
Huntington Beach
Lake Tahoe
Lompoc

Palo Alto
Richmond
Sequoia
Vallejo
Ventura County

246

FOR ADDITIONAL STUDY

Walton Bean, *Boss Ruef's San Francisco* (Berkeley, 1952).

William Bronson, *The Earth Shook, the Sky Burned* (New York, 1959).

Robert G. Cleland and Osgood Hardy, *The March of Industry* (Los Angeles, 1929).

David L. Cohn, *Combustion on Wheels: An Informal History of the Automobile Age* (Boston, 1944).

Spencer C. Olin, Jr., *California's Prodigal Sons: Hiram Johnson and the Progressives, 1911–1917* (Berkeley, 1968).

Upton Sinclair, *I, Candidate for Governor and How I Got Licked* (Pasadena, 1935).

John Steinbeck, *The Grapes of Wrath* (New York, 1939).

•9•

POLITICS, SOCIETY, AND RACE: FROM CONSENSUS TO CONFRONTATION

The decades following the Great Depression brought important changes to life in California. International tensions and technological factors were responsible for continual growth. Later, however, internal demographic patterns, civil rights demonstrations, and ethnic demands accompanied a series of dramatic power conflicts. Newly emergent youth groups also sought control at the expense of "the establishment," with major disruption of the social scene.

CALIFORNIA POLITICS, EARL WARREN TO "JERRY" BROWN

The politicians who led California during this eventful epoch possessed varied personalities and viewpoints. Although many were known beyond the state's boundaries, only a few attained national status. Perhaps the most significant of these was Earl Warren, who dominated California politics from 1942 to 1953. Like Hiram Johnson many years before, he once more brought California to the attention of the nation.

The Warren Era

After serving a four-year term as state attorney general, Earl Warren was elected governor in 1942. A skilled political leader, warm and

249

attractive, Warren was a talented campaigner who, although a progressive-minded Rupublican, stayed clear of factional disputes within his own party. Governor Warren's views were nonpartisan, and he seldom mentioned either of the two leading political parties. Like Governor Johnson, his idol, Warren attracted moderate voters of all parties. When he secured the gubernatorial nominations of both major parties in 1946, embarrassed Democrats vowed to repeal the cross-filing system at the first opportunity.

Informal in manner, Governor Warren projected a reassuring image in difficult times. He was attractive to city workers, middle-class professionals, independent liberals, and conservative farmers alike. Avoiding extremes of either right or left, he gained the support of management and labor. Although the head of the Republican Party in the state, he appointed Democrats to public office and built his administration upon the talents and loyalties of both Republicans and Democrats. The Warren administration secured the enactment of welfare measures that California urgently needed in order to cope with its influx of population. The governor pressed for reform of the state workmen's compensation system, prison conditions, and old-age pension standards. In the enactment of health insurance, Warren was blocked, and then only through the efforts of the powerful California Medical Association. He liked to refer to welfare measures as progressive and middle-of-the-road rather than as liberal.

Warren played an active role in national Republican politics. He led "favorite-son" delegations to three national conventions. In 1948,

Earl Warren, Republican Governor
of California, 1941–1953.

he secured the vice-presidential slot with New York Governor Thomas E. Dewey, who was upset by President Harry S. Truman. This was the only election Warren ever lost. In 1953 President Dwight D. Eisenhower appointed him Chief Justice of the United States, a position which he held for fifteen years. During this period the Warren Court rendered many landmark decisions, including *Brown* v. *Board of Education* (1954), *Engle* v. *Vitale* (1963), the Gideon case (1963), and the Miranda case (1966). Warren was also the chairman of the commission that investigated the assassination of President John F. Kennedy.

After Warren moved to Washington, two ambitious Republicans fought for control of the state. The first of these was former Lieutenant-Governor Goodwin J. Knight, who had succeeded Warren to the governorship and had then been elected to a full term of his own in 1954. The second figure was Senator William F. Knowland, whose father was the owner of the Oakland *Tribune*. After a bitter struggle, Knight, who had continued most of Warren's middle-of-the-road policies, was forced out of the race for reelection in 1958 so that Knowland could seek the governorship. Knight reluctantly ran for the

Edmund G. "Pat" Brown, Democratic Governor of California 1959–1967

Senate. Both lost, and "the Warren era" in California politics came to an end.

The First Governor Brown, "Pat"

Edmund G. "Pat" Brown won a landslide victory over Senator Knowland in 1958. Like Warren, Brown had been state attorney general. He, too, had conducted nonpartisan political campaigns and avoided overly close association with his own Democratic Party. He was a vigorous candidate, a native son, and a Catholic. Brown spoke of liberal reform and attracted thousands of new voters. He garnered not only the support of his own party, but also that of independents tired of Republican rule.

For the first time since 1888, the state legislature was firmly Democratic. Although there had been a Democratic majority of registered voters since 1934, sometimes numbering more than a million, California had elected Republican governors for more than fifty years, except for the Olson regime, elected in 1938.

Brown faced controversial statewide problems, including traffic and smog control, water development, and a debate over capital punishment. The latter issue had become heated because of the case of Caryl Chessman, the "red-light bandit." Chessman's execution had been delayed eight times in twelve years. During this period he argued much of his own defense, claimed mistrials, wrote best-selling books about the injustice of capital punishment, and presented Governor Brown with a first-class legal dilemma. His imprisonment caused worldwide criticism to be focused on the inconsistencies of American legal process and on the state's death penalty. On May 2, 1960, Chessman finally died in San Quentin's gas chamber, after Brown refused him a last stay of execution. Brown opposed capital punishment; however, in the absence of a state law terminating the practice, the governor saw no alternative but to send Chessman to his death. Smarting from criticism over his handling of this case, Brown called an extraordinary session of the legislature to debate the death penalty. The legislature, however, refused to revise the state's laws on this matter.

In the 1960 Democratic National Convention, held in Los Angeles' new Sports Arena, Governor Brown helped to win the presidential nomination for Massachusetts Senator John F. Kennedy. Kennedy went on to fight for the state's political allegiance, campaigning forcefully in California, as did his opponent Richard M. Nixon. Both candidates counted heavily upon California's thirty-two electoral votes. Although Nixon, as a native son, won the state by a narrow margin, his victory proved insufficient to prevent Kennedy's election.

Nixon was, however, encouraged sufficiently by the closeness of the voting to rally Republican forces for the California gubernatorial campaign of 1962. The campaign was bitter. Incumbent Governor Brown contended that Nixon was not really interested in being governor of California, but rather was looking for a power base from which he could launch another presidential campaign. Nixon accused Brown of "being soft on Communists" and of bungling the administration of the state. He pledged the death penalty for "bigtime dope peddlers" and promised to drop "chiselers" from the state welfare rolls. He held out the hope of lower taxes and promised greater efficiency at Sacramento. Brown defended his record on such matters as education, water development, and welfare. Both sides brought lawsuits to stop the circulation of pamphlets described as "smears." When the smoke cleared, Brown had won reelection by a suprisingly wide margin.

Pat Brown's two terms in office were marked by unparalleled economic prosperity, accompanied by huge increases in government spending for highways, universities, and water projects. Brown's leadership, however, was continually undermined by two fellow Democrats, long-time Los Angeles Mayor Sam Yorty and Assembly Speaker Jesse Unruh.

Richard Nixon, a Paradox

Assessing the place of Richard Milhous Nixon in California history is difficult. However, this controversial figure occupied by far the most significant place ever held by a Californian in the realm of national politics and international affairs.

Nixon was born at Yorba Linda and graduated from Whittier College. In 1946, those party leaders who had traditionally opposed Warren selected Nixon, then a young navy veteran, to run for Congress. Nixon had the support of the conservative wing of the Republican Party in the state. After two terms in the House, he won a Senate race against Congresswoman Helen Gahagan Douglas, wife of film star Melvyn Douglas. The Democrats accused Nixon of blatantly unfair tactics in these campaigns. Nixon repeatedly suggested that those opposing him were lacking in patriotism and in anticommunist conviction. He developed a staunch corps of followers and became a national figure, known for his strong stand in matters of internal

253

security and his role in the conviction of former U.S. State Department aide Alger Hiss for perjury in connection with accusations of espionage.

Before Nixon completed his term in the Senate, he was asked to serve as Eisenhower's vice-presidential running mate. The ticket was elected by an overwhelming majority in 1952 and reelected in 1956. Eisenhower's health problems focused unprecedented attention on Nixon because he was only a "heartbeat" away.

Within a two-year period, Nixon lost two major elections. The first, for the presidency in 1960 to John F. Kennedy and the second, for the governorship, in 1962 to Pat Brown. Following the second defeat, he held a bitter "last press conference" at Los Angeles in which he assailed press coverage of the campaign. Most observers considered Nixon "washed-up" on the political scene.

In 1963, Nixon moved to New York and entered a prestigious law firm. He traveled widely and remained active in national political circles, making speeches and campaigning for others including the Republican presidential nominee in 1964, Barry Goldwater. By 1968, the one-time "political corpse" was engaged in a fierce election battle with Lyndon Johnson's vice-president, Hubert Humphrey. This time, Nixon won.

Nixon was at his best in the world of international diplomacy. His "opening toward China" and his policy of détente were widely heralded. But, from his inauguration in 1969 to his resignation in the middle of his second term, the Nixon presidency was one of constant turmoil. The Vietnam War lingered on to divide the nation. Appointments were not confirmed, funds were impounded, and finally the episode called Watergate forced Richard Nixon to leave the White House. In 1974 he returned to a "self-imposed exile" behind the walls of his Mediterranean-style villa overlooking the sea at San Clemente.

Ronald Reagan and the Republican Resurgence

Ronald Reagan, film star and former president of the Screen Actors Guild, also played an active role in Goldwater's 1964 presidential campaign. By 1966, Reagan, who had once been a liberal Democrat, sought the governorship against two-term incumbent Pat Brown. A veteran of more than fifty motion pictures, in which he had frequently played the role of the "nice guy who doesn't get the girl," he projected a relaxed self-possession before television cameras and convinced the electorate that he was a moderate, morally indignant over massive government social welfare programs. While Governor Brown and Assembly Speaker Unruh warred within the Democratic camp, Reagan quieted old disputes inside California's Republican Party.

Despite a continuing Democratic Party advantage in voter registration, Reagan swept into the governorship, defeating Brown by nearly a million votes. In 1967, the Republican Party not only controlled the state but also both national senatorial posts. With the Warren tradition in limbo, the party was dominated by its right wing during the Reagan years.

Reagan began his term by proposing budget slashes of 10 percent in all departments. This caused a storm of demonstrations by students and teachers, as well as mental health and welfare advocates. Reagan's campaign promises had included systematic tax reform, especially for the elderly and for business. Now voters waited for the tax relief their new governor promised. In order not to raise taxes, the administration hoped to make government more frugal. Although Reagan's critics charged him with reaction and negativism, he signed a liberal law on abortion. What seemed like antiintellectualism to academics was applauded by the public at large. Reagan proposed to slice the appropriations for the state college and university systems. Educators remonstrated that the overall effect of such cuts was to injure "quality education." Late in 1967, Reagan proposed to trim 3,700 jobs from state public assistance agencies and to close eight mental health clinics in urban areas. An uproar greeted the curtailments. Ultimately, Reagan did effect significant fiscal cuts, but, in the case of the state's mental health program, he relented.

One of the biggest Reagan economy targets was in funds for medical care of the elderly, the indigent, and other welfare recipients. He proposed slashes in such programs and also called for changes in eligibility requirements. Reagan hoped "to squeeze fraud and abuse out of California's welfare system." He feared the possibility of perpetuating poverty "by substituting a permanent dole for a paycheck." Toll collectors on bridges were forced to surrender revolvers, which were then sold. Travel by state employees was curtailed as were the use of teletype and telephone services and the purchase of major equipment and supplies. The governor's office suspended publication of road maps, brochures, pamphlets, and a recreation magazine. Some $50,000 was saved in typewriter ribbons and $2 million in the state's phone bill during the first few months of Reagan's governorship. He also sold a state-owned airplane.

255

Ronald Reagan, Republican Governor of California 1967–1975

In 1967, Reagan backed six bills to deal with crime control, only one of which was enacted—a law that tripled the minimum penalty for rape, robbery, or burglary in cases where victims were injured. A stronger gun-control law passed the legislature in part because of a national mood toward such controls; also because a Black Panther group, armed with unloaded weapons, stunned the legislature by bursting into that body while the law was being debated. True to his promises, the governor tried but failed to gain repeal of a controversial open-housing law. Governor Reagan also had trouble gaining passage of tighter obscenity laws, or the establishment of county welfare fraud units, or the institution of a merit system for judges. Labor leaders hated Reagan. When farm labor grew short during the 1967 harvest, the governor sent convicts to help harvest crops. He also ordered use of employable welfare recipients where labor shortages existed. Labor, naturally, called such moves a subsidy to growers.

The eight Reagan years can be seen as a checkpoint rather than as a turning point in California's political development. His efforts to stem the growth of government were defeated by a variety of factors. Rampant national inflation lay beyond the control of any state governor. A hostile Democratic legislature was determined to thwart his approach to the issues. Inertia, too, made it difficult to overhaul a lumbering bureaucracy in Sacramento.

Reagan's vetoes against government spending did act as a brake against an even more rapid rate of growth for state services. However, demands for welfare and medical-aid payments grew strident as his term came to an end. Welfare rolls actually increased under Reagan. Reagan's attempts to coax state employees into voluntarily working on holidays only showed how distant he was from entrenched civil servants. He did initiate several worthy measures. His staff computerized some of the most time-consuming state operations. The Reagan administration also stopped construction of a number of new state buildings and facilities that would otherwise have been sanctioned by the legislature. Dissident state college and university personnel were "kept in their place" by a governor who reaped public acclaim by cracking down on unruly students as well.

In 1974, Governor Reagan, who decided not to seek a third term, offered this rambling appraisal of eight years in office:

> "Presuming the historian is objective, I think one thing that we've done —among all the things that we've done—is bring an awareness of state government that people didn't have before. I think they're much more conscious of Sacramento and state government these last few years. I think—also that we proved that so-called conservative principles of common sense and good business practices in government worked—I think there has been a gigantic turnaround in the whole welfare thing —I never in my wildest dreams ever dreamed that I would find myself liking it and as deeply involved in what has been the most fulfilling and exciting thing that I've ever done in my life."

Reagan made two efforts at securing the Republican presidential nomination, the first in 1968 when he made a weak showing against Richard Nixon. In 1976, however, he conducted a grueling battle for the Republican nomination against President Gerald Ford. He came close to capturing the prize in a hotly contested party convention.

The Second Governor Brown, "Jerry"

In the spirit of the 1970s, California's new governor, Edmund G. ("Jerry") Brown, Jr., repeatedly reminded his audiences that there was a limit to what government could undertake. He criticized the "spending philosophy" of old New Dealers like his father. Although an advocate of civil rights, racial integration, and ecology, Brown proved to be a fiscal conservative, like his predecessor, Reagan.

Edmund G. "Jerry" Brown, Jr.,
Democratic Governor of California, 1975–

Only thirty-seven years old and a bachelor who had once studied for the priesthood, Jerry Brown had already served a four-year term as California Secretary of State, a position which gave him an excellent vantage point from which to view the Sacramento political scene. At first, he said that he had no national political aspirations. In 1975, he refused to attend the National Governors Conference, claiming to be more concerned with state problems of unemployment, illegal Mexican immigration, crime, medical insurance, and the plight of the farm workers. Local issues (like fighting the highway and auto lobbies that wanted more freeways) seemed to overwhelm larger national interests, at least at the beginning of his term. Whereas his father, Governor Pat Brown, had dealt with such matters as California's water shortage, even more complex social dilemmas confronted his son.

The wave of fear over mass demonstrations having subsided, Brown spoke to the aspirations of younger educated persons. He seemed to provide the counterculture's response to post-Vietnam disillusionment with big government, big business, and big unions. Half of California's population was under the age of twenty-nine. These products of the 1950s "baby boom" felt comfortable about Brown. In California (which critics have called a "media state") Brown, like Reagan, came off as a good TV performer. His strong flair for manipulating symbols—his refusal to live in a new governor's mansion or to use an executive jet plane and official limousines—struck voters more than favorably.

Press and television were skillfully used by both Brown and Reagan to overcome California's weak party structure. The senatorial election of 1976, which put a virtual nonpartisan, Dr. S. I. Hayakawa, into office, showed how little the rank-and-file voter thought of party loyalty. Hayakawa relied, instead, upon his record in standing up to campus radicals when President of San Francisco State College during the 1960s. The young Governor Brown took little interest in state political contests, claiming to be absorbed with complex problems that suddenly grew to have national implications.

Those Californians who firmly believed that what they think today America does tomorrow saw Brown's political philosophy as the wave of the future. Even in conservative Orange County, Brown was popular. Reminiscent of Reagan, Brown repeated the admonition that his program was "to confront the confusion and hypocrisy of big government, that's what's important."

As young Brown began to think about reelection, cries of "fake" were heard among discontented followers. Willie Brown, a black San Francisco Democrat, said he was tired of being misled by a man who was like "a bowl of Jello." Whatever Jerry Brown's personal inclinations toward welfare programs, he was a shrewd politico who knew that the word "socialism" must never even be whispered before the American people. He, therefore, remained vulnerable to growing disenchantment over his refusal to make ideological commitments. The Brown cult of "creative inaction" caused conventional liberals and fervent reformers to fume. For them, the admonition to lower their expectations "for we are entering an era of limits" was not enough of a program to entice fickle and easily bored voters.

In 1976, young Brown entered several presidential primaries. He offered the nation an appealing style, blending fiscal austerity and idealism. In a year during which Jimmy Carter swept the country to gain the Democratic party nomination, Brown, nevertheless, became the most fashionably refreshing politician in America. The fact that he had defeated Carter in every head-to-head contest was

259

not lost on party leaders. He was viewed as a likely nominee in 1984 should Carter falter. He became as popular in California as Hiram Johnson and Earl Warren had once been. Despite campaign promises, a solid record of achievement did not accompany Brown's presidential bid. While he was off campaigning, former adherents charged that he had abandoned the ship of state in Sacramento.

On occasion, Brown's boyish charm and rhetoric made him sound old-fashioned: "We're going to have to work harder," he stated in a 1976 speech to the California Democratic Council. "It's going to take a lot more pain and suffering before we can get to where we have to go ... The price of democracy is discipline," he said.

Although the second Governor Brown's style seemed to feature decision-making through indecision, protests against his reform record were not entirely fair. Brown did act upon his convictions. A new (1976) state Office of Appropriate Technology was the first such agency in America to advocate climatically and environmentally designed buildings; it sponsored wind power, solar heating, home organic farming, and bioconversion (use of human waste to produce energy). After losing a long battle with the legislature over the death penalty, which ended when his veto was overridden, he stated that he considered it his duty to carry out the law. Brown also appointed unprecedented numbers of women, young, minority members, ecologists, and consumer advocates to state regulatory commissions.

Other Personalities and Events

The careers of several California politicians were closely linked with the Kennedys of Massachusetts. In 1964, Pierre Salinger, who had been President Kennedy's press secretary, defeated Alan Cranston in the Democratic primary contest for the United States Senate nomination. Cranston, one of the founders of the California Democratic Council, was then serving as state controller. In 1970 John Tunney, son of Gene Tunney the former heavyweight boxing champion, became senator.

It was also in California that one of the most shocking events of the Kennedy psychodrama occurred. In June 1968, just moments after acknowledging the applause of the crowd celebrating his victory over Senator Hubert Humphrey in the California presidential primary, Robert F. Kennedy was shot and killed at Los Angeles by a Palestinian refugee.

In September 1975, two unsuccessful assassination attempts were directed at President Gerald Ford in northern California.

Campaign Flyer from RFK's 1968 presidential primary.
(From Dr. Gaines' collection)

Black Politicians

Black representation in the California political process increased dramatically in the sixties. Wilson Riles became the first black to win a statewide office when he was elected superintendent of public instruction in 1970. Reelected in 1974, Riles played an important role in improving early childhood education. He also attempted to restore the California Education Department to the nonpartisan status it had prior to his predecessor's term of office. Mervyn Dymally, a black state senator from Los Angeles, was elected president pro-tempore of the state Senate. Dymally succeeded a Republican lieutenant-governor forced out of office during the Watergate inquiry. Subsequently, he was elected to a full term in 1974. A black former police officer, Tom Bradley, defeated Los Angeles Mayor Sam Yorty in 1973. Mayor Bradley was reelected for a second term in 1977.

Women in California Politics

The increasing importance of the role of women in California politics can be seen by the success of several female office seekers. First to

Wilson Riles, State Superintendent of Public Instruction, 1971–

Dianne Feinstein, elected the 35th Major of the City and County of San Francisco by the Board of Supervisors on December 4, 1978, to fill the unexpired term of the late Mayor George R. Moscone. *(Courtesy of the Office of the Mayor, San Francisco)*

be elected on a statewide ballot was Ivy Baker Priest, a Republican, who served as state treasurer from 1967 to 1973. Mrs. Priest had previously served as treasurer of the United States, a post she had been appointed to by President Eisenhower and which has been held by women ever since. Romana Acosta Banuelos, the owner of a Mexican food-processing firm in Los Angeles, served under President Nixon. In 1974, March Fong Eu, a Chinese-American and former member of the state legislature from Oakland, was elected to the position of secretary of state.

California women have also played notable roles in National party conventions. In 1952, Mildred Younger helped the Eisenhower forces win a pivotal contest in the credentials committee. She later made an unsuccessful try for a seat in Congress. In 1972, Yvonne Brathwaite Burke presided over the Democratic National Convention as temporary chairman. Burke served several terms in Congress. After former child movie star Shirley Temple Black was unsuccessful in a 1970 bid for a seat in the House of Representatives, she held appointive posts in the Nixon and Ford administrations, serving

263

Tom Bradley, Mayor of
Los Angeles, 1973–

successively as a member of the United States delegation to the
United Nations and as ambassador to Ghana.

A Society in Transition

Each generation must deal with some of the continuing problems
that vexed its predecessors. In the 1960s, however, politicians faced
challenges from unexpected quarters. A perplexing "generation
gap" exploded in campus demonstrations and Vietnam War protests.
Long-ignored minorities rioted and made strident demands for immediate justice. The long-standing centrist trend which had characterized California politics for decades was suddenly challenged from
both sides of the political spectrum. Two new parties, the Peace and
Freedom Party, which represented the "New Left," and the American Independent Party, which represented the "Old Right," made
their way onto the ballot. The "old" liberals like Pat Brown were
driven from power. The realigned, much more conservative, Republicans made a comeback under Ronald Reagan. Then a metamor-

Yvonne Brathwaite Burke, Democratic Congresswoman, 1973–1979

phosed Democratic party, led by Jerry Brown, tried its hand at dealing with the realities of the turbulent seventies.

Student Unrest and the Vietnam War

The years from 1963 to 1968 were a period of social and material upheaval possibly never equalled—nationally or in California—during any other five-year span. The 1960s stand out as years of great unrest, violent behavior, and intemperate language. The dominant voices and figures were those of youth. Dissatisfaction with institutions run by "the Establishment" formed the keynote of militants who called themselves the New Left or the Radical Left. The tone of the period was piercingly shrill as colleges, banks, government, and other institutions came under attack, sometimes physically as well as ideologically.

Reflective of the national impatience of students, the mid-1960s stood in contrast to the placidity of "the silent generation" during the 1950s. After 1963, student demonstrations occurred on California's campuses, particularly at the University of California at Berkeley. There were also protest rallies at San Francisco State College and other collegiate centers. A "Free Speech Movement" at Berkeley kept the university in the headlines as "agitator-students" insisted

Ivy Baker Priest, Republican
State Treasurer, 1967–1973

upon a greater voice in university administration. The right of political assembly was particularly dear to activists. Student drama, journalism, and music came to reflect their discontent. Wide-eyed young
fans of the folksingers Bob Dylan and Joan Baez wanted action as
well as words.

Following massive sit-ins during the fall of 1964, the Free
Speech Movement grew unpopular. The blatant use of obscenity by
some of its leaders was particularly unwise. In response to public
demands, local police were called onto the Berkeley campus when
order could not be maintained. More than 700 youths, not all of them
students, were dragged out of Sproul Hall, the administrative center,
and jailed. Almost 600 of these were pronounced guilty of illegal
trespassing and resisting arrest. Conservative leaders spoke of the
need to clean up the Berkeley environment and its "left-wing ex-
tremism."

Contributing to student malaise were stalemates encountered in
both the civil rights struggle and in prosecution of the Vietnam War.
The San Francisco Bay area became a national center of agitation for
black rights and against the war. Students threatened to burn draft
cards, defied law and order, and remonstrated against "the Establish-

ment." At Berkeley, especially, they resented the presence on campus of representatives from napalm-producing firms as well as armed service recruiters. As the war dragged on, student and other rioters blocked the nearby Oakland Induction Center, turning in draft cards and, on occasion, even repudiating educational draft deferments. The student protests spread nationwide, reaching a climax in the tragedy at Kent State University in 1970.

Undergraduates and graduates alike wished to expand the role they played in collegiate government on the campuses of the state university. The wisdom of conservative, business-oriented regents, appointed for sixteen-year terms by past governors, was questioned. Students were impatient also with the depersonalization of academic life, and they argued for decentralization of the state university. The university eventually did take steps to decentralize its campuses; it also strengthened the authority of individual chancellors. Small undergraduate colleges similar to those at Oxford represented a student ideal, only vaguely realized by the founding of new campuses at Santa Cruz and San Diego. At Berkeley, faculty study groups sought to find added ways to reduce mechanization and to disarm hostility and student disloyalty by sharing authority with students.

Under the Reagan administration, public distrust of the state university reached new heights, as did student criticism not only of their authorities but particularly of the governor himself. A ninety-six-page student-faculty (Berkeley) commission report of 1967 read: "The inroads on civil liberties and academic freedom made in the past year are warnings that for the first time in many years we are faced with a consistently unfriendly state administration whose theories of educational financing are a logical accompaniment to its suspicions of this campus."

The dismissal of University of California President Clark Kerr that year highlighted the growing tension between academia and the public at large. California's academic community was clearly in disfavor with a large segment of the electorate. Repeated confrontations between strident demonstrators and university officials had convinced the public that left-wing professors and administrators were spineless allies of student activists. Universities and colleges alike became convenient targets for critics from both the left and the right.

At a time when the tax base staggered under expanding educational budgets (which competed with accelerating welfare and health care costs), disgusted voters began to favor bond issues for police protection rather than for students and their teachers. Falling

University of California, Berkeley. Central campus dominated by its "campanile." *(University of California photograph by Dennis Galloway)*

enrollments, too, forced state officials to pull back from the unrealistic growth projections they had once made.

College campuses became centers of opposition to the Vietnam War as well as of criticism of American society. Taxpayers, confused by the mystique of revolt, believed that the state's colleges and universities should teach students only those skills with which they could make a living, and nothing else. Such critics did not feel that state-operated campuses should become the seats of independent inquiry, public criticism, or distasteful dramatic and artistic productions. At Berkeley, a city in which the university usually dominates the community, the tension between town and "gown" continued unabated.

Civic power remained in the hands of older residents, who showed scant understanding of the radically different younger generations. The "generation gap" was partly related to a difference in goals between new and earlier residents.

The Hippies

In the 1960s the California environment came to reflect the alienation from society of a wide variety of young persons. A new type of rebel called Hippies created an "underground culture." Instead of expressing open aggression against parents, the Hippies took a look at modern life, decided it was beyond hope, and "dropped out." In their refuges located at San Francisco, Oakland, and Venice West, they grew more and more resentful of the war in Vietnam, racial bigotry, the suppression of individuality, and what they considered the shallow materialism and phony morals of adults.

In California, the Hippie generation sought salvation in a new life style that involved the imaginative use of colors—sometimes called psychedelic. To transcend the monotony of ordinary existence, some Hippies used drugs and were preoccupied with the search for "inward values." Hippiedom—the Haight-Ashbury district of San Francisco—became a weird national focal point, and on weekends Haight Street was jammed with curious sightseers, sometimes bringing traffic to a halt.

Magazines and newspapers, as well as radio and television stations, featured descriptions of young rebels. Parents could not understand how their children, who had enjoyed many "advantages," could leave their middle-class homes and, in the language of disillusioned youth "turn on, tune in, and drop out."

Hippies let their hair grow, dressed as they pleased, and often wore no shoes. Parents, however, frequently saw only outward appearances and seldom listened to their ideas, or so their children believed. Young rebels expressed these ideas in what came to be known as the "underground press." The Los Angeles *Free Press* was sold at curbside along the Sunset Strip. In the Bay Area the Berkeley *Barb* and San Francisco *Oracle* also assumed a semisubversive anti-Establishment stance. The *Barb* defined underground people as "that part of the population which lives at odds with the Establishment," and stated that the paper would "push any movement that will push the Establishment in a socially humanistic direction."

The Hippie movement did not seem to diminish inherent avarice, immature aggressiveness, and other personal shortcoming in its adherents. Their ram-shackle neighborhoods were ridden with malnutrition, poverty, theft, murder, suicide, and drug addiction. Distrust arose among those who came to feel that their way of life had proved no better than society's. For the drug user, reentry into the dull routine of one's society proved difficult, for drugs deadened the drive to work and produce. Sociologists and psychologists felt that the Hippies raised valid questions about society's ethics; yet these malcontents did not provide many solutions. Critics of the Hippies believe that they hypocritically refused to face real issues.

Eventually Hippies began to leave the cities and to start communes in rural areas of California. Meditation, taught by advocates of various eastern religions, attracted others. With the end of the draft and the retirement of their arch foes, Nixon and Reagan, most of the former Hippies returned to the mainstream of California society.

An Age of Criminality

In the sixties and seventies a wave of mindless criminality swept over California. Lurid media coverage and sensational trials focused national attention on the Manson "family," the Patty Hearst kidnapping, the Zodiac killer, the Zebra murders, and the Hillside Strangler. Such events are a serious blot on the reputation of the state. Though they cannot be ignored, no constructive purpose is served by recounting the sordid details or giving notoriety to the sociopaths who increasingly blacken our society by criminal acts.

Problems of Race

The state spent millions revamping run-down neighborhoods and improving welfare programs. Although it had no officially sanctioned segregation, deed restrictions and social pressures had produced a segregated society. This was most unjust to those minorities which did not, or in fact could not, easily assimilate into the majority culture —the Orientals, the blacks, the Indians, and the Mexican-Americans. All of these have been dealt with to some extent in earlier chapters, but we must return to the topic in order to consider the Black Power movement and the Brown Revolution.

Mexican-Americans

Mexican-Americans, or Chicanos (the term preferred by most of the younger and more militant members of this minority) are a diverse

270

and misunderstood people. Including a few whose origins coincide with the European occupation of California over 200 years ago and many who have come north from Mexico in recent years, the Mexican-American community is a growing and increasingly important element in California life. The Mexican immigration pattern has been affected by revolutions, inflation, and unemployment in Mexico, which have made refugees out of many dissatisfied persons. Job opportunities, border surveillance, and living conditions north of the border also pose difficult problems, whose solutions have not been easy to find.

Although the Mexican migrant may retain family ties on both sides of the border, he is viewed as a foreigner in Mexico and in the United States as well. The more "Spanish," or fair-skinned, and the less *Indio,* or dark-skinned, the more likely he will be to achieve middle-class status. While nearly all are *mestizos,* or "mixed-bloods," the racial consciousness of Mexico itself is perpetuated in their adopted country. Serious problems of education, housing, and assimilation have developed around California's Mexican minority. Forced to accept unpleasant jobs at low wages, or to remain unemployed, they cling to their language, cluster in their own organizations, and retain strong separate tastes and outlook.

In the 1940s youthful Mexican gangs—known during World War II as *Pachucos*—got into trouble with the police because of fights on the streets of Los Angeles and other communities. Accused of carrying switchblade knives in their trouser pockets, and razor blades in their long hair, they were a source of worry to older and more settled Mexicans, as well as to annoyed *Anglos.* In 1943, discharged navy and marine veterans, in addition to "white hoodlums," rioted against the "zootsuit *Pachucos.* " Intolerant critics shortsightedly associated the *Pachuco* gangland attitude with Mexicans in general.

In the postwar boom period, new jobs became available for Mexican immigrants. Some who came as temporary workers under the *bracero* program decided to stay. Many made their way to the cities where work was plentiful and where they were less likely to be bothered by the immigration service. One Chicano neighborhood just north of the Civic Center was designated as a site for government-owned low-rent housing. The local citizens, who had vigorously protested their eviction and the destruction of their homes, became particularly bitter when after a change in mayors the public housing project plan was abandoned and Chavez Ravine was given to Walter O'Malley for the Dodger Stadium.

271

In 1960 John F. Kennedy campaigned with special vigor among the "Viva Kennedy" clubs organized in the *barrios* (Spanish-speaking neighborhoods) of Los Angeles. Early in 1964, Kennedy's successor, President Lyndon B. Johnson, held a series of conferences in Los Angeles with Mexico's President Lopez-Mateos. These covered the whole range of United States relations with Mexico. In addition to discussing the sharing of Colorado River water and the *bracero* problem, the two chiefs of state dealt with the social reforms championed by Kennedy's Alliance for Progress program throughout the Americas. Astute observers of local politics did not, however, miss the importance of the setting in which the Democratic Party had chosen to hold these talks, or the emerging political role of the Chicanos. Los Angeles contains the largest Mexican population of any city in the United States.

The Californian of Mexican descent continues to live on a smaller per capita income than perhaps any other person in its population, including blacks. *Latino* leaders once referred to the status of their people as *desgraciados,* people "born without grace." For a populace so rich in tradition and so proud of its ancestral heritage, such a condition is humiliating.

Those converts to the *Anglo* social order who were content to move into pleasant grass-green, middle-class neighborhoods were of little help to the Mexican-American leaders who sought to help their people. Among those who furnished leadership was Los Angeles City Councilman Edward Roybal who, in 1962, went on to become a congressman after organizing the Mexican-American Political Association, the most vocal of several such groups. Another leader was Dr. Julian Nava, a history professor who served on the Los Angeles school board. Restiveness among California's Chicanos, however, remained.

Accused of sparking school walkouts were members of a Chicano group called "the Brown Berets," whose leaders sought to unite *La Raza* (the race) in the barrios of California. Wearing clothing reminiscent of other Latin revolutionaries, they carried signs which read *"Viva la Revolucion."* To some, this appeared to be Communist inspired; but to those who were aware of Mexican history, it was less ominous.

After the school boycott in 1968 and a violent protest march in 1970, California's Chicano leaders turned toward the nonglittering but more practical day-to-day organizational process. Hopes to build a new political party, *La Raza Unida,* dissolved into fratricidal disputes as weary activists turned toward the nonviolent ideals of Cesar Chavez, the only nationally known figure of Mexican-American heritage.

Slowly, a new leadership was forged in the bustling barrios of east Los Angeles and south San Francisco. More and more young Chicanos were coming out of the colleges and universities who were anxious to replace the members of the older generation labeled *Tio Tacos*—a parallel for Uncle Tom.

By 1977, an estimated 3.75 million persons of Spanish background lived in California. Of these, 95 percent were Mexican-Americans. Some 1.5 million of them lived in Los Angeles County. That year President Jimmy Carter, like President Johnson earlier, held a series of conferences with Mexico's President Lopez-Portillo. At these sessions Governor Jerry Brown pointed out that as many as 500,000 Mexicans might enter the United States in a given year. In 1978, an estimated 6 million were here illegally—on top of the 6.6 million legal residents numbered by the census bureau.

The Blacks

The inequities that have long faced California's black population continue to cry out for reform. Although California joined the union as a free state, blacks were not allowed to give testimony against whites in a court of law and the Fugitive Slave Act (1852) got applied in such a way as to discriminate against them. They remained clustered mostly in the towns of southern California. The oldest black newspaper in the state, *The California Eagle,* has been published at Los Angeles since 1879. Black communities grew slowly until the 1880s, after which came larger numbers of blacks who found work as custodians, waiters, cooks, railroad porters, and domestics in the homes of the rich. When the restrictive immigration laws of the 1920s went into effect, more jobs opened up.

African-Americans from the southern states flocked to California. World War II added to this in-migration. By 1944, the Japanese district of Los Angeles ("Little Tokyo") felt the inroads of 80,000 new Black residents. Better established blacks moved into Pasadena and into San Francisco from Oakland. But they were conspicuously not welcomed in some "lily-white" suburbs. Blacks, however, founded an all-black community at Val Verde Park in the Tehachapi foothills and an important Los Angeles-based insurance corporation, as well as a few resorts. From the 1950s through the 1960s, about 1,000 blacks per month came into Los Angeles County alone. In that decade California's black populace grew by 91 percent while its overall population increased by only 48 percent. During the same decade over 350,000 blacks moved to California.

273

Middle-class blacks not only moved into white neighborhoods; they also took jobs formerly held by whites. In the professions, in sports, and in the political world they slowly challenged white supremacy, collectively and individually. Dr. Ralph Bunche, a graduate of UCLA, went from a U.S. State Department career to become under secretary at the United Nations; Leslie Brown became postmaster of Los Angeles in 1965; and a number of blacks held elective political offices.

While entertainers like Nat "King" Cole or Sammy Davis, Jr., became well known, relatively few blacks achieved the progress to which they felt entitled. Crowded into dilapidated lower-class neighborhoods, they chafed at prejudice, segregation, and social deprivation. In southeast Los Angeles the sprawling all-black ghetto of Watts became an especially unwholesome sore spot. Although some of its streets were lined with palm trees, crowded slums were bound, eventually, to produce violence, directed against symbolic white oppressors.

The "Black Revolution" that swept across America in the 1960s was to reap tragic repercussions in the riots that broke out during August 1965 at Watts. These violent uprisings epitomized the malaise of disenchanted blacks and deeply upset Californians. Hundreds of rioters, shouting the antiwhite epithets "Burn Baby Burn" and "Get Whitey," looted stores, set buildings afire, and shot at firemen and police. The hurriedly mobilized National Guard troops helped local policemen to restore order and to establish a curfew. The riots, which lasted for several days, caused the deaths of 35 persons (mostly blacks), injury to 600 others, and $40 million in damage. Some 4,000 persons were arrested, mostly in a one square-mile burned-over area. Rioters charged arresting police with brutality in Watts and later at Oakland and San Francisco, where "aftershocks" were felt for several months. The police asserted that criminal elements had taken control of the riots.

These rageful outbursts underscored a sense of hopelessness which grew out of economic misery, a diffuse black family structure, envy of the white man's luxuries, and resentment against "Establishment" forces of law and order. Antiwhite rowdyism, however, made these upheavals only partly racial. The search for material goods led black marauders to sack furniture stores filled with television sets, freezers, and high-fidelity phonographs—as if to defy the traditional white monopoly of "success."

Key phrases repeated after the Watts riots depicted the problems of "inner-city" streets there and elsewhere: discrimination,

274

anarchy, mob violence, looting, illegitimacy, drug addicts, disease, employment inequality, police brutality, attacks on policemen and school teachers, white and nonwhite attitudes toward transportation to schools.

When the rioting ended, Watts lay in ruins, and the anxiety which had been responsible for the outburst remained unsoothed. A number of moves toward racial reform did occur, including the building of a new cultural center at Watts as well as a hospital. Educated blacks from ghetto areas were listened to with greater attention than before; yet there was a continuing failure to delve into the quality of the African past and meaning of race. Local police did attempt to open up a better dialogue with the blacks in order to reduce community tensions. A commission appointed to study the reasons for the riots indicated that Watts needed much better transportation and recreational facilities. White businessmen also tried to widen employment opportunities in order to assuage the distrustful sense of despair of restless young blacks.

Although California's cities long had separate Mexican-American and Chinese sectors, impacted black sections did not emerge until after World War II. Schools, though officially integrated, reflected segregated housing patterns. Blacks blamed the real estate lobby for this situation.

After winning a battle for the enactment of a comprehensive "fair-housing" statute, blacks were outraged when the measure was overturned by an initiative constitutional amendment. The vote occurred almost on the eve of the Watts riots. Even after the courts nullified the initiative measure as unconstitutional in 1966, the issue refused to die. Anti-fair-housing forces made repeated efforts to repeal the original legislation. More importantly, it soon became apparent that legislative remedies for segregation had only a limited effect.

Despite the gains blacks had made, they still lacked full legal and social equality. A rising level of expectations accompanied dissatisfaction over delays in achieving parity with whites. Black Power advocates, particularly Angela Davis and Eldridge Cleaver, stridently reiterated the themes of discrimination and inequality. Meanwhile, a growing population of young blacks longed for the realization of the promises of civil rights legislators and of the sponsors of such national antipoverty measures and education programs as Head Start and Upward Bound.

As late as 1978, the Los Angeles city schools were under court order to come up with a plan to overcome the effects of segregated housing patterns. The unemployment rate of black teenagers is still

275

much higher than that of any other racial group and seems to defy all efforts to reduce it.

In 1978, the United States Supreme Court decided on one of the most important of all civil rights cases. The plaintiff, Alan Bakke, charged that the "affirmative action" admissions policy of the University of California Davis Medical School amounted to "reverse discrimination." The California Supreme Court found in Bakke's favor, holding that the medical school had based its program on the "impermissible grounds of race." When the university appealed, national attention focused on the case. The five-to-four Court ruling also found the Davis plan to be unconstitutional, but on the grounds that it contained a rigid numerical quota. Although it agreed with the California Supreme Court that Bakke should be admitted, it determined that race could be among the factors considered in college admissions procedures. Though disappointing to the advocates on both sides of the hotly contested issue, it was truly a landmark decision.

STUDY SUGGESTIONS

To understand the chapter you should know (1) the meaning and importance of key phrases and terms, (2) the contributions to California history of major personalities, and (3) the location and significance of geographic place names.

1. *Key phrases and terms*

"affirmative action"
American Independent Party
Anglo
the Bakke case
"Black Revolution"
Brown v. *Board of Education*
The California Eagle
Chicano
"the Establishment"
Fair Housing Act

Free Speech Movement
Hippies
La Raza
Latino
mestizo
New Left
Pachucos
Peace and Freedom Party
reverse discrimination
Tio Taco
"underground press"
Vietnam War

2. *Major personalities*

Shirley Temple Black
Tom Bradley

Edmund G. "Jerry" Brown
Edmund G. "Pat" Brown

Yvonne Brathwaite Burke
Caryl Chessman
Angela Davis
Mervyn Dymally
S. I. Hayakawa
Richard M. Nixon
Ivy Baker Priest
Ronald Reagan

Wilson Riles
Edward Roybal
John Tunney
Jesse Unruh
Earl Warren
Sam Yorty
Mildred Younger

3. *Important geographic place names*

Berkeley
Chavez Ravine
Haight-Ashbury district
Oakland
Orange County

San Clemente
Val Verde Park
Venice West
Watts
Yorba Linda

FOR ADDITIONAL STUDY

Paul Bullock, *Watts: The Aftermath* (New York, 1970).
Robert Conot, *Rivers of Blood, Years of Darkness* (New York, 1967).
Arthur G. Coons, *Crisis in California Education* (Los Angeles, 1968).
George E. Frakes and Curtis Solberg (Eds.), *Minorities in California History* (New York, 1971).
Rodolfo Gonzales, *I Am Joaquin: Yo Soy Joaquin* (New York, 1972).
Kenneth Goode, *California's Black Pioneers* (Santa Barbara, 1973).
Joseph Lewis, *What Makes Reagan Run? A Political Profile* (New York, 1968).
Oscar Lewis, *The Children of Sanchez* (New York, 1961).
Seymour M. Lipset and Sheldon S. Wolin (Eds.), *The Berkeley Student Revolt: Facts and Interpretation* (New York, 1965).
Carey McWilliams, *North from Mexico* (Philadelphia, 1949).
Wayne Moquin (Ed.), *A Documentary History of the Mexican Americans* (New York, 1971).
Richard M. Nixon, *Six Crises* (New York, 1962).
Ronald Reagan, *Where's the Rest of Me?* (New York, 1965).
Manuel P. Servin (Ed.), *The Mexican-Americans* (Beverly Hills, 1970).
John D. Weaver, *Warren: The Man, the Court, the Era* (Boston, 1967).
Charles Wollenberg (Ed.), *Ethnic Conflict in California History* (Los Angeles, 1970).

•10•

ALL THAT GLITTERS

Is California still "golden"? To answer this question, we need to examine what has recently come to be known as the "California life style." Rather than attempting to define or describe its confusions, this chapter will provide glimpses of the unique characteristics of modern life in "the Golden State."

CULTURAL ATTAINMENTS

By the late nineteenth century, San Francisco had clearly established itself as the most cosmopolitan American city west of the Mississippi. Since gold rush days it was a center that enthusiastically supported both dramatic and musical theater. Artists from all over the world included "The City" on their annual concert tours. Edwin Booth, Jenny Lind, and Amelita Galli-Curci looked upon "Frisco" as a home away from home. The famed tenor Enrico Caruso sang the role of Don José in Bizet's *Carmen* on the very night of the great 1906 San Francisco earthquake and fire.

Classical Music

At the turn of the century, the most important musical institution in California was the San Francisco Symphony. In 1911, it became the first orchestra in the nation to be assisted regularly by public funds. The San Francisco Opera Company was founded in 1923. Under a succession of talented directors, this organization has beome world famous. After 1932 it had a permanent home, the War Memorial Opera House, the first such municipal structure in the United States.

In southern California, the Los Angeles Philharmonic Orchestra was founded in 1919. In addition, since 1921, the series of open-air concerts at the Hollywood Bowl has given local composers, musicians, and conductors an outlet for their talents. Much later, the Los Angeles Music Center became as well known as the Lincoln Center in New York or the Kennedy Center in Washington, D.C.

Art and Architecture

As early as the 1920s, art colonies at Carmel, Santa Barbara, and Laguna Beach reflected a deepening interest in sculpture, painting, mosaic work, and architectural design. California art institutes, among them Otis, Chouinard, and the Los Angeles Art-Center School, and museums grew in stature. The Huntington Art Gallery in San Marino obtained many paintings of the English Renaissance while the Crocker Art Gallery at Sacramento and the De Young Museum in San Francisco's Golden Gate Park steadily enlarged their collections.

First among California's sculptors was Gutzon Borglum, who began his career as a painter. He studied art at San Francisco in the late 1880s. One of his best paintings was a portrait of the explorer John C. Frémont (now at the Southwest Museum). After a period of residence at Sierra Madre, he was commissioned to carve the features of four American presidents in the granite cliffs of Mount Rushmore, South Dakota; through this work he achieved national fame.

The California photographers best known today are Edward Weston and Ansel Adams. Adams' black-and-white photos are sharp, vivid, and penetrating. Much of his work is devoted to the landscape of the Yosemite Valley. His is a latter-day complement to the superb oil paintings done in the Sierra before World War I by Chris Jorgensen. The majestic spirit of California's land, water, and air governs the artistic impulse of Adams and Weston, and countless professional and amateur painters, water colorists, and etchers follow in this tradition.

Weston achieved an international reputation with his black-and-white photography. Carmel was his home, and his lens explored without rest the landscape of the Monterey peninsula. He died in 1957, having spent fifty years capturing subtleties of light and shadow. "Without ceremony," according to his friend and Carmel neighbor, the poet Robinson Jeffers, Weston "taught photography to be itself, not a facile substitute for painting, or an anxious imitator."

At San Diego, after 1893, Irving Gill built some of that city's most original residences. Utilizing concrete, which he coated with plaster, Gill reduced the use of ornamentation in his buildings. Although the best-known San Diego architect, he was not chosen as a designer for that city's Panama-Pacific International Exposition of 1915. Rather, the honor went to a devotee of Spanish colonial architecture, Bertram Goodhue, whose Balboa Park buildings ushered in a Hispanic revival that profoundly affected the California white stucco and red tile faddism of the period. An exception to this style was his leaner, more angular, Los Angeles Public Library, which most critics consider Goodhue's finest effort.

After 1900, at San Francisco, it was the age of the architects Willis Polk, Bernard Maybeck, and John Galen Howard. Polk designed the Ferry building and became one of the planners of the city's Civic Center. He also constructed the Halidie Building, called

San Diego's Balboa Park covers 1,400 acres within the heart of the city. It is the site of many San Diego cultural and recreational activities as well as the world-famous San Diego zoo. Shown here is the Botanical Garden and lily pond. *(San Diego Convention and Visitors Bureau)*

The Ferry Building. Once a busy terminal for the bay ferry boats, it became San Francisco's World Trade Center after the two great bridges were built. *(San Francisco Visitor's Bureau)*

the world's first glass skyscraper. Maybeck and Howard were the master planners of the University of California at Berkeley. Phoebe Apperson Hearst, William Randolph Hearst's mother, donated huge sums for the development of that campus. Maybeck also collaborated with Polk in designing the 1915 Panama-Pacific International Exposition.

In and around Los Angeles, the architect brothers Greene and Greene created what came to be known as the California bungalow. An elegant example of this style is found in Pasadena's Gamble House (1908).

"Modern" architects, among them Frank Lloyd Wright and Richard Neutra, built some of their first experimental structures in southern California. Wright, who had briefly studied under Chicago's Louis H. Sullivan, built Hollyhock House in Barnsdale Park in 1917. Other notable Wright-designed homes are the Millard House (1923) in Pasadena and the Mayan-motif Ennis House (1924) in Los Angeles.

282

Vienna-born Neutra moved to Los Angeles in 1926. He achieved renown because of his radical building and house designs. By the mid-1930s the Spanish-style house, once almost universally popular in California, had begun to give way to bolder, more functional experiments. Neutra and Wright stressed the importance of the practical in residential construction, especially for "outdoor living." Their modernistic split-level houses offered increased living space, wide windows, and enclosed recreation areas. Admirably suited to the California climate and environment, this architecture dominated many residential neighborhoods and contributed to evolution of the popular ranch-style residence.

A bizarre architectural phenomenon in southern California is the work of an Italian immigrant, Simon Rodia, builder of the Watts Towers. Located near Los Angeles, these novel creations, 99, 97, and 55 feet high, were fashioned out of bits of glass tile and artifacts garnered from nearby junk heaps. Without scaffolding, Rodia built the first of the towers in 1921. Five years later, when Los Angeles annexed the town of Watts, Rodia became involved in a conflict with the city's Department of Building and Safety. He had no building permit, and the towers were considered unsafe. While demolition and condemnation hearings dragged on for years, Rodia, who said he wanted to build something big, went on with his thirty-three years of erecting and defending a "gigantic fantasy of concrete, steel, and rubble." Called a "paramount achievement of twentieth-century folk art in the United States," Rodia's towers were ultimately, and ironically, declared a local monument to be protected by a Los Angeles Cultural Heritage Board. When tested for safety, these filigree-and-mosaic-covered structures proved so strong that they could not be pulled down, even by steel cables attached to tractors. In 1954, at the age of eighty-one, Rodia tired of his project and left Los Angeles permanently. Public bickering over whether the towers were structurally sound left him embittered. He felt rejected by the society for which he had, as a monument of love, built the towers. Rodia never returned to Los Angeles. "Why had he built the towers so strong?" he was once asked. He replied, "If a man no have feet, he no stand."

California Authors

California writers have contributed much to American literature. Some authors were native to the state, while others were attracted by the comfortable climate or lucrative movie contracts. A writer who came to California before World War I and made a sizable fortune was Zane Grey. Prior to settling in Altadena, Grey had been an Ohio dentist with experience as a professional baseball player. In California, he soon was writing at least one and sometimes two western novels per year. The most popular of these was his *Riders of the Purple Sage* (1912). His work achieved vast popularity, and he strongly influenced later writers of western fiction. More than sixty of Grey's books were printed in very large editions.

Robinson Jeffers, the greatest poet California has produced, was educated at Occidental College. He was at his best in long narrative poems such as *Roan Stallion* (1925). In his later years, *Medea* (1947), a new version of a classic Greek tragedy adapted for poetic drama from Euripides, also brought him great acclaim. Jeffers died in his home, Tor House, in Carmel early in 1962.

The previously mentioned progressive reformer, Upton Sinclair, a native of Baltimore, came to southern California after World War I, having already written his best-known novel, *The Jungle* (1906). He has had an extraordinary career, producing numerous books of social criticism while exerting active leadership in countless liberal causes. In later years he wrote the Lanny Budd series.

In addition to the many writers who have moved to California, the state has produced some native-born authors, especially novelists, of the first rank. The best known of the "California novelists" is John Steinbeck, born at Salinas in 1902. Steinbeck's vivid portrayal of the people and the setting of the Salinas Valley frequently reflects the author's anger with social injustice. *The Grapes of Wrath* (1939) is his most important novel and a Pulitzer Prize winner. Steinbeck has continued to produce interesting and successful books over a thirty-year period. The Nobel Prize for Literature, awarded him in 1962, reflected the merits of his earlier work.

As Steinbeck had done, William Saroyan discovered rich literary material in the agricultural area where he was born. Saroyan's work is largely set in the countryside around Fresno, and it reflects his Armenian origins in the San Joaquin Valley. His novels, plays, and short stories present an assemblage of attractive characters, revealing the author's kindly assessment of human nature.

Another successful literary Californian, at least on a commercial level, was the mystery writer, Erle Stanley Gardner. A lawyer by profession, he began writing about criminal topics as a hobby. Gardner remains best known as the creator of Perry Mason, the unbeatable detective-lawyer.

Recent Cultural Activities

Associated with California's educational and scientific institutions are many centers of twentieth-century cultural activity. California possesses two major historical societies, at San Francisco and Los Angeles, both of which produce quarterlies and occasional books for their members. Several research libraries also publish scholarly books and professional journals. In the humanities and social sciences the Henry E. Huntington Library and Art Gallery at San Marino, the Bancroft Library of the University of California at Berkeley, and the Hoover Library of War, Revolution, and Peace at Stanford are internationally known. The Bancroft Library is a research center of western American history and culture. The Huntington Library has become a center for humanistic studies in English and American literature and history. Its treasures include a copy of the *Gutenberg Bible* (1455), and an art collection with a sizable group of paintings by English artists, among them Thomas Gainsborough's "Blue Boy."

The cultural awareness of southern California gained impetus after the mid-1950s, and within a decade Los Angeles took important strides in the development of art and music. In 1964, the city completed a music pavilion, the first structure of a $35 million cultural center. Three years later, the Mark Taper Forum and Ahmanson Theater were added to it. Creation of resident repertory, ballet, and opera companies, as well as the emergence of nineteen symphony orchestras in Los Angeles County by 1967, underscored the rising interest in "culture." The Los Angeles County Art Museum was also completed in 1965. By the 1970s, the benefactions of Norton Simon at Pasadena and of J. Paul Getty in Malibu led to the creation of two major museums named after their benefactors.

Significant cultural developments in San Francisco include the permanent exhibition of the Avery Brundage oriental art collection in Golden Gate Park and the donation, in 1978, of over $100,000 worth of American art by John D. Rockefeller, III, to the city's Fine Arts Museums. Other projects included the restoration of the Palace of Fine Arts, the last remaining remnant of its 1915 Panama-Pacific International Exhibition. Along the Marina shoreline visitors see a 160-foot-high domed rotunda on the east and a semicircular 48-foot-high gallery on the west. Nearby, the Victorian Ghirardelli chocolate factory has also been restored as a place to wine, dine, and shop. Conversion of an adjacent brick cannery near Fisherman's Wharf and of the city's cable-car barn (whose machinery has been repainted

The Getty Museum recreates a Roman Villa destroyed when
Vesuvius erupted in 79 A.D. *(The J. Paul Getty Museum)*

in bright colors) combines preservation of historic sites with today's
recreational tourist needs.

POPULAR CULTURE

California has played a major role in the development of contemporary tastes and interests. It popularized the backyard swimming pool
and barbecue; set trends in sportswear, casual apparel, and hair
styles; and also brought "in" RVs, trail bikes, and customized vans.
It introduced fast-food franchises, "theme parks," retirement villages, and, finally, "slumber rooms" in mortuaries. California as a
major center of the communications media, attracted performers
whose highly publicized activities were assumed to form "the California way of life." The radio, recording, and television industries
have all shared in this phenomenon, but the dominant element has
always been the motion picture business.

286

The Movies

Hollywood, the world's film capital, has drawn California its greatest publicity in modern times, both good and bad. The development of the first motion picture techniques in the United States, however, was not limited to Hollywood or California. About 1907, producers, actors, cameramen, and writers began to swarm toward Hollywood. California's all-year climate and the variety of its scenery made it an ideal location for motion picture production. In 1913, when Samuel Goldwyn, Jesse Lasky, and Cecil B. DeMille came West to produce *The Squaw Man,* they had only a few thousand dollars. This picture and those that followed made millions for the producers as orders poured in from hundreds of former vaudeville houses now transformed into movie parlors.

A sleepy little village founded before the turn of the century, Hollywood had a town ordinance, as late as 1903, which forbade the driving of more than 2,000 sheep down Hollywood Boulevard at any one time. When the first motion picture studios were established there, Hollywood could claim only a few thousand inhabitants; almost overnight it was to be transformed into the film center of the world.

Interior, Norton Simon Museum of Art at Pasadena

Among the most imaginative men who came West to "shoot pictures" was David W. Griffith, producer of *The Birth of a Nation,* a film which eventually grossed $20 million. This was also the first film to be honored with a showing at the White House, where President Wilson is said to have remarked: "It is like writing history with lightning."

With the development of a "star system," the production of films became incredibly expensive. Charlie Chaplin, who became renowned all over the world, was probably the best-known film actor of all time. In two years, Chaplin's salary skyrocketed from $150 to $10,000 a week. Chaplin and "America's Sweetheart," Mary Pickford, soon were receiving salaries in excess of $1 million a year. Theda Bara, Harold Lloyd, Lillian Gish, Rudolph Valentino, and Greta Garbo were other performers whom the fans idolized and wanted to see regularly. Similarly, the cowboys stars William S. Hart, Tom Mix, and Hoot Gibson became the heroes of countless small boys. A few of this group of actors had worked as cowboys and were fine horsemen, as was the comedian Will Rogers. Pearl White left silent-film audiences breathlessly awaiting the next installment of *The Perils of Pauline,* a weekly serial. In 1923, motion pictures already accounted for 20 percent of the annual production of all manufactured products of California. More than 20,000 actors and actresses were by then working before cameras, their weekly payroll amounting to over a million dollars.

The fantastic Hollywood of the 1920s is almost beyond recall today. In those lush years the flow of cash through the box offices was staggering. Movie moguls draped their studios with boastful pennants that read: "More Stars than There Are in Heaven" and "Hollywood, the Greatest Show on Earth." This was the era of matinee idols with sixteen-cylinder racing cars and thirty-room white stucco palaces. Movie queens, such as Pola Negri and Gloria Swanson, spent thousands for perfume alone.

Among the technological improvements that contributed to Hollywood's sucess, one of the most innovative was the addition of sound. The Warner Brothers' production of *The Jazz Singer* was the first motion picture with sound. This "talkie," starring the song-and-dance man Al Jolson, revolutionized the industry when it appeared in 1927. Old stars with squeaky, high-pitched voices vanished and were replaced by others, such as Gary Cooper, Spencer Tracy, Claudette Colbert, and Joan Crawford. Sound pictures, by attracting larger crowds than ever, soon led to the building of bigger and better theaters.

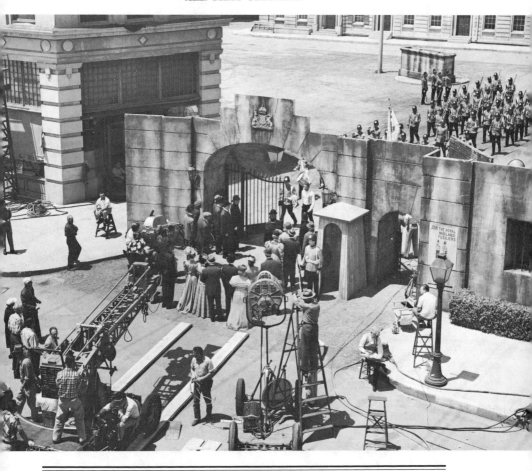

A Hollywood movie set. *(Union Pacific Railroad)*

Commercial considerations almost always triumphed over artistic ones. In those profitable years, director-producer Cecil B. DeMille made "spectacular" films with all-star casts, lavish sets, and thousands of extras. The studios paid large sums of money for movie scripts. Writers drawn to Hollywood included F. Scott Fitzgerald and William Faulkner. Musicians included Carrie Jacobs Bond, George Gershwin, David Rose, and Dimitri Tiomkin.

The best-known movie of the thirties was based upon the novel *Gone With the Wind.* This romanticized story of the Civil War and Reconstruction by Margaret Mitchell provided the characters, setting, and plot for a film that set many firsts and established many standards for future film-making. Starring Clark Gable and Vivien

289

Leigh, it set all-time attendance records and ran off with several Oscars.

Walt Disney, one of Hollywood's most creative and successful personalities, started his long career with the creation of the cartoon character Mickey Mouse. A pioneer of sound movies, he went on to produce the first full-length cartoon, *Snow White,* and the first stereophonic sound film, *Fantasia.* Later he turned to the production of nature films, a television series, and the establishment of the famed amusement center Disneyland at Anaheim.

In later years the term "Hollywood" was misleading because most of the studios had dispersed to other suburbs nearby. Columbia, Warner Brothers, and Universal moved to the San Fernando Valley, while Twentieth-Century-Fox was in Beverly Hills and Metro-Goldwyn-Mayer was in Culver City.

After World War II, gloom settled over Hollywood as it was beset by increased competition for America's leisure time by paperback books, phonograph records, and such developing recreations as bowling, water skiing, and boating. Foreign production of films by American free-lance producers severely curtailed the film-making schedules of the major studios and drastically reduced the employment of local technicians.

At first, Hollywood was also hard hit by television, which offered free home entertainment. In time, however, television became a major source of work for the film industry. In response to successful television stories and techniques, more realistic motion pictures like *Marty* and *Hud* were produced. The seventies brought a new era of sensational films, including *The Godfather, Earthquake, Jaws,* and *Star Wars,* that brought long lines back to the box office. The movies have given many foreigners their main impression of the United States. For better or for worse, the films have reached into the lives of millions, not only as entertainment but also as a means of instruction and confusion.

Tourism Continues

Amusement centers, including Marineland, Disneyland, and other "theme parks" attract hundreds of thousands of customers annually. Two popular tourist attractions are related to the film industry; they are the tour sponsored by Universal Studios and Grauman's Chinese Theater on Hollywood Boulevard with its footprints and signatures of the stars etched in cement.

290

SPORTS IN CALIFORNIA

California's year-round outdoor climate has fostered the development of an assortment of sports and recreation opportunities. Ranging from organized amateur and professional athletics to noncompetitive and leisure activities, they provide fulfillment for participants, entertainment for fans, and enrichment for sponsors, and superstar athletes. Drawing not only from local high school and junior college athletic programs, California's colleges and universities attract additional athletes from across the nation and even from international ranks. Excellent coaches, good facilities, and enthusiastic alumni support all contribute to the success of athletic programs.

College Sports

The premier NCAA (National Collegiate Athletic Association) sport continues to be football, with Pasadena's postseason Rose Bowl the number-one event. University of Southern California's (USC) football team was ranked first in the nation in 1962, 1967, and 1972. Other "big-time" football schools are the University of California, both at Berkeley and at Los Angeles (UCLA), and Stanford. Among the players from these teams who have progressed into the ranks of professional football are Frank Albert and Jim Plunkett from Stanford and O. J. Simpson and Mike Garrett from USC.

College basketball draws more fans in a season than football. No histroy of collegiate basketball can omit the remarkable Coach John Wooden, whose UCLA Bruins won ten NCAA championships between 1964 and 1975. Among those national stars coached by Wooden were Kareem Abdul-Jabbar and Bill Walton. Other national champion teams from California were Stanford (1942), The University of San Francisco with Bill Russell (1955 and 1956), and California (1959).

Professional Sports

In the nineteenth century professional competition in athletics began with boxing and horse racing. Then came golf, auto racing, and minor league baseball. After World War II spectator sports boomed. Professional football reached California in 1946 when the Cleveland Rams moved to Los Angeles. In 1950 the San Francisco Forty-Niners were formed. The two teams won quite a few western division National Football League (NFL) championships and one NFL championship, which was captured by the Rams in 1950. In 1961, the first year for American Football League, the Los Angeles Chargers won the western division. In 1961, the Chargers moved to San Deigo, where they continued to dominate that league until the Oakland Raiders won a string of division championships between 1967 and 1976. In January 1977, they won the Superbowl Championship.

In 1958 "big-league" baseball came to California when the Brooklyn Dodgers moved to Los Angeles and the New York Giants transferred their team, which included homerun-hitter Willie Mays, to San Francisco. The Dodgers won the World Series in 1959, and with the pitching of Sandy Koufax, they won the series again in 1963 and 1965. "Expansion clubs" were formed in Anaheim in 1961 and at San Diego in 1969. The "As" moved to Oakland in 1968; they won three consecutive World Series titles in 1972, 1973, and 1974. Their roster include Reggie Jackson and "Catfish" Hunter. Heading the list of baseball players who came from California were Joe DiMaggio from San Francisco, Jackie Robinson from Pasadena, Ted Williams from San Diego, Casey Stengel from Glendale, and Tom Seaver from Fresno.

National Basketball Association (NBA) basketball arrived in California in the early sixties when the Philadelphia Warriors transferred to San Francisco and the Milwaukee Lakers went to Los Angeles. Wilt Chamberlain led the Warrior's attack for several years. The Lakers, with Jerry West, won the championship playoff in 1972.

The Olympic Games

By far the most prestigious and the most elaborate of all international athletic events are the Olympic Games. Many Olympic athletes and coaches have called California their home. In 1932, the tenth summer Olympiad was held in Los Angeles. Record crowds were thrilled by the performance of a young girl from Texas, Mildred Didrikson, who won two gold medals and one silver medal in field events. Later known as "the Babe" (Zaharias) she became one of the best women golfers of all time and, perhaps the outstanding female athlete of the twentieth century.

In 1960, the Winter Olympics were held in Squaw Valley, California. After bidding for the 1980 games (awarded to Moscow), Los Angeles secured the 1984 Olympics.

Among the Olympic champions from California are decathalon winners Bob Mathias from Stanford (1948 and 1952) and Rafer Johnson from UCLA (1960) as well as Mark Spitz, who captured seven gold medals for swimming in 1972. Other California Olympians are Peggy Fleming the figure skater, Pat McCormick the diver, and Frank Wykoff the sprinter.

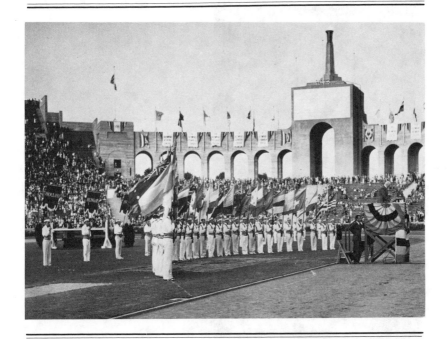

Opening Ceremonies, 1932 Olympics. *(Citizens Savings Athletic Foundation)*

Recent Trends

By the 1970s, various professional team sports vied for attention in the state. Among these were ice hockey, soccer, and softball. Individual professional competitions were staged in the fields of bowling, arm wrestling, weight lifting, surfing, and sky diving. Even tradition-bound tennis entered the commercial market with the advent of open competition. California tennis stars include Elsworth Vines, Don Budge, Pancho Gonzalez, Jack Kramer, Alice Marble, Helen Wills Moody, Maureen Connolly, Rosemary Casals, Billie Jean King, and Tracy Austin.

Professional golfers Gene Littler and Billy Casper come from San Diego while Ken Venturi and Johnny Miller originally lived in the

293

Mildred "Babe" Didrikson.
(Citizens Savings Athletic Association)

The 18th Hole at Pebble Beach. *(Photograph by William C. Brooks, courtesy Northern California Golf Association)*

Bay area. Golf has attracted celebrities from the world of entertainment. Its leaders, among them Bob Hope and Bing Crosby, sponsored tournaments and participated in fund-raising programs. Ex-presidents Eisenhower and Ford established residences in Palm Springs so they could play golf during the winter months.

DEVELOPMENTS IN EDUCATION

The first public school in the state was opened in 1849 at San Francisco. Compulsory attendance laws followed in 1874. California's earliest colleges were private church-related institutions; they all suffered shortages of both funds and qualified faculty staffs. The Catholics established various institutions before the turn of the century, the first of which was Santa Clara University, founded in 1851 as a preparatory school. Later Loyola University, the University of San

Francisco, Saint Mary's, and Immaculate Heart College were established by various Catholic religious orders.

Among the colleges founded by Protestants was the University of the Pacific; today located in Stockton, it was begun at San Jose by the Methodists in 1851. In 1879, the same denomination founded the University of Southern California. Mills College, situated in the Oakland suburbs, traces its history to 1852; it is the oldest women's college in the Far West. At Palo Alto, Stanford University was founded in 1890 by Leland Stanford as a memorial to his only son. It became the most richly endowed of all of the private universities and colleges of the West. Stanford gained early prominence through its first president, David Starr Jordan, who was a nationally known naturalist.

In southern California, Occidental College was opened in 1887 and Pomona College only a few months later. The Associated Colleges of Claremont (including Pomona, Scripps, Claremont University College, Mudd, and Claremont Men's College) grew out of Pomona. In 1901, the Quakers established Whittier College, and in 1909 the Baptists founded a college at Redlands, later called Redlands University. Additional private colleges founded in the twentieth century included the University of San Diego (1949), California Lutheran College (1959), and Pepperdine University (1937).

The privately endowed institutions in California are supplemented by a state university and college system. In 1868, the University of California at Berkeley, was formally created by a bill of the state legislature. In 1919, the State Normal School at Los Angeles became, by legislative act, the University of California, Southern Branch. Ten years later this rapidly growing public institution—now called the University of California at Los Angeles, or UCLA—moved to a beautiful new campus at Westwood, near Beverly Hills. The state university, under the presidencies of Robert Gordon Sproul (1930–1958) and Clark Kerr (1958–1967), improved its faculty, broadened its curriculum, and expanded its multicampus system. By the 1960s, the University of California had campuses at Davis, Santa Barbara, Riverside, La Jolla, Santa Cruz, and Irvine. Since the turn of the century, the state university's professional and graduate schools have grown, with medicine, pharmacy, dentistry, education, business, law, journalism, and music among the disciplines encompassed.

California's state college system, a newer development than its university complex, grew out of a group of loosely related normal schools and teachers' colleges. After the 1940s, eighteen state college campuses were located at Arcata, Chico, Dominguez Hills, Fullerton,

Fresno, Hayward, Long Beach, Los Angeles, Northridge, Oakland, Orange, Rohnert Park, Sacramento, San Bernardino, San Diego, San Francisco, San Jose, and Turlock. Renamed the state college and university system, their scope has widened beyond teacher preparation to include full training in the liberal arts and sciences. Another part of the state college system is its polytechnic colleges at San Luis Obispo, San Dimas, and Pomona. Also participating in public education are some ninety junior colleges.

By 1969, California had almost eighty four-year colleges and universities, both private and public. California's educational offerings include a large-scale "extension" system of training beyond the high school. Utilitarian emphasis upon the applied arts is an important aspect of California's adult education program. The faculties of California's colleges and universities include more than their share of Nobel and Pulitzer prizewinners as well as Fulbright and Guggenheim Foundation fellows. After World War II, the Ford Foundation founded at Palo Alto a Center for Advanced Study in the Behavioral Sciences, which aims to serve behavioral studies as the Institute for Advanced Studies at Princeton, N. J., serves the physical sciences.

Scientific Institutions

In the pure sciences California has shown special prominence during the past half century. The California Institute of Technology, at Pasadena, founded in 1890 as the Polytechnic or Throop College of Technology, was in the 1920s transformed into a virtually new institution by astronomer George Ellery Hale and pioneer physicist Robert A. Millikan and a group of distinguished scientific associates. After Millikan was awarded the Nobel Prize in 1923, he drew around him a coterie of dedicated philanthropists and teachers who lent real distinction to "Caltech." In close cooperation with the Carnegie Institution of Washington, D. C., which operated the nearby Mount Wilson Solar Observatory, Millikan's group created one of the nation's two major national scientific research and technical institutes. The other is the Massachusetts Institute of Technology. Caltech and its scientists have demonstrated brilliance particularly in physics, biology, and genetics. Linus Pauling, a Caltech professor, won two Nobel prizes; the first in 1954 for work in chemistry and then the coveted Peace Prize in 1962 for his stand against nuclear testing. In the late 1950s, Caltech's Jet Propulsion Laboratory designed and supervised the manufacture of the United States's first artificial earth satellites. The institution also became deeply engaged in missile development and on June 2, 1966, achieved the first of many later "soft" landings on the surface of the moon. The Jet Propulsion Laboratory remains a center of research for America's space program in conjunction with the National Aeronautic and Space Administration.

Another research center is the Lawrence Radiation Laboratory of the University of California at Livermore. Cyclotrons exist at both the Berkeley and Los Angeles campuses of the University. Its total scientific facilities, including medical schools, observatories, and institutes, have expanded rapidly. Another university campus specializing in science, the Scripps Institute of Oceanography at La Jolla, regularly charts the ocean's currents and maps its depths; it also operates oceanographic research vessels throughout the Pacific area. Also at La Jolla is the Salk Institute for Biological Studies, founded in the name of Jonas Salk, the research physician who has been given major credit for development of the first poliomyelitis vaccine.

In the field of astronomy the Lick Observatory at Mount Hamilton—technically also a campus of the University of California—was one of the first major observatories established in the United States. It has been in operation since 1874. An even better-known installation is the privately operated Mount Wilson Observatory, whose 100-inch reflecting telescope has been in use since 1917. Its lens is exceeded in size only by the world's largest observatory—also located in California at Mount Palomar in San Diego County. The Mount Palomar facility houses a 200-inch telescope, in operation since 1948. It was installed through the financial aid of the Rockefeller Foundation. The astronomers at Mount Palomar work closely with California Institute of Technology staff members and with astronomers at the Mount Wilson Observatory.

Issues Affecting Education

As tens of thousands of "war babies" reached school age in the 1950s, the state had to provide more schools and teachers for them. The bulge in the school-age population came at a time of increased demand for dams, prisons, hospitals, and parks. Bond issues and "tax overrides" had to be passed in order to provide funds to construct hundreds of new schools and to employ thousands of new teachers. In fact, it was not until the enrollments began to fall in the early seventies that a chronic teacher shortage finally ended. Because of inflation, increases in costs continued even after enrollments stabilized. Some teacher salaries lagged behind those of garbage collectors. Education, however, continued to absorb nearly half of the state's budget and over half of most property taxes. The Serrano case, which challenged the property tax as the primary source of revenue, brought about important changes in the financial support of the schools; this was especially important for districts with a low assessed valuation per pupil.

In June 1978, another major shift in the tax burden occurred when Howard Jarvis, a longtime outspoken advocate of tax limitation, culminated a career of opposition to growth in government with the passage of Proposition 13. This initiative constitutional amendment limited the total property tax on a piece of property to 1 percent of its assessed valuation. It also placed severe restrictions on future assessments and required a two-thirds vote of the legislature for new statewide taxes. The controversial ballot proposition drew a high voter turnout. After the votes were tallied, Jarvis declared: "Tonight we know how our forefathers felt as they hurled the crates of English tea into Boston harbor and paved the way for freedom and liberty in the United States." The two-to-one success of the measure was hailed by the national media as a precursor of a major tax revolt that might soon sweep the nation. Politicians at all levels had to consider redistribution of the tax burden, reductions in programs, job freezes, and layoffs.

Education at the college level became especially difficult to finance. Expansion of California's state college and university system had placed a heavy fiscal responsibility on its taxpayers at a time when the job market for college graduates had softened. Meanwhile, the standards and quality of teaching, from kindergarten through the graduate school years deteriorated. The demands of rebellious youths during the 1960s had produced a serious leveling effect upon the grade system. Colleges and universities found it necessary to reintroduce courses in basic English due to the poor test performances of entering high school graduates.

Other educational trends developed in the 1970s. Bilingual instruction became widespread (most of this was in Spanish). Additionally, all schools were required to admit handicapped students and to provide for their special needs. This period also saw the establishment of minimum-competency tests for graduation from high school and expanded opportunities in girls athletics.

SMOG

Los Angeles and San Francisco have been plagued by one of the most baffling problems that can afflict any city—air pollution in the form of "smog." This term is a combination of the words "smoke" and "fog." The persistent choking, bluish haze grew more uncomfortable each year. It dirtied buildings, reduced visibility, irritated eyes, angered tourists, and created a public furor. Almost every politician promised to do something about the emission of fumes. As early as 1947, Los Angeles organized a County Air Pollution Control District (APCD), which spent millions of dollars trying to banish the fumes. Yet the city banned backyard incinerators only in 1957. Until a state law allowed the APCD to override local jurisdiction, its air pollution ordinances could not be applied to the sixty-three municipalities that surrounded Los Angeles. The control of industries that produced sulphurous petrochemicals became part of the APCD program, as did laboratory investigation to determine the factors responsible for smog. The APCD was succeeded by the Air Quality Management District (AQMD) which had similar but expanded authority.

Los Angeles is unfortunately located in a saucerlike basin which suffers from the lowest wind velocity of any major city of the United States. If the air could escape the surrounding rim of mountains, where the atmosphere grows cooler with altitude, the condition would not be so troublesome. But bright sunshine on hot, sunny days causes photochemical regrouping of exhaust gas molecules. Then smog ozones form, and the sulfurous plumes billowing out of industrial smokestacks refuse to go away. Hydrocarbons from auto exhausts and vapor leaks from gas tanks also contribute to the smog.

Like the San Francisco Bay area, southern California remains a distinct province of the state. Its contrasts are immense as the visitor flies into the Los Angeles Basin on a clear night over an endless network of sparkling lights. Columns of automobiles crowd the freeways. The beauty of this scene obscures the heavy pall of smog that may envelop the region on the next day. Crowding has produced a profligate waste of energy. It is this wastefulness which contributes to high mortality rates from emphysema, bronchitis, lung cancer, and coronary insufficiency. Air pollution has also been related to asthma, acute respiratory infections, allergies, and school children's ailments.

Smog also has become a problem in the north. San Francisco in 1955 organized an Air Pollution Control District. This consisted of nine counties in the Bay area which banned open rubbish fires. Municipal dumps, which deposited layers of filthy air over the bay on windless days, were forced to "cover-and-fill" city refuse. But full smog control was never achieved. An "alert system" inaugurated at Los Angeles after 1956 was, however, helpful. When the concentra-

Los Angeles on a clear day (top); on a smoggy day at 8 A.M. (center) and at 10 A.M. (bottom). *(Courtesy of the Los Angeles Air Pollution Control District)*

tion of pollution reached a prescribed level, local industries were notified by the city's APCD to reduce the burning of fuel. Business firms were forced to burn only natural gas from May through October.

Regulation of automotive exhausts at the state level has given suffering Californians their greatest hope of attacking the problem of smog control. While the legislature patiently awaited development of an effective afterburner, it debated public imposition of such devices after they were made available by the auto industry. Automobiles emitted an estimated 96 percent of Los Angeles toxic air. Each year during the 1960s the "smog season" seemed to lengthen. Californians experienced almost year-round smog conditions, even during the winter months.

In addition to human discomfort, the destructive effects of smog on foliage and flowers are well known. Growers of leafy field crops, including lettuce and spinach, have complained that smog losses have run into the millions. The reduction of fruit and vegetable yields is also demonstrable. The leaves of avocado and orange trees dry up and turn gray and splotchy.

WHO OWNS THE OIL?

California, once second only to Texas as an oil-producing state, has in recent years found its production curve declining while its own comsumption goes on climbing. Californians still prodigally consume all of the oil they produce and more. To outsiders it seemed incredible that a state that still produces a sizable share of the world's oil should be on an import basis.

Despite depletion of the large oil-producing zones at Signal Hill and Santa Fe Springs, new sources of oil continued to be discovered throughout California. During World War II, when the need for oil was vastly increased, exploration was stepped up and prospecting techniques improved. Supervision of drilling to conserve dwindling underground reserves became more common. Both the state and federal governments were drawn into the management of the petroleum industry. As California became an oil-importing state after the war, governmental and private attention was given to its valuable offshore oil resources. This, in turn, gave rise to the tidelands controversy, a battle for jurisdiction over vast deposits, extending outward many miles from the shoreline. Various southern states claimed that historic state limits of jurisdiction extended for ten miles out to sea. Under international law, three miles was the accepted

302

jurisdiction of a nation on the high seas. A further complication involved the fact that California in the 1940s leased tideland drilling rights to private companies and reaped large royalties from these leases. In 1947, furthermore, Supreme Court decisions established the "paramount rights" of the federal government.

The seaboard states, however, continued to maintain rights beyond the federally recognized three-mile limit. Because the offshore jurisdiction of neither state nor federal government was firmly established, California extended its claims as far as thirty miles out to sea. The status of California's tidelands remained nebulous until 1965, when the Supreme Court denied almost all of California's claims to submerged tidelands oil, valued at more than $1 billion.

At Long Beach, city officials after World War II leased offshore reserves to independent oil operators in defiance of both state and federal claims. Only after a lengthy dispute was a three-way agreement reached between the federal government, the state, and various California coastal municipalities. The state had to agree to spend a sizable part of its oil and gas revenues for beautification of polluted beach sites and of cramped picnic and camping areas. Residents and tourists today flock to recreational facilities made possible from these offshore oil funds. Tidelands oil revenues were also earmarked for water development.

Such funds are used for the benefit of the state's people. Care, however, has to be exercised that its shoreline and coastal waters do not become heavily forested with offshore drilling rigs on platforms that rival thirty-story buildings in height. The State Lands Commission limits drilling by operators who have leased thousands of acres of beach land, from north of the Ventura County line beyond Carpinteria to Gaviota. Federal-state tension over offshore oil drilling has grown particularly angry along the Santa Barbara channel. In the 1960s, oil spills led to the formation of a group called GOO (Get Oil Out).

TRANSIT SNAGS AND THE
ENERGY CRISIS

Enamored by the automobile, Californians of the 1970s made little progress in developing mass rapid transit. By 1970, the state's freeway system was in serious trouble. Inflation and lessened tax receipts cut down the amount of roadway that could be built. Yet dependence upon cars remained unabated. While San Francisco did manage to build its BART system, Los Angeles continued to flounder in liberat-

The Richmond Refinery of the Standard Oil Company of California.
(By courtesy of the Standard Oil Company of California)

ing itself from autos. Indifference, poor leadership by its mayors, and public ignorance about the benefits of rapid transit condemned that city to inaction. Bond issue after bond issue was voted down by the electorate. Even urban transit enthusiasts were depressed by the skyrocketing construction and operating estimates.

Related to the failure of mass rapid transit has been the growing scarcity of gasoline in a state which was once its major exporter. The Arab oil boycott of 1973 also partly sidelined the environmental movement which had begun to make important strides toward con-

BART subway station. *(San Francisco Visitors Bureau)*

trolling smog. The Arab boycott had special significance for California's "automobile society." That year there was talk of rationing as motorists lined up at the gas pumps.

A diminished supply of low sulfur fuel oil for heating and generating electricity reminded Californians of their vulnerability and past prodigality. California's oil fields had helped to float World Wars I and II on a sea of surplus oil, which had now vanished. As a result of this profligacy, emergency measures had to be taken, among them allowing cities in the smog-plagued Los Angeles Basin to burn conventional fuel oil until low sulfur fuel became more available. Painful compromises between idealistic environmental goals and the mounting need for energy had a depressive effect upon formerly aggressive ecologists. A no-growth diminished population program had barely gotten underway when the energy crisis broke.

In California the internal combustion engine won an early total victory over electric trains and almost every other means of locomotion. There is some evidence that bus and auto manufacturers, as well as the oil, tire, new- and used-car dealers, helped to destroy the world's largest interurban electric transport system with which southern California was once served. As late as 1945 the Pacific Electric Railway still carried 110 million passengers between fifty-six communities.

When, in the 1970s, the state began to move away from construction of new freeways, northern California legislators and ecologists were accused of politically "ganging up" against southern California.

A BRUTALIZED CALIFORNIA

A widening stain of confusion marred the shift in the postwar years from an agricultural to an industrial way of life. This period of turmoil is difficult to understand. It featured explosive growth, the results of which were not entirely healthy. Vulgarization of the social environment accompanied physical deterioration. California had arrived at a postindustrial stage of economic development.

As frontier rurality developed into an industrial culture, the missions and the ranchos of the Spanish period made way for such new symbols as Hollywood, oil derricks, aircraft factories, steel mills, residential subdivisions, and television studios. The grape vineyards and orange groves of the early twentieth century surrendered to tourist attractions, housing projects, and jet-propulsion laboratories. The noxious fumes of smog, and serious state and municipal problems damaged the charm that California once held for health seekers, tourists, and outdoor lovers. Traffic congestion grew so acute that new freeways were obsolete before they were built. Without helicopter surveillance and air-to-ground radio reports, traffic jams became impossible to control.

Dynamite and bulldozer damaged unique scenic wonders and gouged the landscape with deep scars. In 1963, James K. Carr, a Californian and President Kennedy's under secretary of the interior, took a pessimistic view of this change:

> Smog too often hangs like a pall over all our cities, causing discomfort, damage, and even death. In a single generation we have almost ruined the superb, Mediterranean climate of southern California. Some shore lines foam with detergents, fish and wildlife are threatened, and scenic beauty is destroyed. Cities slobber over into the countryside, cluttered with billboards, spawning sleazy developments that have brought new, ugly words to our California lexicon—slurbs and slurburbia.
>
> The shores of Lake Tahoe, the jewel of the Sierra, already bear the permanent scars of uncontrolled, unplanned commercialism unchecked; this kind of slurbanization can despoil forever our cherished, scenic recreation areas. The redwoods, noble sentries of this "Unique

306

bright land," are increasingly victims of the chain saw, being logged in many places with no other control than the laws of the market place, as though these trees were just another species of timber. In some instances, the logged-over hillsides bleed silt into the streams where fish no longer swim.... We will have to establish Orange Grove State Park in southern California to show future generations a real orange grove.

Lewis Mumford first made us aware of the senseless cannibalism of the modern "gridiron cities." As more freeways are developed, to transport workers in an increasingly hivelike environment, traffic congestion mounts. Not only do California's freeways erase the countryside, they also take valuable land off the public tax rolls. Freeways consume up to twenty-eight acres of land per mile of construction. An interchange uses up to eighty acres. By the late 1960s, the San Francisco Bay area alone lost an estimated twenty-one square miles of countryside every year, while southern California surrendered seventy square miles annually to concrete ribbons and "urban sprawl." When taxes go up, due primarily to shortsighted zoning, farmers are forced to sell valuable agricultural land. The chance for future beautification of the countryside is thus lost.

At Los Angeles, this squandering is at it worst. Perhaps two-thirds of the central part of that city is occupied by streets, freeways, parking facilities, and garages. Regulations require building contractors to furnish one parking space per habitable room. Without autos, however, an even more chaotic urban center would exist. The failure to develop mass transportation into the center of Los Angeles has speeded dispersal of that city to its suburbs.

Several large urban renewal projects radically altered the character of the downtown area of the city. A number of important new public facilities emerged. The Civic Center Mall, with its underground parking and its aboveground tropical plantings and splashing fountains, was one of the most dramatic changes. Another program led to the construction of a huge new Convention Center near the interchange between the Harbor and Santa Monica freeways. Located south of the old focal center of the city, the Convention Center complex represented an expansion as well as an enhancement of the urban nucleus. As land values continued to soar an authentic building boom took place in the newly-enlarged downtown sector. Among the major structures erected in this phase of the city's growth pattern were several new hotels, the 42-story Union Bank building, and the 55-story Richfield-Bank of America complex (planned as a West Coast version of New York's Rockefeller Center). Despite the steadily increasing level of downtown activities, urban areas and to orient their lives around suburban shopping centers rather than revived urban cores.

As the tide of life rushed up through California's valleys, overwhelming the countryside, thousands of new ranch-style houses were hammered together. Peacefulness departed, perhaps forever, from many areas. The whine of rubber tires on concrete and the drone or explosive clatter of overhead aircraft seemed ever present. Repeatedly, engineering-minded planners placed the maintenance of California's scenic beauty low on their order of priorities. The obligation to create and to improve the livability of its communities is, however, at least as important as moving traffic or building new high-tension power lines.

PATTERNS OF POPULATION GROWTH

When admitted to statehood in 1850, California numbered only 92,-597 official residents. The state doubled its residents about every twenty years for more than a century. Growth in the decade 1940–1950 was 53.3 percent—greater than in any other state. From 1950 to 1960, California's expansion accounted for nearly 20 percent of the total United States gain. In that decade the population was growing at a rate of 5 percent a year—as much as five times that of the nation as a whole. Had such growth continued, California would have bypassed the current populations of Great Britain or France or that of many other nations.

By 1969, state population approached 21 million; one American in ten lived there. Demographers predicted that there would be 42 million inhabitants by the year 2000. In 1976, that estimate was revised downward to 29 million because of an abrupt drop in the growth rate during the early seventies. The slowdown was partially the result of the nationwide decline in the birthrate, but it also reflected a reduction in the number of persons moving to California. The peak level of inmigration seems to have been reached in 1962.

What else accounted for California's decline? First, some urban areas attained a relatively mature economy. One result of this was a leveling off of business growth, which adversely affected in-migration. Second, the decline in aerospace employment (which resulted from defense cutbacks after 1970) played a role in the slowdown. During the 1950s and 1960s, the lure of high-paying jobs, mild climate, and informal life style attracted hundreds of thousands of people into California each year. The bulk of these newcomers settled in southern California, where the aerospace industry was booming.

ESTIMATED POPULATION OF SELECTED COUNTIES
IN 1985 AND 2000

County	1985	2000
Alameda	1,194,800	1,358,100
Los Angeles	7,122,900	7,850,400
Orange	2,233,900	2,810,600
San Diego	2,022,400	2,654,100
San Francisco	653,500	656,600
Santa Clara	1,487,800	1,804,900
The State	24,363,000	29,277,000

Population Research Unit of the Department of Finance, Sacramento.

Finally, the negative results of growth—smog, urban sprawl, fear of earthquakes, and congestion—began to dissuade people from moving to the state, influencing some Californians to move elsewhere.

People of affluence and education sought to escape urban problems by a flight to the surburbs. In 1974, Los Angeles County experienced its first population drop in 123 years. Most of that out-migration represented a spill out into Orange and Ventura counties. The Los Angeles County population stabilized at about 7 million persons in 1976 and began to grow again at a modest rate by 1977. Orange County, by contrast, was growing twice as fast as the state's overall 27 percent.

Notable changes in the populations of California's major cities occurred during the 1970s. San Diego, by 1975, had solidified its rank as the second largest city, with a population of 773,400. Third-place San Francisco had dropped to a total of 666,100. San Jose had become number four, while Oakland had been relegated to sixth place, preceded by Long Beach. Sacramento, the capitol, was eighth in population that year, followed by Anaheim, Santa Ana, and Fresno.

Despite a tapering off in the growth rate, California added over 1.5 million residents in the seven years from the census of 1970 to 1977, when it reached a total of 22 million. The late seventies also saw the emergence of a trend of faster growth rates in the northern counties than in the south.

A CLOUDED FUTURE

A central problem of our time is that of mass. From that vortex flows inefficiency and environmental waste. Population growth forces expansion, and society cannot await vital facilities. Even our most mod-

City Center, San Diego. The city's international airport and busy harbor both
adjoin the central business district. A toll bridge spans the bay to link San
Diego with the city of Coronado and the North Island Naval Air Station.
(San Diego Convention and Visitor's Bureau)

ern communication and transport network is hardly suited to the
megalopolis of the future. A cancer of inefficiency, called by some
"metropolitanitis," can undermine California's potential. Inherent in
the planning process is no less than the construction of a healthy
democratic society in the future. Frequently local parochial interests
have impeded progress—in water development, then in smog control, and now in sorely needed municipal transport.

What are the limits of futurism? California and the American
West somehow retain a confidence not found in other parts of the
country. Used to the limitations of water and fertile land, yet possessing lots of space, the western attitude is partly exemplified by an
aggressive sign recently seen hanging on the front of a store which

read: "We can handle it!" The California that has sheltered the altruistic novelist Aldous Huxley and which spawned the mass murderer Charles Manson is not easily tamed by misfortune. It still possesses an euthusiasm which glorifies independence at the expense of unity. Californians too easily boast that what happens in their state will soon be copied elsewhere. Entrepreneurs who want to make a fortune in Europe or Asia (let alone eastern America) do, indeed, study consumer trends in California.

About its potential one English wag remarked, "I have seen the future and it plays." The conversion of the ship *Queen Mary* into a Long Beach hotel or the moving of London Bridge out onto a barren desert have baffled foreigners. The ready acceptance of the unusual is, however, unique rather than universal.

Few other areas share the state's fabulous climate; few can claim to be the world's entertainment center. Detroit, Tokyo, and Calcutta could never become another Los Angeles—the mystique is hardly the same. Fast reflexes and a system open to change have produced a style of life which, for all of its cultural vapidness, attracts adherents and anxious migrants. Technological advance, sexual freedom, and investment capital may not have brought Californians full satisfaction; yet many of them profess to be happy doing what they do. These see the state as a quasi-mecca for all those trying to transcend human limitations whether through drugs, group therapy, or synthetic religions. The absence of tradition and a lack of respect for history seem to point toward a future that is halfway into fantasy. This mixing of the real and the unreal has combined the obsession with making money and the quest for transcendental reality. A superb climate, once seemingly unlimited natural resources, as well as the hopefulness and uplift that accompanies communion with nature, get blurred by business exploitation, pollution, racial tensions, and a range of experimentation and protest, hopeless as well as encouraging.

A significant aspect of California's growth has been in the direction of space technology. This development may offer a clue to future expansion. Californians helped produce the instrumentation that placed astronauts on the moon. Space-age research is performed daily in California's "think factories." These centers for the pursuit of knowledge are bound to influence California's society. The scientists who work in the aerospace industries form a new pool of talent and may alter the state's history culturally as well as materially.

But who will win, people or technology? Will we go on venerating freeways while we surrender to the machine? Or will we con-

311

struct a culture that young people, sickened by falsity and uglification, will not wish to tear apart? We can either go toward orderly growth or on to further blighting of the environment.

Without conforming to rigid patterns, Californians have built a center of political and economic life. This society, with its freer style of work, has attracted international attention. Critics may call Californians sports-mad or loungers in a lotus land, but they also see California as a window into the future. That its expansion will beget cultural depth cannot be forecast. We can only be certain that California's potentialities are vast.

The big, the new, and the innovative do not assure quality. These attributes can actually retard California from maturing into that fusion of culture, will power to excel, and desire for change that characterized fifth-century Greece, Republican Rome, or the Renaissance cities. Motion sometimes defies stability.

California has been likened to Italy in variety: Los Angeles to Rome in amorphousness and San Francisco to Florence in style and atmosphere. Beauty, grace, humor, and wit develop slowly in any civilization. To move from frontier conditions into urban grandeur provides a challenge for any culture. One day a new faith in their future may help Californians to build more than plastic cities pockmarked by ugliness, crowding, and the blight of impersonality. At that point materialist "boosterism" will have given way to the confidence of solid achievement. Beauty lost will have become beauty rewon.

STUDY SUGGESTIONS

To understand the chapter you should know (1) the meaning and importance of key phrases and terms, (2) the contributions to California history of major personalities, and (3) the location and significance of geographic place names.

1. *Key phrases and terms*

AQMD	hydrocarbons
California Institute of	*The Jazz Singer*
Technology	Jet Propulsion Laboratory
freeway system	Lawrence Radiation
GOO	Laboratory
gridiron cities	megalopolis

Mount Wilson Observatory
offshore oil
Olympic Games
Pebble Beach
Rose Bowl

Serrano case
smog
think factories
"war babies"

2. *Major personalities*

Ansel Adams
Gutzon Borglum
Avery Brundage
Charlie Chaplin
Cecile B. DeMille
J. Paul Getty
Howard Jarvis
Robinson Jeffers
David Starr Jordan
Willie Mays
Richard Neutra
Roger Millikan

Linus Pauling
Simon Rodia
Jonas Salk
William Saroyan
John Steinbeck
Norton Simon
O. J. Simpson
Edward Weston
John Wooden
Frank Lloyd Wright
"Babe" Zaharias

3. *Important geographic place names*

Anaheim
Carmel
Hollywood

La Jolla
Long Beach
Mount Palomar

FOR ADDITIONAL STUDY

James A. Baird, Jr., *Time's Wonderous Changes, San Francisco's Architecture, 1776–1915* (San Francisco, 1962).

Reyner Banham, *Los Angeles: The Architecture of Four Ecologies* (Baltimore, 1971).

John W. Caughey and Laree Caughey (Eds.), *Los Angeles: Biography of a City* (Berkeley 1976).

Michael Davie, *In the Future Now* (London, 1972).

Robert Durrenberger, *California: The Last Frontier* (New York, 1969).

Robert Easton, *Black Tide: The Santa Barbara Oil Spill and Its Consequences* (New York, 1972).

F. Scott Fitzgerald, *The Last Tycoon* (New York, 1941).

APPENDIX A:
CITIES OF
LOS ANGELES
COUNTY - 1977

Name of City	Date of Incorporation	Rank	Population
Los Angeles	(1850)	(1)	2,761,805
Pasadena	(1886)	(5)	108,031
Santa Monica	(1886)	(6)	89,166
Monrovia	(1887)	(42)	29,328
Pomona	(1888)	(9)	85,379
Long Beach	(1888)	(2)	341,960
South Pasadena	(1888)	(49)	23,129
San Pedro	(1888–1909)*	—	—
Compton	(1888)	(14)	74,474
Redondo Beach	(1892)	(18)	63,683
Whittier	(1898)	(16)	70,539
Azusa	(1898)	(46)	25,366
Covina	(1901)	(37)	32,684
Alhambra	(1903)	(19)	57,798
Hollywood	(1903–1910)*	—	—
Arcadia	(1903)	(28)	46,236
Venice	(1904–1925)*	—	—
Vernon	(1905)	(79)	239
Wilmington	(1905–1909)*	—	—
Glendale	(1906)	(4)	132,006
Huntington Park	(1906)	(35)	37,590
La Verne	(1906)	(55)	17,983
Sawtelle	(1906–1922)*	—	—
Hermosa Beach	(1907)	(53)	18,523
Sierra Madre	(1907)	(65)	12,189
Watts	(1907–1926)*	—	—
Claremont	(1907)	(47)	25,187
Inglewood	(1908)	(10)	83,796
Belmont Heights	(1908–1909)**	—	—
Eagle Rock	(1911–1923)*	—	—
Tropico	(1911–1918)***	—	—
Burbank	(1911)	(11)	83,330
San Fernando	(1911)	(60)	15,120
Glendora	(1911)	(36)	34,551
El Monte	(1912)	(17)	67,465
Manhattan Beach	(1912)	(38)	32,604
San Gabriel	(1913)	(45)	28,128
San Marino	(1913)	(64)	13,358
Avalon	(1913)	(74)	1,992
Beverly Hills	(1914)	(39)	31,638
Monterey Park	(1916)	(22)	52,022
El Segundo	(1916)	(63)	14,543
Culver City	(1917)	(33)	38,273
Montebello	(1920)	(25)	47,515
Torrance	(1921)	(3)	135,317
Hyde Park	(1921–1923)*	—	—
Lynwood	(1921)	(34)	37,731
Hawthorne	(1922)	(20)	55,592
South Gate	(1923)	(21)	52,711

Name of City	Date of Incorporation	Rank	Population
West Covina	(1923)	(15)	73,291
Signal Hill	(1924)	(72)	5,098
Maywood	(1924)	(57)	16,698
Tujunga	(1925–1932)*	—	—
Barnes City	(1926–1927)*	—	—
Bell	(1927)	(50)	21,838
Gardena	(1930)	(29)	43,265
Palos Verdes Estates	(1939)	(62)	14,803
Lakewood	(1954)	(13)	79,131
Baldwin Park	(1956)	(26)	47,067
Cerritos	(1956)	(27)	46,240
La Puente	(1956)	(41)	30,643
Downey	(1956)	(7)	88,523
Rolling Hills	(1957)	(73)	2,166
Paramount	(1957)	(40)	30,690
Santa Fe Springs	(1957)	(71)	7,398
Industry	(1957)	(78)	717
Bradbury	(1957)	(76)	866
Irwindale	(1957)	(77)	768
Duarte	(1957)	(61)	14,978
Norwalk	(1957)	(8)	85,922
Bellflower	(1957)	(24)	49,122
Rolling Hills Estates	(1957)	(70)	8,881
Pico Rivera	(1958)	(23)	50,818
South El Monte	(1958)	(58)	15,576
Walnut	(1959)	(69)	9,689
Artesia	(1959)	(59)	15,497
Rosemead	(1959)	(32)	39,602
Lawndale	(1959)	(48)	23,588
Commerce	(1960)	(67)	10,196
La Mirada	(1960)	(31)	40,468
Temple City	(1960)	(43)	28,534
San Dimas	(1960)	(54)	18,248
Cudahy	(1960)	(56)	16,949
Bell Gardens	(1961)	(44)	28,237
Hidden Hills	(1961)	(75)	1,730
Palmdale	(1962)	(66)	10,461
Hawaiian Gardens	(1964)	(68)	9,843
Lomita	(1964)	(52)	19,447
Carson	(1968)	(12)	79,556
Rancho Palos Verdes	(1973)	(30)	41,840
La Canada-Flintridge	(1976)	(51)	21,444
Lancaster	(1977)	( )	—

Total Incorporated 6,036,645

Total Unincorporated 1,005,843

County Total 7,042,538

* Consolidated w/Los Angeles
** Consolidated w/Long Beach
*** Consolidated w/Glendale

APPENDIX B: THE GOVERNORS OF CALIFORNIA

SPANISH REGIME, 1767–1821 (Dates of service in the case of each governor are from assumption to surrender of office)

Gaspar de Portolá, November 30, 1767–July 9, 1770
From May 21, 1769, Portolá's position was that of *Comandante-militar* for Alta California. From July 9, 1770, to May 25, 1774, the position of Comandante was filled by Pedro Fages; and from May 25, 1774, to February 1777, by Fernando Rivera y Moncada.
Matías de Armona, June 12, 1769–November 9, 1770
Felipe de Barri, March ?, 1770–March 4, 1775
Governor of *Las Californias,* residing at Loreto.
Felipe de Neve, March 4, 1775–July 12, 1782
In February 1777, Neve arrived from Loreto and took up his residence at Monterey in Alta California. Rivera y Moncada went south to assume the lieutenant-governorship at Loreto. The acting lieutenant-governor, pending Rivera's arrival, was Joaquín Cañete.
Pedro Fages, July 12, 1782–April 16, 1791
On July 18, 1781, Rivera y Moncada was killed on the Colorado River, and Joaquín Cañete served as lieutenant-governor until late in November 1783, when he was succeeded by José Joaquín de Arrillaga.
José Antonio Roméu, April 16, 1791–April 9, 1792
José Joaquí de Arrillaga, April 9, 1792–May 14, 1794
During this period, Arrillaga was lieutenant-governor and Comandante of Lower California, and governor of *Las Californias ad interim.*
Diego de Borica, May 14, 1794–March 8, 1800

319

José Joaquín de Arrillaga, March 8, 1800–July 24, 1814
Until March 11, 1802, when he died, Pedro de Alberni was *Comandante-militar* for Alta California. The decree making Alta California a separate province bore the date August 29, 1804, and it reached Arrillaga November 16.

José Darío Argüello, July 24, 1814–August 30, 1815
Governor *ad interim.*

Pablo Vicente de Solá, August 30, 1815–November 10, 1822
Held over from Spanish regime to November 1822.

MEXICAN REGIME, 1821–1847

Luís Antonio Argüello, November 10, 1822–November ?, 1825
Until April 2, 1823, Argüello's authority was derived from the Spanish Regency. After that date until November 17 it was derived from Iturbide as Agustín I. After November 17 it was derived from the *Congreso Constituyente* (National Congress). In March 1823, Iturbide named Naval Captain Bonifacio de Tosta governor of Alta California. In 1824 José Miñón was appointed governor of Alta California, but he declined the office.

José María de Echeandía, November ?, 1825–January 31, 1831
Antonia García was first appointed as Echeandía's successor, but the Appointment was revoked.

Manuel Victoria, January 31, 1831–December 6, 1831

José María de Echeandía, December 6, 1831–January 14, 1833
De facto *jefe político* and *jefe militar* in the district south of, but not including, Santa Barbara.

Pío Pico, January 27–February 16, 1832
Jefe político by appointment of the *Diputación* for only twenty days.

Agustín Vicente Zamorano, February 1, 1832–January 14, 1833
De facto *jefe militar* only in the district north of and including Santa Barbara.

José Figueroa, January 14, 1833–September 29, 1835
Early in 1833 Figueroa asked to be relieved of office. On July 16, 1833, José María Híjar was appointed *jefe político,* but the appointment was revoked by Mexico's President Santa Anna on July 25. On July 18, 1834, Figueroa withdrew his request to be relieved.

José Castro, September 29, 1835–January 2, 1836
From October 8, 1835, to January 1, 1836, the position of *jefe militar* was held by Nicolás Gutiérrez.

Nicolás Gutiérrez, January 2–May 3, 1836

Mariano Chico, May 3–August 1, 1836
Nicolás Gutiérrez, August 1–November 5, 1836
José Castro, November 5–December 7, 1836
   Castro was *jefe militar* until November 29, when he was suc-
   ceeded by Mariano Guadalupe Vallejo. He then became acting
   governor.
Juan Bautista Alvarado, December 7, 1836–December 31, 1842
   Until August 7, 1839, Alvarado was governor *ad interim.* On June
   6, 1837, Carlos Carillo was appointed governor, and on December
   6 he assumed office at Los Angeles, but he was arrested and
   deposed by Alvarado on May 20, 1838.
Manuel Micheltorena, December 31, 1842–February 22, 1845
Pío Pico, February 22, 1845–August 10, 1846
   By the departmental junta Pío Pico was declared governor *ad
   interim* on February 15, 1845. José Castro served as *jefe militar* for
   the same period.
José María Flores, October 31, 1846–January 11, 1847
Andrés Pico, January 11–January 13, 1847

AMERICAN GOVERNORS UNDER MILITARY RULE

Commodore John D. Sloat, July 7, 1846.
Commodore Robert F. Stockton, July 29, 1846.
Captain John C. Frémont, January 19, 1847.
General Stephen W. Kearny, March 1, 1847.
Colonel Richard B. Mason, May 31, 1847.
General Persifor F. Smith, February 28, 1849.
General Bennett Riley, April 12, 1849.

GOVERNORS OF THE STATE OF CALIFORNIA

Name	Party	Date of Inauguration
Peter H. Burnett	Ind. Dem.	December 20, 1849
John McDougal	Ind. Dem.	January 9, 1851
John Bigler	Dem.	January 8, 1852
John Neely Johnson	Amer.	January 9, 1856
John B. Weller	Dem.	January 8, 1858
Milton S. Latham	Lecomp. Dem.	January 9, 1860
John G. Downey	Lecomp. Dem.	January 14, 1860
Leland Stanford	Rep.	January 10, 1862

Frederick F. Low	Union	December 10, 1863
Henry H. Haight	Dem.	December 5, 1867
Newton Booth	Rep.	December 8, 1871
Romualdo Pacheco	Rep.	February 27, 1875
William Irwin	Dem.	December 9, 1875
George C. Perkins	Rep.	January 8, 1880
George Stoneman	Dem.	January 10, 1883
Washington Bartlett	Dem.	January 8, 1887
Robert W. Waterman	Rep.	September 13, 1887
Henry H. Markham	Rep.	January 8, 1891
James H. Budd	Dem.	January 11, 1895
Henry T. Gage	Rep.	January 4, 1899
George C. Pardee	Rep.	January 7, 1903
James N. Gillett	Rep.	January 9, 1907
Hiram W. Johnson	Prog. Rep.	January 3, 1911
William D. Stephens	Rep.	March 15, 1917
Friend W. Richardson	Rep.	January 8, 1923
Clement C. Young	Rep.	January 4, 1927
James Rolph, Jr.	Rep.	January 6, 1931
Frank F. Merriam	Rep.	January 7, 1935
Culbert L. Olson	Dem.	January 2, 1939
Earl F. Warren	Rep.	January 4, 1943
Goodwin F. Knight	Rep.	October 5, 1953
Edmund G. Brown	Dem.	January 5, 1959
Ronald Reagan	Rep.	January 5, 1967
Edmund G. Brown Jr.	Dem.	January 5, 1975

INDEX

Hoover Library of War,
Revolution, and Peace,
Stanford, 285
Hope, Bob, 295
Hopkins, Mark, 155, 163, 170
Housing
in the future, 307, 308
during the Spanish period, 72
during World War I, 220
after World War II, 242, 243
Howard, John Galen, 281–282
Hughes Aircraft Company, 240
Hughes, Charles Evans, 218
Humphrey, Hubert, 254, 260
Huntington Beach, 224
Huntington, Collis P., 155,
161–163, 164
Huntington, Henry E., 164–165
Huntington Library and Art
Gallery, 165, 280, 285
Hupa Indians, 13, 16, 18
Huxley, Aldous, 311

Ide, William B., 97
Immigration Act of 1965, 208
Imperial Land Company, 190
Imperial Valley, 10, 186, 190–191
Indians, 5, 89
agriculture of, 16–17
attacks on Americans by, 25–26
claims of against federal
government, 27–28
Dawes Act of 1887, 27
and discovery of gold, 24,
103–104
dwellings of, 16
food of, 13, 16–17
general characteristics, 13,
16–21, 36
health of, 20
language of, 21
and missionaries, 13, 16, 45, 57
origin of, 12
population of, 21, 23–24, 26
reaction to explorers, 35, 39, 48,
50

rebellions by, 25–26, 73
religion of, 20–21
and reservations, 24–25
secularization of missions and,
59, 61
and social customs, 17–20
and Treaty of Guadalupe
Hidalgo, 24
as workers, 13, 16, 69
Industrial Workers of the World
(I.W.W.), 208, 226–227
Industry
after Gold Rush, 135–136
effects on society, 306–308
recent, 307
and World War I, 220–221
and World War II, 239–240, 241
International Longshoremen's
Association (I.L.A.), 231, 232
Irish in California, 157–158
Irrigation (*see* water resources)
Irvine, 205, 206, 296
Italian-Swiss Agricultural Colony,
188
Italians in California, 167

Jackson, Andrew, 94
Jackson, Helen Hunt, 26
Japanese, 167, 170–174
Jarvis, Howard, 299
Jeffers, Robinson, 280, 284
Jenkins, John, 127–128
Jet Propulsion Laboratory of
Caltech, 297–298
Johnson, Andrew, 139
Johnson, Hiram, 216, 218, 227,
230, 249, 250, 260
Johnson, John Neely, 139
Johnson, Lyndon B., 254, 272, 273
Johnston, Albert Sidney, 144
Jolson, Al, 288
Jones, Thomas Ap Catesby, 94
Jordan, David Starr, 296
Jorgensen, Chris, 280
Judah, Theodore D., 155
Juno, vessel, 75